PERSONAL REMINISCENCES
OF
HENRY IRVING

THE LAST PICTURE PAINTED OF HENRY IRVING
FROM A PASTEL
BY J. BERNARD PARTRIDGE
(IN THE POSSESSION OF THE AUTHOR)

PERSONAL REMINISCENCES OF
HENRY IRVING

BY

BRAM STOKER

VOLUME I

GREENWOOD PRESS, PUBLISHERS
WESTPORT, CONNECTICUT

Originally published in 1906
by William Heinemann, London

First Greenwood Reprinting 1970

SBN 8371-2845-5 (SET)
SBN 8371-2843-9 (VOL. 1)

PRINTED IN UNITED STATES OF AMERICA

TO

THE MEMORY OF

JOHN LAWRENCE TOOLE

LOVING COMRADE AND TRUE FRIEND

OF

HENRY IRVING

PREFACE

WERE my book a "life" of Henry Irving instead of a grouping of such matters as came into my own purview, I should probably feel some embarrassment in the commencement of a preface. Logically speaking, even the life of an actor has no preface. He begins, and that is all. And such beginning is usually obscure; but faintly remembered at the best. Art is a completion; not merely a history of endeavour. It is only when completeness has been obtained that the beginnings of endeavour gain importance, and that the steps by which it has been won assume any shape of permanent interest. After all, the struggle for supremacy is so universal that the matters of hope and difficulty of one person are hardly of general interest. When the individual has won out from the huddle of strife, the means and steps of his succeeding become of interest, either historically or in the educational aspect—but not before. From every life there may be a lesson to some one; but in the teeming millions of humanity such lessons can but seldom have any general or exhaustive force. The mere din of strife is too incessant for any individual sound to carry far. Fame, who rides in higher atmosphere, can alone make her purpose heard. Well did the framers of picturesque idea understand their work when in her hand they put a symbolic trumpet.

The fame of an actor is won in minutes and seconds, not in years. The latter are only helpful in the recurrence of opportunities; in the possibilities of repetition. It is not feasible, therefore, adequately to record the progress of his work. Indeed that work in its perfection cannot be recorded; words are, and can be, but faint suggestions of awakened emotion. The student of history can, after all, but accept in matters evanescent the judgment of contemporary experience. Of such, the weight of evidence can at best incline in one direction; and that tendency is not susceptible of further proof. So much, then, for the work of art that is not plastic and permanent. There remains therefore but the artist. Of him the other arts can make record in so far as external appearance goes. Nay, more, the genius of sculptor or painter can suggest—with an understanding as subtle as that of the sun-rays which on sensitive media can depict what cannot be seen by the eye—the existence of these inner forces and qualities whence accomplished works of any kind proceed. It is to such art that we look for the teaching of our eyes. Modern science can record something of the actualities of voice and tone. Writers of force and skill and judgment can convey abstract ideas of controlling forces and purposes; of thwarting passions; of embarrassing weaknesses; of all the bundle of inconsistencies which make up an item of concrete humanity. From all these may be derived some consistent idea of individuality. This individuality is at once the ideal and the objective of portraiture.

For my own part the work which I have undertaken in this book is to show future minds something of Heny Irving as he was to me. I have chosen the form of the book for this purpose. As I cannot give the myriad of details and impressions which went to the making up of my own convictions, I have tried to select such instances as were self-sufficient to the purpose. If here and there I have been able to lift for a single instant the veil which covers the mystery of individual nature, I shall have made something known which must help the lasting memory of my dear dead friend. In the doing of my work, I am painfully conscious that I have obtruded my own personality, but I trust that for this I may be forgiven, since it is only by this means that I can convey at all the ideas which I wish to impress.

As I cannot adequately convey the sense of Irving's worthiness myself, I try to do it by other means. By showing him amongst his friends, and explaining who those friends were; by giving incidents with explanatory matter of intention; by telling of the pressure of circumstance and his bearing under it; by affording such glimpses of his inner life and mind as one man may of another. I have earnestly tried to avoid giving pain to the living, to respect the sanctity of the dead; and finally to keep from any breach of trust—either that specifically confided in me, or implied by the accepted intimacy of our relations. Well I know how easy it is to err in this respect; to overlook the evil force of irresponsible chatter. But I have always tried to bear in mind the grim warning of Tennyson's biting words:

> "Proclaim the faults he would not show;
> Break lock and seal; betray the trust;
> Keep nothing sacred; 'tis but just
> The many-headed beast should know."

For nearly thirty years I was an intimate friend of Irving; in certain ways the most intimate friend of his life. I knew him as well as it is given to any man to know another. And this knowledge is fully in my mind, when I say that, so far as I know, there is not in this book a word of his inner life or his outer circumstances that he would wish unsaid; no omission that he would have liked filled.

Let any one who will read the book through say whether I have tried to do him honour—and to do it by worthy means: the honour and respect which I feel; which in days gone I held for him; which now I hold for his memory.

BRAM STOKER.

4 Durham Place,
　Chelsea, London.

CONTENTS

		PAGE
I.	EARLIEST RECOLLECTION OF HENRY IRVING	1
II.	THE OLD SCHOOL AND THE NEW	12
III.	FRIENDSHIP	25
IV.	HONOURS FROM DUBLIN UNIVERSITY	35
V.	CONVERGING STREAMS	42
VI.	JOINING FORCES	55
VII.	THE LYCEUM PRODUCTIONS	70
VIII.	IRVING BEGINS MANAGEMENT	72
IX.	SHAKESPEARE PLAYS—I.	83
X.	SHAKESPEARE PLAYS—II.	93
XI.	SHAKESPEARE PLAYS—III.	107
XII.	SHAKESPEARE PLAYS—IV.	118
XIII.	IRVING'S METHOD	127
XIV.	ART-SENSE	141
XV.	STAGE EFFECTS	156
XVI.	THE VALUE OF EXPERIMENT	173
XVII.	THE PULSE OF THE PUBLIC	185
XVIII.	TENNYSON AND HIS PLAYS—I.	197
XIX.	TENNYSON AND HIS PLAYS—II.	209
XX.	TENNYSON AND HIS PLAYS—III.	224
XXI.	TENNYSON AND HIS PLAYS—IV.	240
XXII.	"WATERLOO"—"KING ARTHUR"—"DON QUIXOTE"	247
XXIII.	ART AND HAZARD	259
XXIV.	VANDENHOFF	276
XXV.	CHARLES MATHEWS	277

CONTENTS

		PAGE
XXVI. CHARLES DICKENS AND HENRY IRVING	. .	280
XXVII. MR. J. M. LEVY		283
XXVIII. VISITS TO AMERICA		285
XXIX. WILLIAM WINTER		289
XXX. PERFORMANCE AT WEST POINT . . .		291
XXXI. AMERICAN REPORTERS		297
XXXII. TOURS-DE-FORCE		304
XXXIII. CHRISTMAS		308
XXXIV. IRVING AS A SOCIAL FORCE . . .		310
XXXV. VISITS OF FOREIGN WARSHIPS . . .		327
XXXVI. IRVING'S LAST RECEPTION AT THE LYCEUM	.	333
XXXVII. THE VOICE OF ENGLAND		343
XXXVIII. RIVAL TOWNS		345
XXXIX. TWO STORIES		346
XL. SIR RICHARD BURTON		350
XLI. SIR HENRY MORTON STANLEY . . .		362
XLII. ARMINIUS VAMBÉRY		371

ILLUSTRATIONS

	To face page
Last Portrait of Irving, Pastel. Coloured. By J. Bernard Partridge	*Frontispiece*
Digby Grant. *Drawing by Fred Barnard*	8
Sketch of Irving as Hamlet. *By Fred Barnard*	13
Henry Irving, 1876	33
Autograph on Tissue	*To face above*
Irving as Hamlet. *Drawing by Fred Barnard*	78
Playbill, Edwin Booth and Henry Irving	87
Suggestion for Iago's Dress. *Drawn by Henry Irving*	89
Irving as Shylock. *Pastel by J. B. Yeats*	86
Autograph Menu	91
Irving as King Lear. *Drawing by J. Bernard Partridge*	119
Irving as Louis XI. *Pastel by J. B. Partridge*	131
Irving as Dubosc. *By James Pryde*	134
Henry Irving as Charles I.	139
Irving as Becket. *From the Painting by Eugene*	242
Ellen Terry as Imogen	261
Irving between England and America. *Drawing by Fred Barnard*	285
Henry Irving on Shipboard	288

I

EARLIEST RECOLLECTIONS OF HENRY IRVING

Earliest Recollection, Dublin, 1867—Captain Absolute— Impersonation — Distinction — Local Criticism—" Two Roses," Dublin, 1871—The Archetype of Digby Grant— Chevalier Wikoff

I

THE first time I ever saw Henry Irving was at the Theatre Royal, Dublin, on the evening of Wednesday, August 28, 1867. Miss Herbert had brought the St. James's Company on tour, playing some of the Old Comedies and Miss Braddon's new drama founded on her successful novel, *Lady Audley's Secret*. The piece chosen for this particular night was *The Rivals* in which Irving played Captain Absolute.

Forty years ago provincial playgoers did not have much opportunity of seeing great acting, except in the star parts. It was the day of the Stock Companies, when the chief theatres everywhere had *good* actors who played for the whole season, each in his or her established class; but notable excellence was not to be expected at the salaries then possible to even the most enterprising management. The " business " — the term still applied to the minor incidents of acting, as well as to the disposition of the various characters and the entrances and exits—was, of necessity, of a formal and traditional kind. There was no time for the exhaustive rehearsal of minor details to which actors are in these days accustomed. When the bill was changed five or six times a week it was only possible, even at the longest rehearsal, to get through the standard outline of action, and the perfection of the cues—in fact those conditions of the interdependence of the actors and mechanics on which the structural excellence of the play depends. Moreover, the system by which great actors appeared as "stars" supported by only one or two players of their own bringing, made it necessary that there should be in the higher order of theatres some kind of standard way of regulating the action of the plays in vogue. It was a matter of considerable interest to me to see, when some fourteen years later Edwin Booth came to play at the Lyceum, that he sent his "dresser" to represent him at the earlier rehearsals so as to point out to the stage management the disposition of the characters and general arrangement of matured action to which he was accustomed. I only mention this here to illustrate the conditions of stage work at an earlier period.

This adherence to standard "business" was so strict, though unwritten, a rule that no one actor could venture to break it. To do so without preparation would have been to at least endanger the success of the play; and "preparation" was the prerogative of the management, not of the individual player. Even Henry Irving, though he had been, as well as a player, the Stage Manager of the St. James's Company and could so carry out his ideas partially, could not have altered the broad lines of the play established by nearly a century of usage.

As a matter of fact *The Rivals* had not been one of Miss Herbert's productions at the St. James's, and so it did not come within the scope of his stage management at all.

Irving had played the part of Captain Absolute in the Theatre Royal, Edinburgh, during the three years of his engagement there, 1856-59, where he had learned the traditional usage. Thus the only possibility open to him, as to any actor with regard to an established Comedy, was to improve on the traditional method of acting it within the established lines of movement; in fact, to impersonate the character to better advantage.

On this particular occasion the play as an entity had an advantage not always enjoyed in provincial theatres. It was performed by a Company of Comedians, several of whom had acted together for a considerable time. The lines of the play being absolutely conventional did not leave any special impress on the mind; one can only recall the actors and the acting.

To this day I can remember the playing of Henry Irving as Captain Absolute, which was different from any performance of the same part which I had seen. What I saw, to my amazement and delight, was a patrician figure as real as the persons of one's dreams, and endowed with the same poetic grace. A young soldier, handsome, distinguished, self-dependent; compact of grace and slumbrous energy. A man of quality who stood out from his surroundings on the stage as a being of another social world. A figure full of dash and fine irony, and whose ridicule seemed to *bite ;* buoyant with the joy of life ; self-conscious ; an inoffensive egoist even in his love-making ; of supreme and unsurpassable insolence, veiled and shrouded in his fine quality of manner. Such a figure as could only be possible in an age when the answer to insolence was a sword-thrust ; when only those dare be insolent who could depend to the last on the heart and brain and arm behind the blade. The scenes which stand out most vividly are the following : His interview with Mrs. Malaprop in which she sets him to read his own intercepted letter to Lydia wherein he speaks of the old lady herself as " the old weather-beaten she-dragon." The manner with which he went back again and again, with excuses exemplified by action rather than speech, to the offensive words —losing his place in the letter and going back to find it—seeming to try to recover the sequence of thought—innocently trying to fit the words to the subject — was simply a triumph of well-bred, easy insolence. Again when Captain Absolute makes repentant obedience to his father's will his negative air of content as to the excellences or otherwise of his suggested wife was inimitable. And the shocked appearance, manner and speech of his hypocritical submission : " Not to please your father, sir ? " was as enlightening to the audience as it was convincing to Sir Anthony. Again the scene in the Fourth Act when in the presence of his father and Mrs. Malaprop he has to make love to Lydia in his own person, was on the actor's part a masterpiece of emotion—the sort of thing to make an author grateful. There was no mistaking the emotions which came so fast, treading on each other's heels: his mental perturbation; his sense of the ludicrous situation in which he found himself; his hurried, feeble, ill-concealed efforts to find a way out of the difficulty. And through them all the sincerity of his real affection for Lydia which actually shone, coming straight and convincingly to the hearts of the audience.

But these scenes were all of acting a part. The reality of his character was in the scene of Sir Lucius O'Trigger's quarrel with him. Here he was real. Man to man the grace and truth of his character and bearing were based on no purpose or afterthought. Before a man his manhood was sincere; before a gallant gentleman his gallantry was without flaw, and, as the dramatist intended, outshone even the chivalry of that perfect gentleman Sir Lucius O'Trigger.

The acting of Henry Irving is, after nearly forty years, so vivid in my memory that I can recall his movements, his expressions, the tones of his voice.

And yet the manner in which his acting in the new and perfect method was received in the local press may afford an object-lesson of what the pioneer of high art has, like any other pioneer, to endure.

During the two weeks' visit to Dublin the repertoire comprised, as well as *The Rivals*, *The School for Scandal, The Belle's Stratagem, The Road to Ruin, She Stoops to Conquer,* and *Lady Audley's Secret.*

Of these other plays I can say nothing, for I did not see them. Lately, however, on looking over the newspapers I found hardly a word of even judicious comment; praise there was not. According to the local journalistic record his Joseph Surface was "lachrymose, coarse, pointless and ineffective. Nothing could be more ludicrously deficient of dramatic power than his acting in the passage with Lady Teazle in the screen scene. The want of harmony between the actual words and gesture, emphasis and expression, was painfully palpable."

And yet to those who can read between the lines and gather truth where truth—though not perhaps the same truth—is meant, this very criticism shows how well he played the hypocrite who meant one thing whilst conveying the idea of another. Were Joseph's acts and tones and words all in perfect harmony he would seem to an audience not a hypocrite but a reality.

Another critic considered him "stiff and constrained, and occasionally left the audience under the impression that they were witnessing the playing of an amateur."

The only mention of his Young Marlow was in one paper that it was "carefully represented by Mr. Irving"; and in another that it was "insipid and pointless."

Of young Dornton in *The Road to Ruin* there was one passing word of praise as an "able impersonation." But of *The Rivals* I could find no criticism whatever in any of the Dublin papers when more than thirty-eight years after seeing the play I searched them hoping to find some confirmation of my vivid recollection of Henry Irving's brilliant acting. The following only, in small type, I found in the *Irish Times* more than a week after the play had been given :

> "Of those who support Miss Herbert, Mr. and Mrs. Frank Matthews are, undoubtedly, the best. Mr. Stoyle is full of broad comedy, but now and then he is not true to nature. Mr. Irving and Mr. Gaston Murray are painstaking and respectable artists."

It is good to think that the great player who, as the representative actor of his nation—of the world—for over a quarter of a century was laid to rest in Westminster Abbey to the grief of at least two Continents, had after eleven years of arduous and self-sacrificing work during which he had played over five hundred different characters and had even then begun quite a new school of acting, been considered by at least one writer for the press " a painstaking and respectable artist."

II

I did not see Henry Irving again till May 1871, when with the Vaudeville Company he played for a fortnight at the Theatre Royal Albery's Comedy, *Two Roses*. Looking back to that time the best testimony I can bear to the fact that the performance interested me is that I went to see it three times. The company was certainly an excellent one. In addition to Henry Irving it contained H. J. Montague, George Honey, Louise Claire, and Amy Fawsitt.

Well do I remember the delight of that performance of Digby Grant and how well it foiled the other characters of the play.

Amongst them all it stood out star-like. An inimitable character which Irving impersonated in a manner so complete that to this day I have been unable to get it out of my mind as a reality. Indeed it was a reality though at that time I did not know it. Years afterwards I met the original at the house of the late Mr. James McHenry—a villa in a little park off Addison Road.

This archetype was the late Chevalier Wikoff, of whom in the course of a friendship of years I had heard much from McHenry, who well remembered him in his early days in Philadelphia, in which city Wikoff was born. In his youth he had been a very big, handsome man; in the days when men wore cloaks used to pass down Chestnut Street or Locust Street with a sublime swagger. He was a great friend of Edwin Forrest the actor, and a great "ladies' man." He had been a friend and lover of the celebrated dancer Fanny Elsler, who was so big and yet so agile that, as my father described to me, when she bounded in on the stage seeming to light from the wings to the footlights in a single leap, the house seemed to shake. Wikoff was a pretty hard man, and as cunning as men are made. When I knew him he was an old man, but he fortified the deficiencies of age with artfulness. He was then a little hard of hearing; but he simulated complete deafness, and there was little said within a reasonable distance that he did not hear. For many years he had lived in Europe chiefly in London and Paris. There was one trait in his character which even his intimate friends did not

HENRY IRVING AS DIGBY GRANT IN "TWO ROSES"
Drawing made in his dressing-room by Fred Barnard, 1870

suspect. Every year right up to the end of his long life he disappeared from London at a certain date. He was making his pilgrimage to Paris where on a given day he laid some flowers on a little grave long after the child's mother, the dancer, had died. Wikoff was a trusted agent of the Bonaparte's and he held strange secrets of that adventurous family. He it was, so McHenry told me, who had brought in secret from France to England the last treasures of the Imperial house after the *débâcle* following Sedan.

This was the person whom Irving had selected as the archetype of Digby Grant. Long before, he had met him at McHenry's; with that "seeing eye" of his had marked his personality down for use; and with that marvellous memory which, in my long experience of him never failed him, was able to reproduce with the exactness of a "Chinese copy" every jot and tittle appertaining to the man, without and within. His tall gaunt, slightly stooping figure; his scanty hair artfully arranged to cover the ravages of time; the cunning, inquisitive eyes; the mechanical turning of the head which becomes the habit of the deaf. The veiled voice which can do everything but express truth—even under stress of sudden emotion. Years after *Two Roses* had had its run at the Vaudeville and elsewhere I went to see Wikoff when he was ill in a humble lodging. In answer to my knuckle-tap he opened the door himself. For an instant I was startled out of my self-possession, for in front of me stood the veritable Digby Grant. I had met him already a good many times, but always in the recognised costume of morning or evening. Now I saw him as Irving had represented him; but I do not think he had ever seen him as I saw him at that moment. I believe that the costume in which he appeared in that play was the result of the actor's inductive ratiocination. He had studied the individuality so thoroughly, and was so familiar with not only his apparent characteristics but with those secret manifestations which are in their very secrecy subtle indicators of individuality grafted on type, that he had re-created him—just as Cuvier or Owen could from a single bone reconstruct giant reptiles of the Palæozoic age. There was the bizarre dressing-jacket, frayed at edge and cuff; with ragged frogs and stray buttons. There the three days' beard, white at root and raven black at point. There the flamboyant smoking-cap with yellow tassel which marks that epoch in the history of ridiculous dress out of which in sheer revulsion of artistic feeling came the Pre-Raphaelite movement.

Irving had asked me to bring with me to Wikoff some grapes and other creature comforts for which the poor old man was, I believe, genuinely grateful; but in the course of our chat he told me that Irving had "taken him off" for "that fellow in the *Two Roses*." It was strange how the name of that play was so often given wrong; most people spoke of it and wrote of it as *The Two Roses;* I have known even Irving himself to make the mistake! Wikoff did not seem displeased at the duplication of his identity. To me he conveyed the idea of being in some degree proud of it.

This wonderful creation in the play "took the town," as the phrase is, and for some time the sayings of the characters in it were heard everywhere. It was truly a "creation"; not merely in the actor's sense where the first player of a character in London is deemed its "creator" but in the usual meaning of the word. For it is not enough in acting to know what to do; it must be done! All possible knowledge of Wikoff, from his psychical identity to his smoking-cap, could not produce a strong effect unless the actor through the resources of his art could transform reality to the appearance of reality—a very different and much more difficult thing.

When Irving played in *Two Roses* in Dublin in 1872 there was not a word in any of the papers of the acting of any of the accomplished players who took part in it; not even the mention of their names.

What other cities may have said of him in these early days I know not; but I take it that the standard of criticism is generally of the same average of excellence, or its opposite, according to the assay of the time. In the provinces the zone of demarcation between bad and good varies less, in that mediocrity qualifies more easily, and superexcellence finds a wider field for work. Of one thing we may be sure: that success has its own dangers. Self-interest and jealousy and a host of the lesser and meaner vices of the intellectual world find their opportunity.

When the floodgates of Comment are opened there comes with the rush of clean water all the scum and rubbish which has accumulated behind them drawn into position by the trickling stream.

II

THE OLD SCHOOL AND THE NEW

Irving's Early Experience in Dublin—A Month of Hisses —The Old School of Acting and the New—Historical Comparison—From Edmund Kean to Irving—Irving's Work—The Thoughtful School

I

MORE than five years elapsed before I saw Henry Irving again. We were both busy men, each in his own way, and the Fates did not allow our orbits to cross. He did not come to Dublin; my work did not allow my going to London except at times when he was not playing there. Those five years were to him a triumphant progress in his art and fame. He rose; and rose; and rose. *The Bells* in 1871 was followed in 1872 by *Charles I.*, in 1873 by *Eugene Aram* and *Richelieu*, in 1874 by *Philip* and *Hamlet*, in 1875 by *Macbeth*, and in 1876 by *Othello* and *Queen Mary*.

For my own part, being then in the Civil Service, I could only get away in the " prime of summer time " as my seniors preferred to take their holiday in the early summer or the late autumn. I had, when we next met, been for five years a dramatic critic. In 1871 my growing discontent with the attention accorded to the stage in the local news-

SKETCH FOR IRVING AS HAMLET
By Fred Barnard

papers had culminated with the neglect of *Two Roses*. I asked the proprietor of one of the Dublin newspapers whom I happened to know, Dr. Maunsell, an old contemporary and friend of Charles Lever, to allow me to write on the subject in the *Mail*. He told me frankly that the paper could not afford to pay for such special work, as it was in accordance with the local custom of the time done by the regular staff who wrote on all subjects as required. I replied that I would gladly do it without fee or reward. This he allowed me to carry out.

From my beginning the work in November 1871 I had an absolutely free hand. I was thus able to direct public attention, so far as my paper could effect it, where in my mind such was required. In those five years I think I learned a good deal. As Bacon says, "Writing maketh an exact man," and as I have always held that in matters critical the critic's personal honour is involved in every word he writes I could always feel that the duty I had undertaken was a grave one. I did not shirk work in any way; indeed, I helped largely to effect a needed reform as to the time when criticism should appear. In those days of single printings from slow presses "copy" had to be handed in very early. The paper went to press not long after midnight, and there were few men who could see a play and write the criticism in time for the morning's issue. It thus happened that the critical article was usually a full day behind its time. Monday night's performance was not generally reviewed till Wednesday at earliest; the instances which I have already given afford the proof. This was very hard upon the actors and companies making short vists. The public *en bloc* is a slow-moving force; and when possibility of result is cut short by effluxion of time it is a sad handicap to enterprise and to exceptional work.

I do not wish to be egotistical and I trust that no reader may take it that I am so, in that I have spoken of my first experiences of Henry Irving and how, mainly because of his influence on me, I undertook critical work with regard to his own art. My purpose in doing so is not selfish. I merely wish that those who honour me by reading what I have written should understand something which went before our personal meeting; and why it was that when we did meet we came together with a loving and understanding friendship which lasted unbroken till my dear friend passed away.

Looking back now after an interval of nearly forty years, during which time I was mainly too busy to look back at all, I can understand something of those root-forces which had so strange an influence on both Irving's life and my own, though at the first I was absolutely unconscious of even their existence. Neither when I first saw Irving in 1867, nor when I met him in 1876, nor for many years after I had been his close friend and fellow worker did I know that his early experiences of Dublin had been painful to the last degree. I thought from the way in which the press had ignored him and his work that they must have been bad enough in 1867 and 1871. But later on, when in the prolonged sweetness of years of success the bitterness of that early chagrin had passed away, he told me the story to this effect:

A MONTH OF HISSES

Quite early in his life as an actor—when he was only twenty-one—in an off season when the "resting" actor grasps at any chance of work, he received from Mr. Harry Webb, then Manager of the Queen's Theatre, Dublin, with whom he had played at the Edinburgh Theatre, an offer of an engagement for some weeks. This he joyfully accepted and turned up in due course. He did not know then, though he learned it with startling rapidity, that he was wanted to fill the place of a local favourite who had been, for some cause, summarily dismissed. The public visited their displeasure on the new-comer, and in no uncertain way. From the moment of his coming on the stage on the first night of his engagement until almost its end he was not allowed to say one word without interruption. Hisses and stamping, cat-calls and the thumping of sticks were the universal accompaniments of his speech.

Now to an actor nothing is so deadly as to be hissed. Not only does it bar his artistic effort but it hurts his self-esteem. Its manifestation is a negation of himself, his power, his art. It is present death to him *quâ* artist, with the added sting of shame. Well did the actors who crowded the court at Bow Street when the vanity-mad fool who murdered poor William Terriss know it. The murderer was an alleged actor, and they wanted to punish him. When he was placed in the dock, with one impulse they *hissed* him!

In Irving's case at the Queen's the audience with some shameful remnant of fair play treated him well the last two nights of his performance and cheered him. It was manifestly intended as a proof that it was not against the man that their protest was aimed—though he was the sufferer by it; but against *any one* who might have taken the place of their favourite whom they considered had been injured. It could not have been the *actor* on whom they lavished either hisses or cheers for they had never even heard the sound of his voice, except in the pauses of their own tumult. But to him the effect was the same.

That early visit to Dublin has so many interesting points that it may be worth while to go into it in detail.

The actor who had been dismissed was Mr. Vincent. He had played on the Saturday night, March 3, up to which time Irving had been giving Readings. On the sudden summons he came quickly, and on the first night of his engagement, Monday, March 5, played to the Othello of Mr. T. C. King the part of Cassio with which he was already familiar.

On the 8th was given Gerold Griffin's play *Gisippus; or, The Forgotten Friend*, in which Irving took the part of Titus Quintus Fulvius lately vacated by Mr. Vincent.

The engagement was for four weeks terminating on Saturday, March 31; and during the remainder of that time he played the following parts: Laertes in *Hamlet*—the only play of which any press notice was taken of his performance, the *Freeman's Journal* speaking of it as "a clever and judicious performance"; Florizel in *A Winter's Tale;* Frank Fairplay in *Boots at the Swan*—another of Mr. Vincent's parts; Colonel Davenport in *The British Legion* (called at other times

The Volunteers); Lucien de Nerval in *Pauline;
or, A Night of Terror;* Didier in *The Courier of
Lyons;* and Dangle in *The Critic*. From which
it will be seen that there were varied opportunities
of judging of an actor's talents.

Of this engagement Irving spoke to an interviewer in 1891 *apropos* of an outrage, unique to him, inflicted on Toole shortly before at Coatbridge—a place of which the saying is : " There is only a sheet of paper between Hell and Coatbridge."

" Did you ever have any similar experience in your own career, Mr. Irving ? "

" . . . I did have rather a nasty time once, and suffered much as Mr. Toole has done from the misplaced emotions of the house. It was in this way—when I was a young man—away back about 1859 " (should be 1860) " I should say it was—I was once sent for to fulfil an engagement of six weeks at the Queen's Theatre, a minor theatre in the Irish capital. It was soon after I had left here, Edinburgh. I got over all right, and was ready with my part, but to my amazement, the moment I appeared on the stage I was greeted with a howl of execration from the pit and gallery. There was I standing aghast, ignorant of having given any cause of offence, and in front of me a raging Irish audience, shouting, gesticulating, swearing probably, and in various forms indicating their disapproval of my appearance. I was simply thunderstruck at the warmth of my reception. . . . I simply went through my part amid a continual uproar—groans, hoots, hisses, catcalls, and all the appliances of concerted opposition. It was a roughish experience that ! "

" But surely it did not last long ? "

" That depends," replied the player grimly, " on what you call long. It lasted six weeks. . . . I was as innocent as yourself of all offence, and could not for the life of me make out what was wrong. I had hurt nobody; had said nothing insulting; I had played my parts not badly for me. Yet for the whole of that time I had every night to fight through my piece in the teeth of a house whose entire energies seemed to be concentrated in a personal antipathy to myself."

It was little wonder that the actor who had thus suffered undeservedly remembered the details though the time had so long gone by that he made error as to the year. No wonder that the time the Purgatorial suffering seemed 50 per cent. longer than its actual duration. Other things of more moment had long ago passed out of his mind— he had supped full of success and praise; but the bitter flavour of that month of pain hung all the same in his cup of memory.

An actor *never* forgets a hiss! Collot d'Herbois was once hissed at Lyons. Did *he* forget? Read history for the effect it had on him—and on others—in the massacre of Brumaire in the Year II. of the Republic (November 1793). The historical episode was typical, though happily on that occasion the effect was out of the usual proportion to the cause.

How his own painful episode hung in Irving's mind can hardly be expressed in words. For years he did not speak of it even to me when telling me of how on March 12, 1860, he played Laertes to the Hamlet of T. C. King. It was not till after more than a quarter of a century of unbroken success that he could bear even to speak of it. Not even the consciousness of his own innocence in the whole affair could quell the mental disturbance which it caused him whenever it came back to his thoughts.

II

When, then, Henry Irving came to Dublin in 1876, though it was after a series of triumphs in London running into a term of years, he must have had some strong misgivings as to what his reception might be. It is true that the early obloquy had lessened into neglect; but no artist whose stock-in-trade is mainly his own personality could be expected to reason with the same calmness as that Parliamentary candidate who thus expressed the grounds of his own belief in his growing popularity:

"I am growing popular!"

"Popular!" said his friend. "Why last night I saw them pelt you with rotten eggs!"

"Yes!" he replied with gratification, "that is right! But they used to throw bricks!"

In London the bricks had been thrown, and in plenty. There are some persons of such a temperament that they are jealous of any new idea— of any thing or idea which is outside their own experience or beyond their own reasoning. The new ideas of thoughtful acting which Irving introduced won their way, in the main, splendidly. But it was a hard fight, for there were some violent and malignant writers of the time who did not hesitate to stoop to any meanness of attack. It is extraordinary how the sibilation of a single hiss will win through a tempest of cheers! The battle, however, was being won; when Irving came to Dublin he brought with him a reputation consolidated by the victorious conclusions of five years of strife. The new method was already winning its way.

It so happens that I was myself able through a "fortuitous concourse" of facts to have some means of comparison between the new and the old.

My father, who was born in 1798 and had been a theatre-goer all his life, had seen Edmund Kean in all his Dublin performances. He had an immense admiration for that actor, with whom none of the men within thirty years of his death were, he said, to be compared. When the late Barry Sullivan came on tour and played a range of the great plays he had enormous success. My father, then well over seventy, did not go to the play as often as he had been used to in earlier days; but I was so much struck with the force of Barry Sullivan's acting that I persuaded him to come with me to see him play Sir Giles Overreach in *A New Way to Pay Old Debts*—one of his greatest successes, as it had been one of Kean's. At first he refused to come, saying that it was no use his going as he had seen the greatest of all actors in the part and did not care to see a lesser one. However, he let me have my way, and went; and we sat together in the third row of the pit which had been his chosen locality in his youth. He had been all his life in the Civil Service serving under four Monarchs—George III., George IV., William IV. and Victoria—and retiring after fifty years of service. In those days, as now, the home Civil Service was not a very money-making business, and it was just as well that he preferred the pit. I believed then that I preferred it also; for I too was then in the Civil Service!

He sat the play out with intense eagerness; and

as the curtain fell on the frenzied usurer driven mad by thwarted ambition and the loss of his treasure, feebly spitting at the foes he could not master as he sank feebly into supporting arms, he turned to me and said:

"He is as good as the best of them!"

Barry Sullivan was a purely traditional actor of the old school. All his movements and gestures, readings, phrasings, and times were in exact accordance with the accepted style. It was possible, therefore, for my father to judge fairly, though *longo intervallo*. I saw Barry Sullivan in many plays: *Hamlet, Richelieu, Macbeth, King Lear, The Gamester, The Wife's Secret, The Stranger, Richard III., The Wonder, Othello, The School for Scandal*, as well as playing Sir Giles Overreach, and some more than once; I had a fair opportunity of comparing his acting over a wide range with the particular play by which my father judged. *Ab uno disce omnes* is hardly a working rule in general, but one example is a world better than none. I can fairly say that the actor's general excellence was fairly represented by his characterisation and acting of Sir Giles. I had also seen Charles Kean, G. V. Brook, T. C. King, Charles Dillon and Vandenhoff. I had therefore in my own mind some kind of a standard by which to judge of the worth of the old school, tracing it back to its last great exemplar. When, therefore, I came to contrast it with the new school of Irving I was building my opinion not on sand but upon solid ground. Let me say how the change from the old to the new affected me; it is allowable, I suppose, in matters of reminiscence to take personal example. Hitherto I had only seen

Irving in two characters, Captain Absolute and Digby Grant. The former of these was a part in which for at least ten years—for I was a playgoer very early in life—I had seen other actors all playing the part in a conventional manner. As I have explained, I had only in Irving's case been struck by his rendering of his own part within the conventional lines. The latter part was of quite a new style—new to the world in its essence as its method, and we of that time and place had no standard with regard to it, no means or opportunity of comparison. It was, therefore, with very great interest that we regarded the playing of this actor who was accepted in the main as a new giant. To me as a critic, with the experience of five years of the work, the occasion was of great moment; and I am free to confess that I was a little jealous lest the new-comer—even though I admired so much his work as I had seen—should overthrow my friend and countryman. For at this time Barry Sullivan was more than an acquaintance; we had spent a good many hours together talking over acting and stage history generally. Indeed I began my critical article thus:

> "When an actor has arrived at the distinction which Mr. Henry Irving has undoubtedly achieved, he must not be judged by the same rules of praise and blame as hold good in the judgment of less distinguished performers. Mr. Irving holds in the minds of all who have seen him a high place as an artist, and by some he is regarded as the Garrick of his age; and so we shall judge him by the highest standard which we know."

At the first glance, after the lapse of time, this seems if not unfair at least hard upon the actor; but the second thought shows a subtle, though

ILLUSTRATION OF THE OLD SCHOOL

unintentional compliment: Henry Irving had already raised in his critic, partly by the dignity of his own fame and partly through the favourable experience of the critic, the standard of criticism. He was to be himself the standard of excellence! His present boon to us was that he had taught us to *think*. Let me give an illustration.

Barry Sullivan was according to accepted ideas a great Macbeth. I, for one, thought so. He had great strength, great voice, great physique of all sorts; a well-knit figure with fine limbs, broad shoulders and the perfect back of a prize-fighter. He was master of himself and absolutely well versed in the parts which he played. His fighting power was immense and in the last act of the play good to see. The last scene of all, when the "flats" of the penultimate scene were drawn away in response to the usual carpenter's whistle of the time, was disclosed as a bare stage with wings of wild rock and heather. At the back was Macbeth's Castle of Dunsinane seen in perspective. It was supposed to be vast, and occupied the whole back of the scene. In the centre was the gate, double doors in a Gothic archway of massive proportions. In reality it was quite eight feet high, though of course looking bigger in the perspective. The stage was empty, but from all round it rose the blare of trumpets and the roll of drums. Suddenly the Castle gates were dashed back and through the archway came Macbeth, sword in hand and buckler on arm. Dashing with really superb vigour down to the footlights he thundered out his speech:

"They have tied me to a stake; I cannot fly."

Now this was to us all very fine, and was vastly exciting. None of us ever questioned its accuracy to nature. That Castle with the massive gates thrown back on their hinges by the rush of a single man came back to me vividly when I saw the play as Irving did it in 1888; though at the time we never gave it a thought. Indeed we gave thought to few such things; we took them with simplicity and as they were. Just as we accepted the conventional scenes of the then theatre, *the Palace Arches, the Oak Chamber, the Forest Glade* with its added *wood wings* and all the machinery of tradition. With Irving all was different. That "easy" progress of Macbeth's soldiers returning tired after victorious battle, seen against the low dropping sun across the vast heather studded with patches of light glinting on water; the endless procession of soldiers straggling, singly, and by twos and threes, filling the stage to the conclusion of an endless array, conveyed an idea of force and power which impressed the spectator with an invaluable sincerity. In fact Irving always helped his audience to think.

III

FRIENDSHIP

*Criticism—My Meeting with Irving—A Blaze of Genius
—The Friendship of a Life*

I

THAT Irving was, in my estimation, worthy of the test I had lain down is shown by my article on the opening performance, *Hamlet*, and in the second article written after I had seen him play the part for the third time running. That he was pleased with the review of his work was proved by the fact that he asked on reading my criticism on Tuesday morning that we should be introduced. This was effected by my friend Mr. John Harris, Manager of the Theatre Royal.

Irving and I met as friends, and it was a great gratification to me when he praised my work. He asked me to come round to his room again when the play was over. I went back with him to his hotel and with three of his friends supped with him.

We met again on the following Sunday when he had a few friends to dinner. It was a pleasant evening and a memorable one for me; for then began the close friendship between us which only terminated with his life—if indeed friendship, like any other form of love, can ever terminate. In the meantime I had written the second notice of his Hamlet. This had appeared on Saturday, and when we met he was full of it. Praise was no new thing to him in those days. Two years before, though I knew nothing of them at that time, two criticisms of his Hamlet had been published in Liverpool. One admirable pamphlet was by Sir (then Mr.) Edward Russell, then, as now, the finest critic in England; the other by Hall Caine—a remarkable review to have been written by a young man under twenty. Some of the finest and most lofty minds had been brought to bear on his work. It is, however, a peculiarity of an actor's work that it never grows stale; no matter how often the same thing be repeated it requires a fresh effort each time. Thus it is that criticism can never be stale either; it has always power either to soothe or to hurt. To a great actor the growth of character never stops and any new point is a new interest; a new lease of intellectual life.

II

Before dinner Irving chatted with me about this second article. In it I had said:

"There is another view of Hamlet, too, which Mr. Irving seems to realise by a kind of instinct, but which requires to be more fully and intentionally worked out. . . . The great, deep, underlying idea of Hamlet is that of a mystic. . . . In the high-strung nerves of the man; in the natural impulse of spiritual susceptibility; in his concentrated action spasmodic though it sometimes be, and in the divine delirium of his perfected passion, there is the instinct of the mystic which he has but to render a little plainer, in order that the less susceptible senses of his audience may see and understand."

He was also pleased with another comment of mine. Speaking of the love shown in his parting with Ophelia I had said:

"To give strong grounds for belief, where the instinct can judge more truly than the intellect, is the perfection of suggestive acting; and certainly with regard to this view of Hamlet Mr. Irving deserves not only the highest praise that can be accorded, but the loving gratitude of all to whom his art is dear."

There were plenty of things in my two criticisms which could hardly have been pleasurable to the actor, so that my review of his work could not be considered mere adulation. But I never knew in all the years of our friendship and business relations Irving to take offence or be hurt by true criticism —that criticism which is philosophical and gives a reason for every opinion adverse to that on which judgment is held. When any one could let Irving believe that he had either studied the subject or felt the result of his own showing he was prepared to argue to the last any point suggested, on equal terms. I remember at this time Edward Dowden the great Shakespearean critic, then, as now, Professor of English literature in Dublin University, saying to me in discussing Irving's acting:

" After all an actor's commentary is his acting ! " —a remark of embodied wisdom. Irving had so thoroughly studied every phase and application and the relative importance of every word of his part that he was well able to defend his accepted position. Seldom indeed was any one able to refute him; but when such occurred no one was more ready to accept the true view—and to act upon it.

Thus it was that on this particular night my host's heart was from the beginning something toward me, as mine had been toward him. He had learned that I could appreciate high effort; and with the instinct of his craft liked, I suppose, to prove himself again to his new, sympathetic and understanding friend. And so after dinner he said he would like to recite for me Thomas Hood's poem *The Dream of Eugene Aram*.

That experience I shall never—can never—forget. The recitation was different, both in kind and degree, from anything I had ever heard; and in those days there were some noble experiences of moving speech. It had been my good fortune to be in Court when Whiteside made his noble appeal to the jury in the Yelverton Case; a speech which won for him the unique honour, when next he walked into his place in the House of Commons, of the whole House standing up and cheering him.

I had heard Lord Brougham speak amid a tempest of cheers in the great Round Room of the Dublin Mansion House.

I had heard John Bright make his great oration on Ireland in the Dublin Mechanics' Institute, and had thrilled to the roar within and the echoing roar from the crowded street without which followed his splendid utterance. Like all the others I was touched with deep emotion. To this day I can

A WONDERFUL RECITATION

remember the tones of his organ voice as he swept us all—heart and brain and memory and hope—with his mighty period; moving all who remembered how in the Famine time America took the guns from her battleships to load them fuller with grain for the starving Irish peasants.

These experiences and many others had shown me something of the power of words. In all these and in most of the others there were natural aids to the words spoken. The occasion had always been great, the theme far above one's daily life. The place had always been one of dignity; and above all, had been the greatest of all aids to effective speech, that which I heard Dean (then Canon) Farrar call in his great sermon on Garibaldi " the mysterious sympathy of numbers." But here in a hotel drawing-room, amid a dozen friends, a man in evening dress stood up to recite a poem with which we had all been familiar from our schooldays, which most if not all of us had ourselves recited at some time.

But such was Irving's commanding force, so great was the magnetism of his genius, so profound was the sense of his dominance that I sat spellbound. Outwardly I was as of stone; nought quick in me but receptivity and imagination. That I knew the story and was even familiar with its unalterable words was nothing. The whole thing was new, re-created by a force of passion which was like a new power. Across the footlights amid picturesque scenery and suitable dress, with one's fellows beside and all around one, though the effect of passion can convince and sway it cannot move one personally beyond a certain point. But here was incarnate power, incarnate passion, so close to one that one could meet it eye to eye, within touch of one's outstretched hand. The surroundings became non-existent; the dress ceased to be noticeable; recurring thoughts of self-existence were not at all. Here was indeed Eugene Aram as he was face to face with his Lord; his very soul aflame in the light of his abiding horror. Looking back now I can realise the perfection of art with which the mind was led and swept and swayed, hither and thither as the actor wished. How a change of tone or time denoted the personality of the "Blood-avenging Sprite"—and how the nervous, eloquent hands slowly moving, outspread fanlike, round the fixed face—set as doom, with eyes as inflexible as Fate—emphasised it till one instinctively quivered with pity. Then the awful horror on the murderer's face as the ghost in his brain seemed to take external shape before his eyes, and enforced on him that from his sin there was no refuge. After the climax of horror the Actor was able by art and habit to control himself to the narrative mood whilst he spoke the few concluding lines of the poem.

Then he collapsed half fainting.

III

There are great moments even to the great. That night Irving was inspired. Many times since then I saw and heard him—for such an effort eyes as well as ears are required—recite that poem and hold audiences, big or little, spellbound till

A GREAT MOMENT

the moment came for the thunderous outlet of their pent-up feelings; but that particular vein I never met again. Art can do much; but in all things even in art there is a summit somewhere. That night for a brief time in which the rest of the world seemed to sit still, Irving's genius floated in blazing triumph above the summit of art. There is something in the soul which lifts it above all that has its base in material things. If once only in a lifetime the soul of a man can take wings and sweep for an instant into mortal gaze, then that "once" for Irving was on that, to me, ever memorable night.

As to its effect I had no adequate words. I can only say that after a few seconds of stony silence following his collapse I burst out into something like a violent fit of hysterics.

Let me say, not in my own vindication, but to bring new tribute to Irving's splendid power, that I was no hysterical subject. I was no green youth; no weak individual, yielding to a superior emotional force. I was as men go a strong man, strong in many ways. If autobigraphy is allowable in a work of reminiscence let me say here what I was:

I was a very strong man. It is true that I had known weakness. In my babyhood I used, I understand to be, often at the point of death. Certainly till I was about seven years old I never knew what it was to stand upright. I was naturally thoughtful and the leisure of long illness gave opportunity for many thoughts which were fruitful according to their kind in later years.

This early weakness, however, passed away in

time and I grew into a strong boy and in time enlarged to the biggest member of my family. When I was in my twentieth year I was Athletic Champion of Dublin University. When I met Irving first I was in my thirtieth year. I had been for ten years in the Civil Service and was then engaged on a dry-as-dust book on *The Duties of Clerks of Petty Sessions*. I had edited a newspaper, and had exercised my spare time in many ways—as a journalist; as a writer of short and serial stories; as a teacher. In my College days I had been Auditor of the Historical Society—a post which corresponds to the Presidency of the Union in Oxford or Cambridge—and had got medals, or certificates, for History, Composition and Oratory. I had been President of the Philosophical Society; had got Honours in pure Mathematics. I had won numerous silver cups for races of various kinds. I had played for years in the University football team, where I had received the honour of a "cap!" I was physically immensely strong. In fact I feel justified in saying I represented in my own person something of that aim of university education *mens sana in corpore sano*. When, therefore, after his recitation I became hysterical, it was distinctly a surprise to my friends; for myself surprise had no part in my then state of mind. Irving seemed much moved by the occurrence.

On piecing together the causes of his pleasure at finding an understanding friend, and his further pleasure in realising that that friend's capacity for receptive emotion was something akin in forcefulness to his power of creating it, I can now have some glimpse of his compelling motive when he

My dear friend Stoker
 "God bless you!
God bless you"
 Hy Irving

Dublin
3 Dec 1876

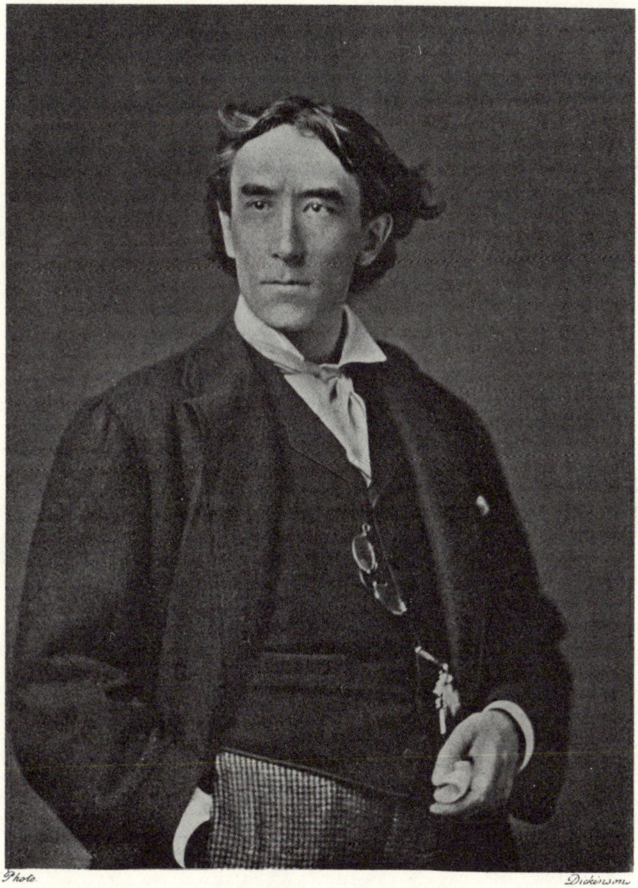

Photo. *Dickinson.*

Henry Irving. 1876.

A DEAR INSCRIPTION

went into his room and after a couple of minutes brought me out his photograph with an inscription on it, the ink still wet:

"My dear friend Stoker. God bless you! God bless you!! Henry Irving. Dublin, December 3, 1876."

In those moments of our mutual emotion he too had found a friend and knew it. Soul had looked into soul! From that hour began a friendship as profound, as close, as lasting as can be between two men.

He has gone his road. Now he lies amongst the great dead; his battle won; the desire of his heart for the advancement of his chosen and beloved art accomplished; his ambition satisfied; his fame part of the history and the glory of the nation.

And the sight of his picture before me, with those loving words, the record of a time of deep emotion and full understanding of us both, each for the other, unmans me once again as I write.

* * * * *

I have ventured to write fully, if not diffusely, about not only my first meeting with Irving but about matters which preceded it and in some measure lead to an understanding of its results.

When a man with his full share of ambition is willing to yield it up to work with a friend whom he loves and honours, it is perhaps as well that in due season he may set out his reasons for so doing. Such is but just; and I now place it on record for the sake of Irving as well as of myself, and for the friends of us both.

For twenty-seven years I worked with Henry Irving, helping him in all honest ways in which one man may aid another—and there were no ways with Irving other than honourable.

Looking back I cannot honestly find any moment in my life when I failed him, or when I put myself forward in any way when the most scrupulous good taste could have enjoined or even suggested a larger measure of reticence.

By my dealing with him I am quite content to be judged, now and hereafter. In my own speaking to the dead man I can find an analogue in the words of heartbreaking sincerity :

> "Stand up on the jasper sea,
> And be witness I have given
> All the gifts required of me!"

IV

HONOURS FROM DUBLIN UNIVERSITY

Public Address—University Night—Carriage Dragged by Students

DURING that visit to Dublin, 1876, Irving received at the hands of the University two honours, one of them unique. Both were accorded by all grades of the College—for Dublin University is the University of the College.

Both honours were unofficial and yet both entirely representative. Both were originated by a few of us the morning after his first performance of *Hamlet*—before I had the honour of knowing him personally. The first was an Address to be presented in the Dining Hall by the Graduates and Undergraduates of the University. The movement came from a few enthusiasts of whom the late G. F. Shaw and Professor R. Y. Tyrrell, both Fellows of the University, were included. As I had originated the idea I was asked by the Committee to write the draft address.

One of the paragraphs, when completed, ran as follows :

> " For the delight and instruction that we (in common with our fellow citizens) have derived from all your impersonations, we tender you our sincere thanks.

But it is something more than gratitude for personal pleasure or personal improvement that moves us to offer this public homage to your genius. Acting such as yours ennobles and elevates the stage, and serves to restore it to its true function as a potent instrument for intellectual and moral culture.

"Throughout your too brief engagement our stage has been a school of true art, a purifier of the passions, and a nurse of heroic sentiments; you have even succeeded in commending it to the favour of a portion of society, large and justly influential, who usually hold aloof from the theatre."

The Address was signed with the names necessary to show its scope and wide significance.

To this Irving replied suitably. I give some passages of his speech; for the occasion was a memorable one, with far-reaching consequences to himself and his art and calling:

"I believe that this is one of the very rare occasions on which public acknowledgment has been given by an Academic body to the efforts of a player, and this belief impresses me with the magnitude of the honour which you have conferred. . . . I feel not merely the personal pride of individual success which you thus avow, but that the far nobler work which I aim at is in truth begun. When I think that you, the upholders of the classic in every age, have thus flung aside the traditions of three centuries, and have acknowledged the true union of poet and actor, my heart swells with a great pride that I should be the recipient of such acknowledgment. I trust with all my soul that the reform which you suggest may ere long be carried out, and that that body to whom is justly entrusted our higher moral education may recognise in the Stage a medium for the accomplishment of such ends. What you have done to-day is a mighty stride in this direction. In my profession it will be hailed with joy and gladness—it must elevate, not only the aims of in-

UNIVERSITY HONOURS

dividual actors, but our calling in the eyes of the world. Such honour as you have now bestowed enters not into the actor's dreams of success. Our hopes, it is true, are dazzling. We seek our reward in the approval of audiences, and in the tribute of their tears and smiles; but the calm honour of academic distinction is and must be to us, as actors, the Unattainable, and therefore the more dear when given unsought. . . .

"It is only natural in the presence of gentlemen whose *Alma Mater* holds such state among institutes of learning that I should feel embarrassed in the choice of words with which to thank you; but I beg you to believe this. For my Profession, I tender you gratitude; for my Art I honour you; for myself, I would that I could speak all that is in my soul. But I cannot; and so falteringly tender you my most grateful thanks."

The second honour given on the same day—December 11, 1876—was a "University Night." Trinity had taken all the seats in the theatre and these had been allotted in a sort of rough precedence, University dignitaries coming first, and public men of light and leading—alumni of the University—next and so on to the undergraduates who occupied pit and gallery. An announcement had been made by the Management of the theatre that only those seats not required by the University would be available on the evening for the public. What follows is from the account of the affair written by myself for the Dublin *Mail*.

"The grand reception given to Mr. Irving in Trinity College during the day had increased the interest of the public, and vast crowds had assembled to await the opening of the doors. A little before seven the sound of horns was heard in the College, and from the gate in Brunswick Street swept a body of five hundred students, who took the seats reserved for them in the pit of the theatre. Then gradually the boxes began to fill, and as each Fellow and Professor and well-known University character made his appearance, he was cheered according to the measure of his popularity. . . . All University men, past and present, wore rosettes. Long before the time appointed for beginning the play the whole house was crammed from floor to ceiling; the pit and galleries were seas of heads, and the box lobbies were filled with those who were content to get an occasional glimpse of the stage through the door. When Mr. Irving made his appearance the pit rose at him, and he was received with a cheer which somewhat resembled a May shower, for it was sudden, fierce, and short, as the burst of welcome was not allowed to interrupt the play. The Duke of Connaught arrived during the second act, and received a hearty and prolonged cheer, but not till the scene was ended. Mr. Irving's performance was magnificent. It seemed as though he were put on his mettle by the University distinction of the day to do justice to the stateliness of his mighty theme, and, at the same time, was fired to the utmost enthusiasm—as it was, indeed, no wonder—at the warmth of his reception. In the philosophic passage 'To be or not to be,' and the advice to the players, there was a quiet, self-possessed dignity of thought which no man could maintain if he did not know that he had an appreciative audience, and that he was not talking over their heads. In the scene with Ophelia he acted as though inspired, for there was a depth of passionate emotion evident which even a great actor can but seldom feel; and in the play scene he stirred the house to such a state of feeling that there was a roar of applause. During the performance he was called before the drop-scene several times; but it was not till the green curtain fell that the pent-up enthusiasm burst forth. There was tremendous applause, and when the actor came forward the whole house rose simultaneously to their feet, and there was a shout that made the walls ring again. Hats and handkerchiefs were waved, and cheer upon cheer swelled louder and louder as the player stood proudly before his audience, with a light upon his face such as never shone from the floats. It was a pleasant sight to behold—the sea of upturned faces in the pit, clear, strong young faces, with broad foreheads and bright eyes—the glimpse of colour as the crimson rosettes which the students wore flashed with their every movement—the gleaming jewels of the ladies in the boxes—the moving mass of hats and handkerchiefs, and above all the unanimity with which everything was done. It was evident that in the theatre this night was a body moved by a strong *esprit de corps*, for without any fugleman every movement was simultaneous. They took their cue from the situation, moved by one impulse to do the same thing. It was, indeed, a tribute of which any human being might be proud. For many minutes the tempest continued, and then, as one man, the house sat down, as Mr. Henry Irving stepped forward to make his speech, which was as follows :

"'Ladies and Gentlemen,—Honest steadfast work in any path of life is almost sure to bring rewards and honours ; but they are rewards and honours so unexpected and so unprecedented that they may well give the happy recipient a new zest for existence. Such honours you have heaped upon me. For the welcome you have given me upon these classic boards—for the proud distinction your grand old University has bestowed upon me—a distinction which will be remembered as long as the annals of our stage will last—for these honours accept the truest, warmest, and most earnest thanks that an overflowing heart tries to utter, and you cannot think it strange that every fibre of my soul throbs and my eyes are dim with emotion as I look upon your faces and know that I must say "Goodbye." Your brilliant attendance on this, my parting performance, sheds a lustre upon my life. I only hope that I have your " God's blessing," as you have mine.'

" At the close of his speech Mr. Irving seemed much affected, as, indeed, it was no wonder, for the memory of Saturday night is one which he will carry to his grave. Not Mr. Irving alone, but the whole of the profession should be proud of such a tribute to histrionic genius, for the address in the University and the assemblage at the theatre not only adds another sprig to the actor's well-won crown of laurel, but it marks an era in the history of the stage."

When the performance was over a vast crowd of young men, nearly all students, waited outside the stage door to escort the actor to his hotel, the Shelbourne, in St. Stephen's Green. This they did in noble style. They had come prepared with a long, strong rope, and taking the horses from the carriage harnessed themselves to it. There were over a thousand of them, and as no more than a couple of hundred of them could get a hand on the rope the rest surrounded us—for I accompanied my friend on that exciting progress—on either side a shouting body. The street was a solid moving mass and the wild uproar was incessant. To us the street was a sea of faces, for more than half the body were turning perpetually to have another look at the hero of the hour. Up Grafton Street we swept, the ordinary passengers in the street falling of necessity back into doorways and side streets; round into St. Stephen's Green, where the shouting crowd stopped before the hotel. Then the cheering became more organised. The desultory sounds grew into more exact and recurring volume till the cheers rang out across the great square and seemed to roll away towards the mountains in the far distance. Irving was greatly moved, almost overcome; and in the exuberance of his heart asked me seriously if it would not be possible to ask all his friends into the hotel to join him at supper. This being manifestly impossible, as he saw when he turned to lift his hat and say good-night and his eyes ranged over that seething roaring crowd, he asked could he not ask them all to drink a health with him. To this the hotel manager and the array of giant constables—then a feature of the Dublin administration of law and order, who had by this time arrived, fearing a possibility of disorder from so large a concourse of students—answered with smiling headshake a *non possumus*. And so amid endless cheering and relentless hand-shaking we forced a way into the hotel.

That the occasion was marked by rare orderliness—for in those days town and gown fights were pretty common—was shown by the official Notice fixed on the College gate on Monday morning:

> " At Roll-call to-night the Junior Dean will express his grateful sense of the admirable conduct of the Students on Saturday last, at Mr. Irving's Reception in Trinity College, and subsequently at the performance in the Theatre Royal."

After that glorious night Henry Irving with brave heart and high hopes, now justified by a new form of success, left Ireland for his own country, where fresh triumphs awaited him.

V

CONVERGING STREAMS

A Reading in Trinity College—James Knowles—Hamlet the Mystic — Richard III. — The Plantagenet Look— "Only a Commercial" — True Sportsmen — Coming Events

I

IN June 1877 Henry Irving paid a flying visit to Dublin in order to redeem his promise of giving a Reading in Trinity College. It must have been for him an arduous spell of work. Leaving London by the night mail on Sunday he arrived at half-past six in the morning of Monday, June 18, at Kingstown, where I met him. He had with him a couple of friends: Frank A. Marshall, who afterwards edited Shakespeare with him; and Harry J. Loveday, then and afterwards his stage manager. The Reading was in the Examination Hall; on the wall of which is the portrait of Queen Elizabeth, Founder of the College, and in the gallery of which is a fine old organ said to have been taken from one of the galleons of the Armada wrecked on the Irish coast. The hall was crowded in every corner and there was much enthusiasm. He read part of *Richard III.*, part of *Othello*, Calverley's *Gemini et Virgo*, and Dickens' *Copperfield and*

A READING IN TRINITY COLLEGE

the Waiter, and recited *The Dream of Eugene Aram.*

He was wildly cheered in the Hall; and in the Quadrangle when he came out, he was "chaired" on men's shoulders all round the place. Knowing that particular game is best played by the recipient of the honour and surmising what the action of the crowd would be, I was able to help him. I had already coached him when we had breakfasted together at the hotel as to how to protect himself; and in the rush I managed to keep close to him to see that the wisdom of my experience was put in force. Being chaired is sometimes dangerous from the fact that some of the young enthusiasts who do it are not experts in the game. Often they do not know or realise the necessity of holding to one another as well as to their victim, and so in the whirl they get pulled in different ways and lose their feet. Now the way to secure safety in such cases—in all cases of chairing—is for the one chaired to at once twist the fingers of each hand in the hair of the bearers closest to him, right and left. If all goes well there is no harm done, and even the hair-pulling is not painful. But if there be an accident the danger is averted, for it is not possible that the victim can fall head down; feet down does not matter. The instant the pull comes on the hair of the bearers they resist it; bad for them, but safety for the one in danger. Years afterwards, in 1894, I saw Irving saved by this means from possibly a very nasty accident when, at his being chaired in the Quadrangle of the Victoria University of Manchester, the bearers got pulled in different ways and he was falling head down; his legs being safe held tight in the clutches of two strong young men.

That night he dined in Hall with the Fellows at the High Table and was afterwards in the Commination Room where I too was a guest, and where we remained till it was time for him to leave for London by the night mail. Edward Lefroy, brother of the present Dean of Norwich—a brilliant and most promising young journalist, who unhappily died a few years afterwards—and I saw him off from Kingstown.

His reading that day of *Richard III.* gave me a wonderful glimpse of his dealing with that great character. There was something about it so fine —at once so subtle and so masterly—that it made me long to see the complete work.

II

Thirteen days afterwards, I was in London and saw him at the Lyceum in *The Lyons Mail*, I sat in his dressing-room between the acts. My visit to London was my holiday for that year and took in the Handel Festival. I saw a good deal of Irving, meeting him on most days.

I may here give an instance of his thoughtful kindness. Since our first meeting the year before, he had known of my wish to get to London where as a writer I should have a larger scope and better chance of success than at home. One morning, July 12, I got a letter from him asking me to call at 17 Albert Mansions, Victoria Street, at half-past one and see Mr. Knowles. I did so, and on arriving

ADVICE FROM JAMES KNOWLES

found that it was the office of the *Nineteenth Century*. There I saw the Editor and owner, Sir (then Mr.) James Knowles, who received me most kindly and asked me all sorts of questions as to work and prospects. Presently whilst he was speaking he interrupted himself to say:

"What are you smiling at?" I answered:

"Are you not dissuading me from venturing to come to London as a writer?"

After a moment's hesitation he said with a smile:

"Yes! I believe I am."

"I was smiling to think," I said, "that if I had not known the accuracy and wisdom of all you have said I should have been here long ago!"

That seemed to interest him; he was far too clever a man to waste time on a fool. Presently he said:

"Now, why do you think it better to be in London? Could you not write, to me for instance, from Dublin?"

"Oh! yes I could write well enough, but I have known that game for some time. I know the joy of the waste-paper basket and the manuscript returned—unread. Now Mr. Knowles," I went on, "may I ask you something?"

"Certainly!"

"You are, if I mistake not, a Scotchman?" He nodded acquiescence, keeping his eyes on me and smiling as I went on:

"And yet you came to London. You have not done badly either, I understand! Why did you come?"

"Oh!" he answered quickly, "far be it from

me to make little of life in London or the advantages of it. Now look here, I know exactly what you feel. Will you send me anything which you may have written, or which you may write for the purpose, which you think suitable for the *Nineteenth Century?* I promise you that I shall read it myself; and if I can I will find a place for it in the magazine!"

I thanked him warmly for his quick understanding and sympathy, and for his kindly promise. I said at the conclusion:

"And I give you my word that I shall never send you anything which I do not think worthy of the *Nineteenth Century!*"

From that hour Sir James and I became close friends. I and mine have received from him and his innumerable kindnesses; and there is for him a very warm corner in my heart.

Strange to say that the next time we spoke of my writing in the *Nineteenth Century* was when in 1881 he asked me to write an article for him on a matter then of much importance in the world of the theatre. I asked him if it was to be over my signature. When he said that was the intention I said:

"I am sorry I cannot do it. Irving and I have been for now some years so closely associated that anything I should write on a theatrical subject might be taken for a reflex of his opinion or desire. Since we have been associated in business I have never written anything regarding the stage unless we shared the same view. And whilst we are so associated I want to keep to that rule. Otherwise it would not be fair to him, for he might get odium in some form for an opinion which he did not hold! As a matter of fact we join issue on this particular subject!"

The first time I had the pleasure of writing for him was when in 1890 I wrote an article on "Actor-Managers" which appeared in the June number. Regarding this, Irving's opinion and my own were at one and I could attack the matter with a good heart. I certainly took pains enough for I spent many, many hours in the Library of my Inn, the Inner Temple, reading all the "Sumptuary" laws in the entire collection of British Statutes. Irving himself followed my own article with a short one on the subject of the controversy on which we were then engaged.

III

In the Autumn of that year, 1877, Irving again visited Dublin, opening in *Hamlet* on Monday, November 19. The year's work had smoothed and rounded his impersonation, and to my mind, improved even upon its excellence. I shall venture to quote again some sentences from my own criticism upon it. Not that I mean to set myself up as an infallible authority, but it is as well to place on record here the evidence of an independent and sincere opinion. What one wrote at the time has in its own way its historical value. I should say that in the year not only the public had learned something—much; but that he too had learned also, even of his own instinctive ideas —up to then not wholly conscious. We all had learned, acting and reacting on each other. We had followed him. He, in turn, encouraged and aided by the thought as well as the sympathy of others and feeling justified in further advance, had let his own ideas grow, widening to all the points of the intellectual compass and growing higher and deeper than had been possible to his unaided efforts. For original thought must, after all, be in part experimental or tentative. It is in the consensus of many varying ideas, guesses and experiences—reachings out of groping intelligences into the presently dark unknown—that the throbbing heart of true wisdom is to be found. In my criticism I said:

> "Mr. Irving has not slackened in his study of Hamlet, and the consequence is an advance. All the little fleeting subtleties of thought and expression which arise from time to time under slightly different circumstances have been fixed and repeated till they have formed an additional net of completeness round the whole character. To the actor, art is as necessary as genius, for it is only when the flashes of genius evoked by occasion have been studied as facts to be repeated, that a worthy reproduction of effect is possible. . . . Hamlet, as Mr. Irving now acts it, is the wild, fitful, irresolute, mystic, melancholy prince that we know in the play; but given with a sad, picturesque gracefulness which is the actor's special gift. . . . In his most passionate moments with Ophelia, even in the violence of his rage, he never loses that sense of distance—of a gulf fixed—of that acknowledgment of the unseen which is his unconscious testimony to her unspotted purity. . . ."

The lesson conveyed to me by his acting of which the above is the expression was put by him into words in his Preface to the edition of Diderot's *Paradox of Acting* translated by Walter Pollock and published in 1883—six years after he had been practising the art by which he taught and illuminated the minds of others.

During this engagement Irving played *Richard III.*, and his wonderful acting satisfied all the hopes aroused by sample given in his Reading at the University. For myself I can say truly that I sat all the evening in a positive quiver of intellectual delight. His conception and impersonation of the part were so "subtle, complete and masterly" —these were the terms I used in my criticism written that night—that it seemed to me the power of acting could go no further; that it had reached the limit of human power. Most certainly it raised him still higher in public esteem. Its memory being still with me, I could fully appreciate the power and fineness of Tennyson's criticism which I heard long afterwards. When the poet had seen the piece he said to Irving:

"Where did you get that Plantagenet look?"

IV

In those days a small party of us, of whom Irving and I were always two, very often had supper in those restaurants which were a famous feature of men's social life in Dublin. There were not so many clubs as there are now, and certain houses made a speciality of suppers—Jude's, Burton Bindon's, Corless's. The latter was famous for "hot lobster" and certain other toothsome delicacies and had an excellent grill, and so we often went there. By that time Irving had a great vogue in Dublin, and since the Address in College and the University night in 1876 his name was in the public mind associated with the University. All College men were naturally privileged persons with him, so that any one who chose to pass himself off as a student could easily make his acquaintance. The waiters in the restaurant, who held him in great respect, were inclined to resent this, and one night at Corless's when a common fellow came up and introduced himself as a Scholar of Trinity College—he called it " Thrinity "—Irving, not suspecting, was friendly to him. I looked on quietly and enjoyed the situation, hoping that it might end in some fun. The outsider having made good his purpose wished to show off before his friends, men of his own style who were grinning at another table. When he went over towards them, our waiter who had been hovering round us waiting for his chance—his napkin taking as many expressive flickers as the tail of Whistler's butterfly in *The Gentle Art of Making Enemies*—stooped over to Irving and said in a hurried whisper :

"He said he was a College man, sur ! He's a liar ! He's only a Commercial ! "

V

During his fortnight in Dublin I drove one Sunday with Irving in the Phœnix Park, the great park near Dublin which measures some seven miles in circumference. Whilst driving through that section known as the " Nine Acres " we happened on a scene which took his fancy hugely. In those days wrestling was an amusement much in vogue in Ireland, chiefly if not wholly amongst the labouring class. Bouts used to be held on each Sunday afternoon in various places, and naturally the best of the wrestlers wished to prove themselves in the Capital. Each Sunday some young man who had won victory in Navan, or Cork, or Galway, or wherever exceptional excellence had been manifested, would come up to town to try conclusion in the "Phaynix" generally by aid of a subscription from his fellows or his club, for they were all poor men to whom a long railway journey was a grave expense. There was no prize, no betting; it was Sport, pure and simple; and sport conducted under fairer lines I have never seen or thought of. We saw the gathering crowd and joined them. They did not know either of us, but they saw we were gentlemen, strangers to themselves, and with the universal courtesy of their race put us in the front when the ring had been formed. This forming of the ring was a unique experience. There were no police present, there were no stakes or ropes; not even a whitened mark on the grass. Two or three men of authority amongst the sportsmen made the ring. It was done after this fashion: One man, a fine, big, powerful fellow, was given a drayman's heavy whip. Then one of those with him took off his cap and put it before the face of the armed man. Another guided him from behind in the required direction. Warning was called out lustily, and any one not getting at once out of the way had to take the consequence of that fiercely falling whip. It was wonderful how soon and how excellently that ring was formed. The manner of its doing, though violent exceedingly, was so conspicuously and unquestionably fair that not even the most captious or quarrelsome could object.

Then the contestants stepped into the ring and made their little preparations for strife. Two splendid young men they were—Rafferty of Dublin and Finlay of Drogheda—as hard as nails and full of pluck. The style of wrestling was the old-fashioned "collar and elbow" with the usual test of defeat : both shoulders on the ground at once. It was certainly a noble game. A single bout sometimes lasted for over a quarter of an hour ; and any one who knows what the fierce and unrelenting and pauseless struggle can be, and must be in any kind of equality, can understand the strain. What was most noticeable by us however was the extraordinary fairness of the crowd. Not a word was allowed ; not a hint of method of defence or attack ; not an encouraging word or sign. The local men could have cheered their own man to the echo ; but the stranger must of necessity be alone or with only a small backing at best. And so, as encouragement could not be equal for the combatants, there should be none at all !

It was a lesson in fair play which might have shone out conspicuously in any part of the civilised world—or the uncivilised either if we do not "count the grey barbarian lower than the Christian child."

Irving was immensely delighted with it and asked to be allowed to give a prize to be divided equally between the combatants ; a division which showed the influence on his mind of the extraordinary fairness of the conditions of the competition. In this spirit was the gift received. Several of the men came round me whom they had by this time recognised as an old athlete of "the College"—now a "back number" of some ten years' standing. When I told them who was the donor they raised a mighty cheer.

The only difficulty we left behind us was that of "breaking" the bank-note which had been given. We saw them as we moved off producing what money they had so as to make up his half for the stranger to take with him to Drogheda.

VI

One evening in that week Irving came up to supper with me in my rooms after *The Bells*. We were quite alone and talked with the freedom of understanding friends. He spoke of the future and of what he would try to do when he should have a theatre all to himself where he would be sole master. He was then in a sort of informal partnership with Mrs. Bateman and had of course the feeling of limitation of expansive ideas which must ever be when there is a sharing of interests and responsibilities. He was quite frank as to the present difficulties, although he put them in the most kindly way possible. I had a sort of dim idea that events were moving in a direction which within a year became declared. He had spoken of a matter at which he had hinted shortly after our first meeting: the possibility of my giving up the post I then occupied in the Public Service and sharing his fortunes in case he should have a theatre quite his own. The hope grew in me that a time might yet come when he and I might work together to one end that we both believed in and held precious in the secret chamber of our hearts. In my diary that night, November 22, 1877, I wrote:

" London in view ! "

VI

JOINING FORCES

"Vanderdecken"—Visit to Belfast—An Irish Bull—I join Irving—Preparations at the Lyceum—The Property Master "getting even"

I

HENRY IRVING produced Wills's play *Vanderdecken* at the Lyceum on June 8, 1878. I had arrived in London the day before and was able to be present on the occasion. The play was a new version of the legend of the " Flying Dutchman " and was treated in a very poetical way. Irving was fine in it, and gave one a wonderful impression of a dead man fictitiously alive. I think his first appearance was the most striking and startling thing I ever saw on the stage. The scene was of the landing-place on the edge of the fiord. Sea and sky were blue with the cold steely blue of the North. The sun was bright and across the water the rugged mountain-line stood out boldly. Deep under the shelving beach, which led down to the water, was a Norwegian fishing-boat whose small brown foresail swung in the wind. There was no appearance anywhere of a man or anything else alive. But suddenly there stood a mariner in old-time dress of picturesque cut and faded colour of brown and peacock blue with a touch of red. On his head was a sable cap. He stood there, silent, still and fixed, more like a vision made solid than a living man, realising well the description of the phantom sailor of whom Thekla had told in the ballad spoken in the first act:

> "And the Captain there
> In the dismal glare
> Stands paler than tongue can tell
> With clenchéd hand
> As in mute command
> And eyes like a soul's in Hell!"

It was marvellous that any living man should show such eyes. They really seemed to shine like cinders of glowing red from out the marble face. The effect was instantaneous and boded well for the success of the play. In my criticism I wrote:

> "In his face is the ghastly pallor of the phantom Captain and in his eyes shines the wild glamour of the lost—in his every tone and action there is the stamp of death. Herein lies the terror—we can call it by no other name—of the play. The chief actor is not quick but dead. Twice only does he sound the keynote to the full. In the third act, when before fighting with Olaf he curses him for 'trifling with my eternal happiness,' and again in the last act when he answers to Thekla's question: 'Where are we?':
> "'Between the living and the dead!'"

But the play itself wanted something. The last act, in which Thekla sails away with the phantom lover whose soul had been released by her unselfish love, was impossible of realisation by the resources of stage art of the time. Nowadays, with calcium lights and coloured "mediums" and electricity, and all the aids to illusion which Irving had himself created or brought into use, much could be done.

For such acting the play ought to have been a great one; but it fell short of excellence. It was a great pity; for Irving's appearance and acting in it were of memorable perfection.

On the next day, Sunday, I spent hours with Irving in his rooms in Grafton Street helping him to cut and alter the play. We did a good deal of work on it and altered it considerably for the better I thought.

The next morning I breakfasted with him in his rooms; and, after another long spell of work on the play, I went with him to the Lyceum to attend rehearsal of the altered business.

That evening I attended the Lyceum again and thought the play had been improved. So had Irving too, so far as was possible to a performance already so complete. I supped with him at the Devonshire Club, where we talked over the play and continued the conversation at his own rooms till after five o'clock in the morning.

The next day I went to Paris, but on my return saw *Vanderdecken* again and thought that by practice it had improved. It played " closer " and the actors were more at ease—a most important thing in an eerie play!

II

In August of the same year, 1878, Henry Irving paid another visit to Ireland. He had promised to give a Reading in the Ulster Hall for the benefit of the Belfast Samaritan Hospital, and this was in the fulfilment of it. By previous arrangement the expedition was enlarged into a holiday. As the Reading was to be on the 16th he travelled from London on the night mail of the 12th. I met him on his arrival at Kingstown in the early morning. He was to stay with my eldest brother, Sir Thornley Stoker (he was in great spirits—something like a schoolboy off on a long-expected holiday). Here he spent three very enjoyable days, a large part of which were occupied in driving-excursions to Lough Bray and Leixlip. On the 15th Irving and Loveday and I went to Belfast. After having a look at the Ulster Hall, a huge hall about as big as the Manchester Free Trade Hall, we supped with a somewhat eccentric local philanthropist, David Cunningham. Mr. Cunningham was a large man, tall and broad and heavy and with great bald head which rose dome-shaped above a massive frontal sinus. He was the best of good fellows, the mainstay of the Samaritan Hospital, and a generous helper of all local charities.

The Reading was an immense success. Over three thousand persons were present, and at the close was a scene of wild enthusiasm. We supped again with David Cunningham—he was one of the " Christian name" men whose surname is seldom heard and never alone. A good many of his friends were present and we had an informal and joyous time. There were, of course lots of speeches. Belfast is the very home of fiery and flamboyant oratory and all our local friends were red-hot Orangemen.

On this occasion, however, we were spared any contentious matter, though the harmless periods of the oratory of the " Northern Acropolis," as some of them called their native city, were pressed

into service. One speaker made as pretty an
"Irish Bull" as could be found—though the "bull"
is generally supposed to belong to other provinces
than the hard-headed Ulster. In descanting on
the many virtues of the guest of the evening he
mentioned the excellence of his moral nature and
rectitude of his private life in these terms:

"Mr. Irving, sir, is a gentleman what leads a life
of unbroken blemish!"

Years afterwards when at a large and fashionable
luncheon-party at Chicago, given in honour of
Washington's birthday, I, as one of the strangers,
was asked to speak of Washington, I got out of my
difficulties by relating, after saying that I would
apply to the Father of his Country the words used to
the actor, the incident of that notable speech. The
fun of it was instantaneously received; I was able
to sit down amidst a burst of laughter and applause.

We sometimes kept late hours in the seventies.
That night we left our host's house at three o'clock
A.M. On our return to the hotel Irving and I sat
up talking over the events of the day. The sun
was beginning to herald his arrival when we
began, but in spite of that we sat talking till the
clock struck seven.

I well understood even then, though I understand it better now, that after a hard and exciting
day or night—or both—the person most concerned
does not want to go to bed. He feels that sleep is
at arm's-length till it is summoned. Irving knew
that the next day he would have to start at three
o'clock on a continuous journey to London, which
would occupy some fifteen hours; but I did not
like to thwart him when he felt that a friendly chat

of no matter how exaggerated dimensions would rest him better than some sleepless hours in bed.

III

Irving's visit to Dublin as an actor began in that year, 1878, on September 23, and lasted a fortnight. During this time I was a great deal with him, not only in the theatre during rehearsals as well as at the performances, but we drove almost every day and dined and supped at the house of my brother and sister-in-law, with whom he was great friends; at my own lodgings or his hotel; at restaurants or in the houses of other friends. It was a sort of gala time to us all, and through every phase of it —and through the working time as well—our friendship grew and grew.

We had now been close friends for over two years. We understood each other's nature, needs and ambitions, and had a mutual confidence, each towards the other in his own way, rare amongst men. It did not, I think, surprise any of us when six weeks after his departure I received a telegram from him from Glasgow, where he was then playing, asking me if I could go to see him at once on important business.

I was with him the next evening. He told me that he had arranged to take the management of the Lyceum into his own hands. He asked me if I would give up the Civil Service and join him; I to take charge of his business as Acting Manager.

I accepted at once. I had then had some thirteen years in the public service, a term entitling me to pension in case of retirement from ill-health (as distinguished from "gratuity" which is the rule for shorter period of service); but I was content to throw in my lot with his. In the morning I sent in my resignation and made by telegram certain domestic and other arrangements of supreme importance to me at that time—and ever since. We had decided that I was to join him on December 14 as I should require a few weeks to arrange matters at home. I knew that as he was to open the Lyceum on December 31 time was precious, and accordingly did all required with what expedition I could.

I left Glasgow on November 25, and took up my work with Irving at Birmingham on December 9, having in the meantime altered my whole business life, arranged for the completion of my book on *The Duties of Petty Sessions Clerks*, and last, not least, having got married—an event which had already been arranged for a year later.

Irving was staying at the Plough and Harrow, that delightful little hotel at Edgbaston, and he was mightily surprised when he found that I had a wife—*the* wife—with me.

IV

We finished at Birmingham on Saturday December 14, and on Sunday he went on with the company to Bristol whilst we came on to London. The week at Birmingham had been a heavy time. I had taken over all the correspondence and the letters were endless. It was the beginning of a vast experience of correspondence, for from that on till the day of his death I seldom wrote, in working times, less than fifty letters a day. Fortunately—for both myself and the readers, for I write an extremely bad hand—the bulk of them were short. Anyhow I think I shall be very well within the mark when I say that during my time of working with Henry Irving I have written in his name nearer half a million than a quarter of a million letters!

But the week in Birmingham was child's play compared with the next two weeks in London. The correspondence alone was greater; but in addition the theatre which was to be opened was in a state of chaos. The builders who were making certain structural alterations had not got through their work; plasterers, paper-hangers, painters, upholsterers were tumbling over each other. The outside of the building was covered with men and scaffolding. The whole of the auditorium was a mass of poles and platforms. On the stage and in the paint-room and the property-rooms, the gas-rooms and carpenter's shop and wardrobe-room, the new production of *Hamlet* was being hurried on under high pressure.

On the financial side of things too, there were matters of gravity. Irving had to begin his management without capital—at least without more than that produced by his tour and by such accommodation as he could get from his bankers on the security of his property.

These were matters of much work and anxiety, for before the curtain went up on the first night of his management he had already paid away nearly ten thousand pounds, and had incurred liability for at least half as much more on the structure and what the lawyers call "beautifyings" of the Lyceum.

He had taken over the theatre as from the end of August 1878, so that there was a good deal of extra expense even whilst the theatre was lying idle; though such is usual in some form in the "running" of a theatre.

In another place I shall deal with Finance. I only mention it here because at the very start of his personal enterprise he had to encounter a very great difficulty.

Nearly all the work was new to me, and I was not sorry when on the 19th my colleague, Mr. H. J. Loveday, the stage manager, arrived and took in hand the whole of the stage matters. When Irving and the company arrived four days after, things both on the stage and throughout the house were beginning to look more presentable. When the heads of departments came back to work, preparations began to hum.

V

One of these men, Arnott, the Property Master and a fine workman, had had an odd experience during the Bristol week. Something had gone wrong with the travelling "property" horse used in the vision scene of *The Bells*, and he had come up to town to bring the real one from the storage. In touring it was usual to bring a "profile" representation of the gallant steed. "Profile" has in theatrical parlance a special meaning other than its dictionary meaning of an "outline." It is thin wood covered on both sides with rough canvas carefully glued down. It is very strong and can be cut in safety to any shape. The profile horse was of course an outline, but the art of the scene-painter had rounded it out to seemingly natural dimensions. Now the "real" horse, though a lifeless "property," had in fact been originally alive. It was formed of the skin of a moderately sized pony; and being embellished with picturesque attachments in the shape of mane and tail was a really creditable object. But it was expensive to carry as it took up much space. Arnott and two of his men ran up to fetch this down as there was not time to make a new profile horse. When they got to Paddington he found that the authorities refused to carry the goods by weight on account of its bulk, and asked him something like £4 for the journey. He expressed his feelings freely, as men occasionally do under irritating circumstances, and said he would go somewhere else. The clerk in the office smiled and Arnott went away; he was a clever man who did not like to be beaten, and railways were his natural enemies. He thought the matter over. Having looked over the time-table and found that the cost of a horse-box to Bristol was only £1 13s., he went to the department in charge of such matters and ordered one, paying for it at once and arranging that it should go on the next fast train. By some manœuvring he so managed that he and his men took Koveski's horse into the box and closed the doors.

When the train arrived at Bristol there had to be some shunting to and fro so as to place the horse-box in the siding arranged for such matters. The officials in charge threw open the door for the horse to walk out. But he would yield to no blandishment, nor even to the violence of chastisement usual at such times. A little time passed and the officials got anxious, for the siding was required for other purposes. The station at Bristol is not roomy and more than one line has to use it. The official in charge told him to take out his damned horse!

"Not me!" said he, for he was now seeing his way to "get back" at the railway company, "I've paid for the carriage of the horse and I want him delivered out of your premises. The rate I paid includes the services of the necessary officials."

The porters tried again, but the horse would not stir. Now it is a dangerous matter to go into a horse-box in case the horse should prove restive. One after another the porters declined, till at last one plucky lad volunteered to go in by the little window close to the horse's head. Those on the platform waited in apprehension, till he suddenly ran out from the box laughing and crying out:

"Why you blamed fools. He ain't a 'orse at all. He's a stuffed 'un!"

VI

As I have said, Arnott always got even in some way with those who tried to best him. I remember once when a group of short lines, now amalgamated into the Irish Great Northern Railway and worked in quite a different way, did what we all considered rather too sharp a thing. We had to have a special train to go from Dublin to Belfast on Sunday. For this they charged us full fare for every person and a rate for the train as well. Then when we were starting they took, at the ordinary rate, other passengers in *our* train for which we had paid extra. This, however, was not that which awoke Arnott's ire. The *causa teterrima belli* was that whilst they gave us only open trucks for goods they charged us extra for the use of tarpaulins, which are necessary in railway travelling where goods are inflammable and sparks many. Having made the arrangement I had gone back to London on other business, and did not go to Belfast so I did not know what had happened later till after the tour had closed. When I was checking the accounts in my office at the Lyceum, I found that though the railway company had charged us what we thought was an exorbitant price, still the cost of the total journey compared favourably with that of other journeys of equal length. I could not understand it until I went over the accounts, comparing item by item with the other journeys. Thus I "focussed" the difference in the matter of "goods." Then I found that whereas the other railways had charged us on somewhere about nineteen tons weight this particular line had only assessed us at seven. I sent for Arnott and asked him how could the difference be, as on the first journey I had verified the weight as I usually did, such saving much trouble throughout a tour as it made the check easier. He shook his head and said that he did not know. I pressed him, pointing out that either this railway had underweighed us or that others had overweighed.

WEIGHING SCENERY

"Oh, the others were all right, sir," he said. "I saw them weighed at Euston myself!"

"Then how on earth can there be such a difference?" I asked. "Can't you throw any light on it?" He shook his head slowly as though pondering deeply and then said with a puzzled look on his face:

"I haven't an idea. It must have been all right for the lot of them was there, and the lot of us, too. There couldn't have been any mistake with them *all* looking on. No, sir, I can't account for it; not for the life of me!" Then seeing that I turned to my work again he moved away. When he was half way to the door he turned round, his face brightening as though a new light had suddenly dawned upon him. He spoke out quite genially as though proud of his intellectual effort:

"Unless it was, sir, that there was some mistake about the weighin'. You see, while the weighin' was goin' on we was all pretty angry about things. We because they was bestin' of us, and they because we was tellin' 'em so, and rubbin' in what we thought of 'em in a general way. Most of us thought that there might have been a fight and we was all ready —the lot of us—on both sides. We was standin' close together for we wouldn't stir and they had to come to us. . . . An'—it might have been that me and the boys was standin', before they came to join us on the platform with the weights! I dare say we wasn't so quarrelsome when we moved a bit away for there was more of them than of us; an' they stood where we had been. They didn't want to follow us. An'—an'—the weighin' was done by them!"

VII

One more anecdote of the Property Master.

We were playing in Glasgow at the Theatre Royal, which had just been bought by Howard and Wyndham. J. B. Howard was a man of stern countenance and masterful manner. He was a kindly man, but Nature had framed him in a somewhat fierce mould. His new theatre was a sacred thing, and he liked to be master in his own house. We were playing an engagement of two weeks; and on the first Saturday night it was found that a certain property—a tree trunk required for use in *Hamlet*, which was to be played on Tuesday night— was not forthcoming. So Arnott was told to make another at once and have it ready, for it required time to dry. Accordingly he went down to the theatre on Sunday morning with a couple of his men. There was no one in the theatre; in accordance with the strict Sabbath-keeping then in vogue at Glasgow, local people were all away—even the hall-keeper. Such a small matter as that would never deter Arnott. He had his work to do, and get in he must. So he took out a pane of glass, opened a window, and went in. In the property shop he found all he required; wood, glue, canvas, nails, paint; so the little band of expert workmen set to work, and having finished their task, came away. They had restored the window pane, and came out by the door. On Monday morning there was a hub-bub. Some one had broken into the theatre and taken store of wood and canvas, glue, nails and paint and there in the shop lay a fine property log already " set "

A ZEALOUS SERVANT

and drying fast. Inquiry showed that none of the local people were to blame. So suspicion naturally fell on our men, and we did not deny the soft impeachment. Howard was fuming; he sent for the man to have it out with him. Arnott was a fine, big, well-featured north-countryman, with large limbs and massive shoulders—such a man as commanded some measure of respect even from an angry manager.

"I hear that you broke into my theatre yesterday and used up a lot of my stores?"

"Yes sir! The theatre was shut up and there was no time."

"Time has nothing to do with it, sir. Why did you do it?"

"Well, Mr. Howard, the governor ordered it and Mr. Loveday told me not to lose any time in getting it ready as we had to rehearse to-day." This accounted to Mr. Howard, the man, for the breach of decorum; but as the manager he was not satisfied. He was not willing to relinquish his grievance all at once; so he said, and he said it in the emphatic manner customary to him:

"But sir, if Mr. Loveday was to tell you to take down the flys of my theatre would you do that, too?"

The answer came in a quiet, grave voice:

"Certainly, sir!"

Howard looked at him fixedly for a moment and then raising both hands in front of him said, as he shrugged his shoulders:

"In that case I have nothing more to say! I only wish to God that my men would work like that!" And so the quasi-burglar went unreproved.

VII

THE LYCEUM PRODUCTIONS

DURING Henry Irving's personal management of the Lyceum he produced over forty plays, of which eleven were Shakespeare's; *Hamlet, The Merchant of Venice, Othello, Romeo and Juliet, Much Ado About Nothing, Twelfth Night, Macbeth, Henry VIII., King Lear, Cymbeline,* and *Richard III. Coriolanus* was produced during his agreement with the Lyceum Company. He also reproduced six plays which he had before presented during his engagement by and partnership with the Batemans: *Eugene Aram, Richelieu, Louis XI., The Lyons Mail, Charles I., The Bells.* He also produced the following old plays, in most of which he had already appeared at some time: *The Lady of Lyons, The Iron Chest, The Corsican Brothers, The Belle's Stratagem, Two Roses, Olivia, The Dead Heart, Robert Macaire,* and a good many "curtain-raisers" whose excellences were old and tried.

The new plays were in some instances old stories told afresh, and in the remainder historic subjects treated in a new way or else quite new themes or translations. In the first category were *Faust, Werner, Ravenswood, Iolanthe* (one act). In the second were: *The Cup, The Amber Heart, Beckett, King Arthur, Madame Sans-Gêne, Peter*

IRVING'S "PRODUCTIONS"

the Great, The Medicine Man, Robespierre and the following one-act plays: *Waterloo, Nance Oldfield,* and *Don Quixote. Dante* was produced after the Lyceum Company had been unable to carry out their contract with him.

This gives an average of two plays, "by and large" as the sailors say, for each year from 1878 to 1898, after which time he sold his rights to the Lyceum Theatre Company, Limited. Regarding some of these plays are certain matters of interest either in the preparation or the working. I shall simply try, now and again, to raise a little the veil which hangs between the great actor and the generations who may be interested in him and his work.

VIII

IRVING BEGINS MANAGEMENT

The "Lyceum Audience"—"Hamlet"—A Lesson in Production—The Chinese Ambassador—Catastrophe averted—The Responsibility of a Manager—Not Ill for Seven Years

I

THE first half-year of Irving's management was, in accordance with old usage, broken into two seasons, the first ending on May 31 and the second beginning on June 1. This was the last time except in the spring of 1881 that such an unnatural division of natural periods took place. After that during the entire of his management the "season" lasted until the theatre closed. And as the coming of the hot weather was the time when, for the reason that the theatre-going public left London, the theatre had to be closed, about the end of July became practically the time for recess. It had become an unwritten law that Goodwood closed the London theatre season, just as in Society circles the banquet of the Royal Academy, on the first Saturday in May, marked the formal opening of the London "season." This made things very comfortable for the actors who by experience came to count on from forty-six to forty-eight weeks salary in a year. This was certainly so in the Lyceum, and in some other theatres of recognised position.

II

The first season made great interest for the public. It was all fairly new to me, for except when I had been present at the first night of Wills's *Medea* played by Mrs. Crowe (Miss Kate Bateman) in July 1872 and had seen Irving in *The Lyons Mail* in 1877 and had been at the performance and rehearsal of *Vanderdecken* in 1878, I had not been into the theatre till I came officially. As yet I knew nothing at all of the audiences, from the management point of view. I soon found an element which had only anything like a parallel in the enthusiasm of the University in Dublin. Here was an audience that *believed* in the actor whom they had come to see; who took his success as much to heart as though it had been their own; whose cheers and applause—whose very presence, was a stimulant and a help to artistic effort.

This was the audience that he had won—had made; and I myself, as a neophyte, was in full sympathy with them. With such an audience an artist can go far, and in such circumstances there seems nothing that is not possible on the hither side of life and health. The physicists tell us that it is a law of nature that there must be two forces to make impact; that the anvil has to do its work as well as the hammer. And it is a distinguishing difference between scientific and other laws that the former has no exceptions.

So it is in the world of the theatre. Without an audience in sympathy no actor can do his best. Nay more, he should have the assurance of approval, or else sustained effort at high pitch becomes impossible. Some people often think, and sometimes say, that an actor's love of applause is due to a craving vanity. This may be in part true, and may even be wholly true in many cases; but those who know the stage and its needs and difficulties, its helps and thwarting checks, learn to dread a too prolonged stillness. The want of echoing sympathy embarrasses the player. For my own part, having lived largely amongst actors for a quarter of a century; having learned to understand their motives, to sympathise with their aims, and to recognise their difficulties, I can understand the basic wisdom of George Frederick Cook when on the Liverpool stage he stopped in the middle of a tragic part and coming down to the footlights said to the audience:

"Ladies and gentlemen, if you don't applaud I can't act!"

It was from Irving I heard the story; and he certainly understood and felt with that actor of the old days. If the members of any audience understood how much better value they would get for their money—to put the matter on its lowest basis—when they show appreciation of the actor's efforts, they would certainly now and again signify the fullest recognition of his endeavour.

This "Lyceum audience," whose qualities endeared them to me from that first night, December 30, 1878, became a quantity to be counted on for twenty-four years of my own experience. Nay more, for when the Lyceum came as a theatre to an end, the audience followed Irving to Drury Lane. They or their successors in title were present on that last night of his season, June 10, 1905, that memorable night when he said farewell, not knowing that it would be the last time he should ever appear in London as a player.

III

The production with which the season of 1878-9 opened was almost entirely new. When Irving took over the Lyceum the agreement between him and Mrs. Bateman entitled him to the use of certain plays and *matériel* necessary for their representation. But he never contented himself with the scenery, properties or dresses originally used. The taste of the public had so improved and their education so progressed, chiefly under his own influence, that the perfection of the seventies would not do for later days. For *Hamlet* new scenery had been painted by Hawes Craven, and of all the dresses and properties used few if any had been seen before. What we had seen in the provinces was the old production. I remember being much struck by the care in doing things, especially with reference to the action. It was the first time that I had had the privilege of seeing a play " produced." I had already seen rehearsals, but these except of pantomime had generally been to keep the actors, supers and working staff up to the mark of excellence already arrived at. But now I began to understand *why* everything was as it was. With regard to stagecraft it was a liberal education. Often and often in the years since then, when I have noticed the thoughtless or careless way in which things were often done on other stages, I have wondered how it was that the younger generation of men had not taken example and reasoned out at least the requirements of those matters incidental to their own playing. Let me give an example:

"In the last act, the cup from which Gertrude drinks the poison is an important item inasmuch as it might have a disturbing influence. In one of the final rehearsals, when grasped by Hamlet in a phrenzy of anxiety lest Horatio should drink: 'Give me the cup; let go; by heaven, I'll have it!' the cup, flung down desperately rolled away for some distance and then following the shape of the stage rolled down to the footlights. There is a sort of fascination in the uncertain movement of an inanimate object and such an occurrence during the play would infallibly distract the attention of the audience. Irving at once ordered that the massive metal goblet used should have some bosses fixed below the rim so that it could not roll. At a previous rehearsal he had ordered that as the wine from the cup splashed the stage, coloured sawdust should be used—which it did to exactly the same artistic effect.

In another matter of this scene his natural kindness made a sweet little episode which he never afterwards omitted. When he said to the pretty little cup-bearer who offered him the poisoned goblet: "Set it by awhile!" he smiled at the child and passed his hand caressingly over the golden hair.

Certain other parts of his Hamlet were unforgettable. His whirlwind of passion at the close of the play scene which, night after night, stirred the whole audience to frenzied cheers. The extraordinary way in which by speech and tone, action and time, he conveyed to his auditory the sense of complex and entangled thought and motive in his wild scene with Ophelia. His wonderment at the announcement of Horatio:

" I think I saw him yester-night."
Hamlet. "Saw who?"
Horatio. "My Lord, the King your Father."
Hamlet. "The King—my father?"

And the wonderful way in which he conveyed his sense of difference of the subjective origin of the ghost at its second appearance at which Shakespeare hinted, following out Belleforest's remark on the novel: "in those days, the northe parts of the worlde, living as then under Sathans lawes, were full of inchanters, so that there was not any young gentleman whatsoever that knew not something therein sufficient to serve his turne, if need required. . . . Hamlet, while his father lived, had been instructed in that devilish art, whereby the wicked spirite abuseth mankind, and advertiseth him (as he can) of things past."

Of things past! Hamlet could know of things that had been though he could not read the future. This it was which was the essence of his patient acquiescence in the ways of time—half pagan fatalism, half Christian belief, as shown in that pearl amongst philosophic phrases:

"If it be now, 'tis not to come; if it be not to come, it will be now; if it be not now, yet it will come; the readiness is all."

IV

Hamlet was played ninety-eight nights on that first season. Four of them hang in my mind for very different reasons. The first was that wonderful opening night when the great audience all aflame with generous welcome and exalted by ready sympathy lifted us to unwonted heights.

The second was on January 18, the eighteenth night of *Hamlet*. The Chinese Ambassador, the Marquis Tsêng, came to see the play and with him came Sir Halliday Macartney.

After the third act the Ambassador and Sir Haliday Macartney came to see Irving in his dressing-room, where they stayed some time talking. It was interesting to note—Sir Halliday translated his remarks verbally—how accurately the Ambassador followed the play, which he had not read nor heard of. Where he failed was only on some small points of racial or theological difference. He seemed to be absolutely correct on the human side.

Presently we all went down on the stage whilst Ellen Terry as Ophelia was in the midst of her mad scene. Irving and Sir Halliday and I were talking and, in the interest of the conversation, we all temporarily overlooked the Ambassador. Presently I looked round instinctively and was horrified to see that he had moved in on the stage and was then close to the edge of the arch at the back of the scene where Ophelia had made her entrance and would make her exit. He was in magnificent robes of Mandarin yellow and wore such adornments as are possible to a great official who holds

HENRY IRVING AS HAMLET

Copy of drawing made in his dressing-room by Fred Barnard, 1874

the high grade and honour of the Peacock's Feather. I jumped for him and just succeeded in catching him before he had passed into the blaze of the limelight. I could fancy the sudden amazement of the audience and the wild roar of laughter that would follow when in the midst of this most sad and pathetic of scenes would enter unheralded this gorgeous anachronism. Under ordinary circumstances I think I should have allowed the *contretemps* to occur. Its unique grotesqueness would have ensured a widespread publicity not to be acquired by ordinary forms of advertisement. But there was greater force to the contrary. The play was not yet three weeks old in its run; it was a tragedy and the holy of holies to my actor-chief to whom full measure of loyalty was due; and beyond all it was Ellen Terry who would suffer.

V

The third was a very sad occasion, but one which showed that the manager of a theatre must have "nerve" to do the work entailed by his high responsibility. He remained in the wings O.P. ("Opposite Prompt" in stage parlance) after scene ii of Act I. The following scene (iii), is a front scene ready for the change to the "front scene" where Polonius gives good advice to his children Laertes and Ophelia. After the few words between the brother and sister on the cue of Laertes: "here my father comes," Polonius enters speaking quickly as one in surprise: "Yet here Laertes! Aboard, aboard, for shame!"

Irving instinctively turned on hearing the intonation of the voice, and after one lightning glance signed to the prompter to drop the act-drop, which was done instantly. I was standing beside him at the time talking to him and was struck by the marvellous rapidity of thought and action; of the decision which seemed almost automatic. Then the curtain having been drawn back sufficiently to let him pass he stepped to the footlights and said:

"Ladies and gentlemen, I regret to have to tell you that something has happened which I should not like to tell you; and will ask you to bear in patience a minute. We shall, with your permission, go on from the beginning with the third scene of Act I." He stepped back amid instantaneous and sympathetic applause. Perhaps some knew; some few must have seen for themselves what had occurred, and many undoubtedly guessed. But all recognised the mastery and decision which had saved a very painful and difficult situation. The curtain straightened behind him as he passed in on the stage.

In an incredibly short time all was ready, for stage workmen as well as actors are adepts at their trade. Within seven or eight minutes the curtain went up afresh and the play began anew—with a different Polonius.

That night a call went up for the whole company and employees—"Everybody concerned on the stage" at noon the next day.

It was a grave and solemn gathering; and all were there except one who had received a kindly intimation that he need not attend. Irving came on the stage from the office on the stroke of the hour. Loveday and I were with him. He stood in front of the footlights with his back to the auditorium. He spoke for a few minutes only; but that speech must have sunk deeply into the hearts of every listener. He reminded them of the loyalty which is due from craftsmen to one another. Of the loyalty which is due to a manager who has to think for all. And finally of the loyalty which is due—and was on the unhappy occasion to which he referred—due to their own comrade. " By that want of loyalty," he said, " in any of the forms, you have helped to ruin your comrade. Some of you *must* have noticed; at least those who dressed in the room with him or saw him in the Green Room. Had I been told—had the stage manager had a single hint from any one, we could, and would, have saved him. The lesson would perhaps have been to him a bitter one, but it would have saved him from worse disaster. As it is, no other course was open to me to save him from public shame. As it is, the disaster of last night may injure him for life. And it is *you* who have done this. Now, my dear friends and comrades, let this be a lesson to us all. We must be loyal to each other. That is to be helpful, and it is to the honour of our art and our calling! "

There he stopped and turned away. No one said a word. For a short space they stood still and then melted slowly away in silence like the multitude of a dream.

VI

The fourth occasion was on the night of March 27 when Irving, having been taken with a serious cold, was unable to play—the first time he had been out of the bill for seven years! The note in my diary runs:

> "Stage very dismal. Ellen Terry met me in the passage and began to cry! I felt very like joining her!"

I instance this as a fair illustration of how Irving was loved by all with whom he came in personal contact.

IX

SHAKESPEARE PLAYS—I

"The Merchant of Venice"—Preparation—The Red Handkerchief—Booth and Irving—"Othello"—A Dinner at Hampton Court—The Hat

I

IRVING did not think of playing *The Merchant of Venice* until he had been to the Levant. The season of 1879–80 had been arranged before the end of the previous season. We were to commence with *The Iron Chest;* Irving had considerable faith in Colman's play and intended to give it a run. It was to be followed in due course, as announced in his farewell speech at the end of the second season, by *The Gamester, The Stranger, Coriolanus,* and *Robert Emmett*, a new play by Frank Marshall. It was rather a surprise, therefore, when on October 8 before the piece had run two weeks, he broached the subject of a new production. It had been apparent to us since his return from a yachting-trip in the Mediterranean that he was not so much in love with the play as he usually was with anything which he had immediately in hand. Even if a play did not seem to fill him, I never saw him show the slightest sign of indifference to it in any other case.

On that particular evening he asked Loveday and me if we could stay and have a chop in the Beefsteak Room. He was evidently full of something of importance; it seemed a relief to him when supper was finished and the servant who waited had gone. When we had lit our cigars he said quietly:

"I am going to do *The Merchant of Venice*." We both waited, for there was nothing to say until we should know a little more. He went on:

"I never contemplated doing the piece which did not ever appeal very much to me until when we were down in Morocco and the Levant. You know the *Walrus*" (that was the fine steamer which the Baroness Burdett Coutts had chartered for her yachting party) "put into all sorts of places. When I saw the Jew in what seemed his own land and in his own dress, Shylock became a different creature. I began to understand him; and now I want to play the part—as soon as I can. I think I shall do it on on the first of November! Can it be done?"

Loveday answered it would depend on what had to be done.

"That is all right," said Irving. "I have it in my mind. I have been thinking it over and I see my way to it. Here is what I shall have in the 'Casket' scene." He took a sheet of notepaper and made a rough drawing of the scene, tearing out an arch in the back and propping another piece of paper in it with a rough suggestion of a Venetian scene. "I will have an Eastern lamp with red glass—I know where is the exact thing. It is, or used to be two or three years ago, in that furniture shop in Oxford Street, near Tottenham Court Road."

THE "RED HANDKERCHIEF"   85

Then he went on to expound his idea of the whole play; and did it in such a way that he set both Loveday and myself afire with the idea. We talked it out till early morning. Indeed the Eastern sun was outlining the beauty of St. Mary's-le-Strand as the time-roughened stone stood out like delicate tracery against the blush of the sunrise. Then and often since have I thought that Sir Christopher Wren must have got his inspiration regarding St. Mary's on returning late—or early in the morning from a supper in Westminster. The church is ugly enough at other times, but against sunrise it is a picturesque delight.

As we parted Irving smiled, as he said:

"Craven had better get out that red handkerchief, I think."

Therein lay a little joke amongst us. Hawes Craven who was—as happily he still is—a great scene-painter and could work like a demon when time pressed. Ordinarily he wore when at work in those days a long coat once of a dark colour, and an old brown bowler hat, both splashed out of all recognition with paint. Scene-painting is essentially a splashy business, the drops of paint from the great brushes, of necessity vigorously used to cover the acres of canvas, " come not in single spies but in battalions." But when matters got desperate, when the pressure of the time-gauge registered not in hours but in minutes, the head-gear was changed for a red handkerchief which twisted round the head made a sort of turban. This became in time a sort of oriflamme. We knew that there was to be no sleep, and precious little pause even for food, till the work was all done.

Of course no mortal man could do the whole of the scenery in the three weeks available. Scenes had to be talked over, entrances and exits fixed and models made. Four scene-painters bent their shoulders to the task. Craven did three scenes, Telbin three, Hann three and Cuthbert one. The whole theatre became alive with work. Each night had its own tally of work with the running play; but from the time the curtain went down at night till when the doors were opened the following night work at full pressure never ceased. Properties and dresses and " appointments " came in completed every day. Rehearsals went on all day. On Saturday night, November 1, just over three weeks after he had broached the idea, and less than three from the time the work was actually begun—the curtain went up on *The Merchant of Venice*.

It had an unbroken run of two hundred and fifty nights; the longest run of the play ever known.

It is a noteworthy fact that one of the actors, Mr. Frank Tyars, who played the Prince of Morocco, after being perfect for two hundred and forty-nine nights forgot some of his words on the two hundred and fiftieth.

For twenty-six years that play remained in the working *répertoire* of Henry Irving. He played Shylock over a thousand times.

II

The occasion of Irving's producing *Othello* during his own management was due to his love and remembrance of Edwin Booth. In 1860, at the

Henry Irving as Shylock.
from a Pastel by J. B. Yeats, 1880.
in the possession of the Author

PLAY-BILL: FECHTER AND IRVING, BIRMINGHAM, 1865

PLAY-BILL: BOOTH AND IRVING, MANCHESTER, 1861

Theatre Royal, Manchester, Irving began a long engagement. In the bill his name is announced: "His first appearance." In November of the following year Booth appeared as a star, playing *Othello*, Irving being the Cassio; *Hamlet*, Irving being the Laertes; *A New Way to Pay Old Debts*, he of course taking Sir Giles Overreach, and Irving Wellborn. For his benefit he gave on Friday night *Romeo and Juliet*, in which Irving played Benvolio to his Romeo. Often, when we talked of Booth some twenty years afterwards, he told me of the extraordinary alertness of the American actor; of his fierce concentration and tempestuous passion; of the blazing of his remarkable eyes. It will be seen from the comparison of their respective parts in the plays set out that the difference between them in the way of status as players was marked. The theatre has its own etiquette, and stars were supposed to have a stand-off manner of their own. These things have changed a good deal in the interval, but in the early sixties it was a real though an impalpable barrier, as hard to break through as though it were compact of hardier material than shadowy self-belief. Naturally the men did not have much opportunity for intimacy, but Irving never forgot the bright young actor who had won his heart as well as his esteem. Twenty years afterwards, when the younger man had won his place in the world, and when his theatre was becoming celebrated as a national asset, Booth again visited England. Whoever had arranged his business did not choose the best theatre for him. For in those days the Princess's in Oxford Street did not have a high dramatic *cachet*. He got a good reception of course;

but the engagement was not a satisfactory one, and Booth was much chagrined. I was there myself on the night of his opening, November 6, 1880, on which he played *Hamlet*. I was much disappointed with the *ensemble*; for though Booth was fine neither the production nor the support was worthy of his genius and powers. The management was a new one and the manager a man who had been used to a different class of theatre. Also there were certain things which jarred on the senses of any one accustomed to a finer order. This was none of Booth's doing; he was the sufferer by it. Booth and Irving had met at once after the former had come to London, and had renewed their old acquaintance but on a more intimate basis. In those days there was a certain class of busybodies who tried always to make mischief between Americans and English; twenty-five years ago the *entente cordiale* was not so marked as became noticeable after the breaking out of the war between America and Spain. There were even some who did not hesitate to say that Booth had not been fairly received in London. Irving jumped to the difficulty, went at once to Booth and said to him:

"Why don't you come and play with me at the Lyceum? I'll put on anything you wish; or if there is any play in which we can play together, let us do that."

Booth was greatly delighted, and took the overture in the same good spirit in which it was meant. He at once told Irving that he would like to appear in *Othello*. Irving said:

"All right! You decide on the time; and I'll get the play ready, if you will tell me how you would like it arranged."

SUGGESTION FOR IAGO'S DRESS

Drawn by Henry Irving, 1881

Booth said he would like to leave all that to his host, as he had not himself taken a part in the production of plays for years and did not even attend rehearsals. So Irving took all the task on himself. When he asked Booth whether he would like to play Othello or Iago—for he played both—he said he would like to begin with Othello and that it would, he thought, be well if they changed week about; and so it was arranged. The performance began on May 2, 1881.

By Booth's wish *Othello* was only to be played three times a week, as he was averse from the strain of such a heavy part every night. The running bill —*The Cup* and *The Belle's Stratagem*—kept its place on the other three. For the special performances some of the prices were altered, stalls nominally ten shillings becoming a guinea, the dress-circle seats being ten shillings instead of six. The prices for the off night remained as usual.

The success of *Othello* was instantaneous and immense. During the seven weeks the arrangement lasted the houses were packed. And strange to say the takings of the off nights were not affected in any way.

III

The two months thus occupied made a happy time for Booth. He came down to rehearsal early in the week before the production and was so pleased that he never missed a rehearsal during the remainder of the time. He said more than once that it had given him a new interest in his work. In social ways too the time went pleasantly. Several of his distinguished countrymen were then staying in London, and no matter how strenuous work might be, time was found for enjoyment though the days had to be stretched out in the manner suggested in Tommy Moore's ballad :

"For the best of all ways to lengthen our days
Is to steal a few hours from the night, my dear!"

On Sunday, June 12, John McCullough gave a party at Hampton Court, where we dined at the Greyhound. We drove down in four-in-hand drags and spent the late afternoon walking through the beautiful gardens of Hampton Court. June in that favoured spot is always delightful.

There was an amusing episode on our dilatory journeying among the flowers. One of the gardeners, a bright-faced old fellow for whom Nature had been unkind enough to use the mould wrought for the shaping of Richard III., on being asked some trivial question gave so smart an answer that we all laughed. Then began a hail of questions; the old man, smiling gleefully, answered them as quick as lightning. One by one nearly all the party joined in; but to one and all a cunnning answer was given without slack of speed, till the whole crowd was worsted. One of the party asked the gardener if he would lend him his hat for a minute. The old man handed it, remarking in a manifestly intended stage aside :

"It'll be no use to him. The brains don't go with it!" The man who had borrowed it, "Billy" Florence, put it on the grass, open side up, and said :

"Now boys!"

Instantly a rain of money, more of it gold than silver and some folded notes fell into the hat. Then

MENU OF McCULLOUGH'S DINNER AT HAMPTON COURT,
JUNE 12, 1881

with a handshake all round the clever old fellow toddled off. The names of that party will show most people of the great world, even twenty years afterwards, that there was no lack of "brains" in that crowd, even enough possibly to answer effectually to the sallies of one old man. Most of them may be seen on the obverse of the dinner *menu* which they signed:

John McCullough
Henry Irving
Arthur Cecil
J. L. Toole
Ernest Bendall.
Edmund Yates
Lewis Wingfield
Charles Dickens (the younger)
John Clayton
Edwin Booth

C. A. Whittier
F. C. Burnand
W. J. Florence
W. W. Tucker
Bram Stoker
George Augustus Sala
Whitelaw Reid (now the United States Ambassador to England)
Lord Mandeville (afterwards Duke of Manchester)

One night at supper in the Beefsteak Room, Irving told me an amusing occurrence which took place at Manchester when Booth played there. He said it was "about 1863," so it may have been that of which I have written, of 1861. *Richard III.* was put up, Charles Calvert, the manager, playing Richmond, and Booth Gloster. Calvert determined to make a brave show of his array against the usurper, and being manager was able to dress his own following to some measure of his wishes. Accordingly he drained the armoury of the theatre and had the armour furbished up to look smart. Richard's army came on in the usual style. They were not much to look at though they were fairly comfortable for their work of fighting. But Richmond's army enthralled the senses of the spectators, till those who knew the play began to wonder how such an army *could* be beaten by the starvelings opposed to them. They were not used to fight, or even to move in armour, however; and the moment they began to make an effort they one and all fell down and wriggled all over the stage in every phase of humiliating but unsuccessful effort to get up; and the curtain had to be lowered amidst the wild laughter of the audience.

X

SHAKESPEARE PLAYS—II

"Romeo and Juliet"—Preparation—Music—The Way to carry a corpse—Variants of the Bridal Chamber—"Much Ado About Nothing" John Penberthy—Hypercriticism—Respect for feelings

I

Romeo and Juliet was the first great Shakespearean production which Irving made under his own management. *Hamlet* had been done on very simple lines; the age in which it is set not allowing of splendour. *The Merchant of Venice* had been entirely produced and rehearsed within three weeks. But the story of "Juliet and her Romeo," perhaps the greatest and most romantic love-story that ever was written, is one which not only lends itself to, but demands, picturesque setting. For its tragic basis the audience must understand the power and antiquity of the surroundings of each of these unhappy lovers. Under conditions of humbler life the tragedy would not have been possible; in still loftier station, though there might have been tragedy, it would have been wrought by armed force on one of the rival Houses or the other. It is necessary to give something of the luxury, the hereditary feud of two dominant factions represented by their chiefs, of the ingrained bloodthirstiness of the age of the Italian petty States. Irving knew this well, and with his superlative stage instinct grasped the picturesque possibilities The Capulets and the Montagues must be made not only living forces, but typal.

What Irving's intention was may be seen in the opening words which he wrote himself in the short preface to the published Acting Version of the play:

> "In producing this tragedy, I have availed myself of every resource at my command to illustrate without intrusion the Italian warmth, life, and romance of this enthralling love-story."

It was produced on May 8, 1882, and ran for one hundred and sixty-one nights, the summer vacation intervening.

Extraordinary care was taken in the preparation of the play. In the beginning Irving had asked Mr. Alfred Thompson, known as a popular designer of dresses for many plays, to design the costumes. This he did; but as they were not exactly what was wanted, not a single one of them was used in the piece. Irving himself selected the costumes from old pictures and prints, and costume books. He chose and arranged the colours and stuff to be used. Nevertheless, with his characteristic generosity, he put in the playbill and advertisements Mr. Thompson's name as designer. For the scenery also he made initial suggestions, all in reference to exactness of detail and the needs of the play in the way of sentiment as well as of action. The scenery was really most beautiful and poetic and won much κυδος for the painters, Hawes Craven, William Telbin and Walter Hann.

In another way too a new departure was made. Hitherto it had been a custom in theatres that the musical director should compose or select whatever incidental music was necessary. In every great theatre might be found a really good musician in charge of the orchestra; and on him the management wholly relied for musical help and setting. But with regard to *Romeo and Juliet* Irving thought that the theme was a tempting one for a composer of note to take in hand. If this could be arranged not only would the play as a whole benefit enormously, but even its business aspect would be greatly enhanced by the addition of the new strength. He wished that Sir Julius Benedict should compose special music for the new production. We were then on a provincial tour; but I ran up to London and saw Sir Julius, who was delighted to undertake the task. In due time charming music was completed.

So long before as June 1880, on two different nights, 14th and 16th, Irving and I supped alone in the Beefsteak Room and on each occasion talked of *Romeo and Juliet*. For a long time the play had been in Irving's mind as one to be produced when the proper opportunity should come. In his early days in the "fifties" he had played both Paris and Tybalt; and we may be sure that in his ambitious soul and restless eager brain the tragic part of Romeo was shaping itself for future use. More than twenty years afterwards, when the dreams of power to do as he wished on the stage had grown first to possibilities and then to realities, he certainly convinced me that his convictions of the phases of character were quite mature. He had followed

Romeo through all his phases, both of character and emotion. He seemed to have not only the theory of action and pose and inflection of voice proper for every moment of his appearance, but the habit of doing it, which is the very stronghold of an actor's art. To me his conception was enlightening with a new light.

The words: "Thou canst not teach me to forget" he took to strike a key-note of the play. He rehearsed them over and over again, not only on the stage but on several occasions when we were alone, or when Loveday was also with us. I well remember one night when we three were alone and had supped after the running play, *Two Roses*, when he was simply bubbling over with the new play. Over and over again he practised the action of leaning on Benvolio, and the tone and manner of the speech. In it there was a distinct duality of thought—of existence. He managed to convey that though his mind was to a measure set on love with a definite object, there was still a sterner possibility of a deeper passion. It seemed to show the heart of a young man yearning for all-compelling love, even at the time when the pale phantom of such a love claimed his errant fancy.

Once he was started on this theme he went on with fiery zeal to other passages in the play, till at last the pathos of the end touched him to his heart's core. I find an entry in my diary:

"H. much touched at tragedy of last act, and in speaking the words wept."

That night too, we practised carrying the body of Paris into the tomb. In the first instance he asked me, as one who had been an athlete, to show him how I would do it. Accordingly Loveday lay on the floor on his back whilst I lifted him, Irving keenly watching all the time. Standing astride over the body I took it by the hinches—as the wrestlers call the upper part of the hips—and bending my legs whilst at the same moment raising with my hands, keeping my elbows down, and swaying backwards I easily flung it over my shoulder. Irving thought it was capital, and asked me to lift him so that he could understand the motion. I did so several times. Then I lay down and he lifted me, easily enough, in the same way. It must have required a fair effort of strength on his part; for he was a thin, spare man whilst I was over twelve stone. He said that that method would do very well and looked all right, but that it might prove too much of a strain in the stress of acting. So we put off other experiments till another evening.

Some ten days after, my brother George, who had been all through the Russo-Turkish war as a surgeon in the Turkish service, was in the theatre. He had been Chief of Ambulance of the Red Crescent and had been in the last convoy into Plevna and had brought to Philippopolis all the Turkish wounded from the battle at the Schipka Pass, and had had about as much experience in the handling of dead bodies as any man wants. Irving thought it might be well to draw on his expert knowledge, and after supper asked him what was the easiest way of carrying a dead body, emphasising the " easiest "; accordingly I, who was to enact the part of " body," lay down again. George drew my legs apart, and stooping very low with his back to me, lifted the legs in turn so that the inside of my knees rested on his shoulders. Then, catching one of my ankles in each hand, he drew my body up till the portion of my anatomy where the back and legs unite was pressed against the back of his neck. He then straightened his arms and rose up, my body, face outward, trailing down his back and my arms hanging limp. It was just after the manner of a butcher carrying the carcase of a sheep. It was most certainly the "easiest" way to carry a body —there was no possible doubt about that; but its picturesque suitability for stage purpose was another matter. Irving laughed consumedly, and when next we discussed the matter he had come to the conclusion that the best way was to *drag* the body into the entrance of the monument. He would then appear in the next scene dragging the body down the stone stair to the crypt. To this end a body was prepared, adjusted to the weight and size of Paris so that in every way *vraisemblance* was secured.

That production was certainly wonderfully perfect. Some of the scenes were of really entrancing beauty, breathing the Italian atmosphere. Even the supers took fire with the reality of all around them. No matter how carefully rehearsed, they would persist in throwing into their work a martial vigour of their own. The rubric of the scene, as printed from the original, does not give the slightest indication of the wonderful stress of the first scene :

> "Enter Several Persons of both Houses, who join in the Fray: then enter Citizens and Peace Officers, with their Clubs and Partisans."

The scene was of the market-place of Verona with

side streets and at back a narrow stone bridge over a walled-in stream. The "Several Persons," mostly apprentices of the Capulet faction, entered, at first slowly, but coming quicker and quicker till quite a mass had gathered on the hither side of the bridge. The strangers were being easily worsted. Then over the bridge came a rush of the Montagues armed like their foes with sticks or swords according to their degree. They used to pour in on the scene down the slope of the bridge like a released torrent, and for a few minutes such a scene of fighting was enacted as I have never elsewhere seen on the stage. The result of the mighty fight was that during the whole time of the run of the play there was never a day when there was not at least one of the young men in hospital. We tried to make them keep to the business set down for them, for on the stage even a fight between supers is so carefully arranged that no harm can come if they keep to their instructions. But one side or the other would grow so ardent that a nightly trouble of some kind had to be counted upon.

When I look back upon other presentations of *Romeo and Juliet* I can see the exceeding value of all the picturesque realism of Irving's production. I have in my mind's eye two others in London, one of which I saw and the other of which I heard, for we were then in America, where tragedy was lost in the mirth of the audience.

The former was held in the old Gaiety Theatre then under the management of the late John Hollingshead. It was at a *matinée* given by a lady who was ambitious of beginning her theatrical career as Juliet. Of course on such an occasion one has to be contented with the local scenery;

either such as is used in the running play or can be easily taken from and to the storage. The play went fairly well until the third act; William Terriss was the Romeo, and his performance, if not subtle, was full of life and go. But when the scene went up on Juliet's chamber there was a sudden and wild burst of laughter from every part of the house. The stage-management had used a picturesque scene without any idea of suitability. Juliet's bed was set right in the open, on a wide marble terrace with steps leading to the garden!

The other occasion was when the Property Master, with a better idea of customary utility than of picturesque accuracy, had set out for Juliet's bed one of double width—a matrimonial couch with *two* pillows!

II

Much Ado About Nothing followed close after *Romeo and Juliet*, the theatre being closed for three nights to allow of full-dress rehearsals. It began on October 11, 1882, and had an unbroken run of two hundred and twelve nights, being only taken off because the other plays of the *répertoire* for the coming American tour had to be made ready and rehearsed by playing them. This was not only the longest run the play had ever had, but probably the only real run it had ever had at all. It was always one of those plays known as "ventilators" which are put up occasionally with hope on the part of the management that they *may* do something this time, and a moral conviction that they can't in any case do worse than the plays that have already been tried.

AN ENCHANTING PERSONALITY

But Irving had faith in it, and in his own mind saw a way of doing it which would help it immensely. It was beautifully produced and carefully rehearsed. The first act was all brightness and beauty. The cathedral was such as was never before seen on the stage. Even the cathedral servants were new, their brown dresses giving picturesque sombre richness to the scene. Irving had seen such dresses in the cathedral of Seville or Burgos—I forget which—and had noted and remembered. Ellen Terry was born for the part of Beatrice. It was almost as though Shakespeare had a premonition of her coming.

Don Pedro. "Out of question, you were born in a merry hour."

Beatrice. "No, sure, my lord, my mother cried; but then there was a star danced, and under that was I born."

Surely never such a buoyant, winsome, merry, enchanting personality was ever seen on the stage—or off it. She was literally compact of merriment till when her anger with Claudio blazed forth in a brief tragic moment half passion and whole pathos that carried everything before it. And as for tragic strength, none who have ever seen or may ever see it can forget her futile helpless anger, the surging, choking passion in her voice, as striding to and fro with long paces, her whirling words won Benedick to her as in answer to his query: "Is Claudio thine enemy," she broke out:

"Is he not approved in the height a villain, that hath slandered, scorned, dishonoured my kinswoman?—O, that I were a man!—what? bear her in hand until they come to take hands; and then with public accusation, uncovered slander, unmitigated rancour—O God, that I were a man! I'd—I'd—I'd eat his heart in the market-place!"

And then after some combative words with her lover:

"I cannot be a man with wishing, therefore I will die a woman with grieving."

It was that last feminine touch that won Benedick to her purpose of revenge. All the audience felt that he could do no less.

III

By the way, a curious evidence of the truth of its emotional effect came one night, not very long after the play began its long career. I was in my office just after the curtain had gone up on the fourth act, when I was sent for to the front of the house to see some one. In the vestibule I found a tall, powerful, handsome man. He had masterful eyes, a resonant voice and a mouth that shut like steel. A most interesting personality I thought. I introduced myself, and as I had been told he had expressed a wish to see Irving I asked him if he could wait a little as the curtain had gone up. He was very cheery and friendly and he said at once:

"Of course I'll wait. I've just come to London and I came at once to see my cousin Johnny. I haven't seen him since we were boys." I had been trying to place him. This gave me the clue I wanted.

"Are you John Penberthy?" I asked. This delighted him and he shook my hand again as I said that I had often heard of him. From the moment of our meeting we became friends.

JOHN PENBERTHY

John Penberthy was one of the sons of Sarah Behenna, sister of Irving's mother, who had married Captain Isaac Penberthy, a famous mining captain of his time in Cornwall. Whilst a very young man John had gone to South America and had soon become, by his courage and forceful character as well as by his gifts and skill as a miner himself, a great mining captain. He was mostly in the silver mines; he it was who had developed and worked the great Huanchaca mine in Bolivia. For some twenty or more years he had lived in a place and under conditions where a quick eye and a ready hand were the surest guarantees of long life—especially to a man who had to control the fierce spirits of a Spanish mine.

I took him round on the stage, thinking what a surprise as well as a pleasure it would be to Irving to find him there when he came off after the scene. He at once got deeply interested in the scene going on, and now and again as I stood beside him I could see his strong hands closed and hear him grind his teeth. When the scene was over and Irving and Ellen Terry were bowing in the glare of the footlights amid a storm of applause, Captain Penberthy turned to me, his face blazing with generous anger, and said in his native Cornwall accent which he had never lost:

"It was a damned good job for that cur Claudio that I hadn't my shootin' irons on me. If I had I'd soon have blasted hell out of him!"

IV

An instance of the interest of the public in a Lyceum production was shown by a letter received by Irving a few nights after the play had been produced. For one of the front scenes the scene-painter, Hawes Craven, had been given a free hand. He chose for the subject a walk curving away through giant cedars, brown trunks and twisted branches—a noble spot in which to muse. Irving's correspondent pointed out, as well as I remember, that whereas the period is set in the third quarter of the fifteenth century, the cedar was not introduced into Messina until the middle of that century and could not possibly have attained the stature shown in the scene.

Perhaps I may here mention that Irving had some other experiences of the same kind:

When he reproduced *Charles I.* in June 1879, some critical observer called attention to the fact that the trees in the Hampton Court scene, having been planted in the time of Charles, could not possibly have grown within his reign to the size represented.

Again, whilst in Philadelphia in 1894, where we had played *Becket*, the secretary of a Natural History Society wrote a letter—a really charming letter it was too—pointing out that Tennyson had made a mistake in that passage of the last act of the play where Becket speaks of finding a duck frozen on her nest of eggs. Such might certainly occur in the case of certain other wild birds; but not in the case of a duck whose habits made such a tragedy impossible. Irving replied in an equally courteous letter, saying, after thanking him for the interest displayed in the play and for his kindness in calling attention to the alleged error, that there must have been some misreading of the poet's words as he did not mention a duck at all!

> ". . . we came upon
> A wild-fowl sitting on her nest . . ."

V

It may be well to mention here the way in which Irving cared always and in every way for the feelings of the public. In religious matters he was scrupulous against offence. When the church scene of *Much Ado About Nothing* was set for the marriage of Claudio and Hero, he got a Catholic priest to supervise it. He listened carefully whilst the other explained the emblematic value of the points of ritual. The then Property Master was a Catholic and had taken some pains to be correct as to details. When the reverend critic pointed out that the white cloth spread in front of the Tabernacle on the High Altar meant that the Host was within, Irving at once ordered that a piece of cloth of gold should be spread in its place. Again, when he was told that the cross on the ends of the stole of the marrying priest was emblematical of the Sacrament he ordered a fleur-de-lis to be embroidered instead. In the same way, on knowing that the red lamp, hung over the altar-rail by his direction for purely scenic effect, was a sacramental sign he had it altered and others placed to destroy the significance. But not so when as Becket he put on even the pall to go into the cathedral where the murderous huddle of knights awaited him. There he wore the real pall. There were no feelings to be offended then, though the occasion was in itself a sacrament—the greatest of all sacraments—martyrdom. All sensitiveness regarding ritual was merged in pity and the grandeur of the noble readiness :

"I go to meet my King."

XI

SHAKESPEARE PLAYS—III

"Macbeth"—An Amateur Scene-Painter—Sir Arthur Sullivan—A Lesson in Collaboration—"Henry VIII."—Lessons in Illusion—Stage Effects—Reality v. Scenery—A Real Baby and its Consequences

I

OF all the plays of which Irving talked to me in the days of our friendship when there was an eager wish for freedom of effort, or in later times when a new production was a possibility rather than an intention, I think *Macbeth* interested me most. When I met him in 1876 he had already played it at the Lyceum; but somehow it was borne in on me that what had been done was not up to his fullest sense of truth. His instinctive idea of treatment —that which is the actor's sixth sense regarding character—was correct. So much I could tell, for the conviction which was in him came out from him to others. But I do not think that at that time his knowledge of the part was complete. In the consideration of such a play it has to be considered what was Shakespeare's knowledge of its origin; for it is by this means that we can get a guiding light on his intention. That he had studied Wintown and Holinshed is manifest to any one who has read the " Cronykil " of the former or the Chronicle of the latter. Now Irving had got hold of the correct idea of Macbeth's character, and from his own inner consciousness of its working out, combined with the enlightenment of the text, knew that Macbeth had thought of and intended the murder of Duncan long before the opening of the play, and that he and his wife had talked it over. But I think that not at first, nor till after he had re-studied the play, was he aware of the personal relationship between Macbeth and Duncan : that after the King and his sons Macbeth was the next successor to the crown of Scotland. This is according to history, and Shakespeare knew it from Holinshed. But even Shakespeare is somewhat wanting in his way of setting it forth in the play. I know that I myself had from my earliest recollection been always puzzled by the passage in Act I, scene iv, where Macbeth in an aside says :

" The Prince of Cumberland ! that is a step
On which I must fall down, or else o'erleap,
For in my way it lies."

Nothing that has gone before in the play can afford to any unlearned member of an audience any possible clue as to how Macbeth could have been injured or thwarted by an honour shown to his own son by the King who had already showered honours and thanks upon his victorious general. In his Address at Owens College, Manchester, six years after his second production of the play, Henry Irving set forth this and many other critical points with admirable lucidity.

To me Irving's intellectual position with regard to the character from the first was irrefragable. He added scholarship as the time went on; but every addition was an added help to understanding. Between the time when I had first heard him talk over the play and the character in 1876 and when I saw him play it twelve years elapsed. In all that time it was a favourite subject to talk between us, and I think it was one evening in February 1887, on which after he and I having supped alone in the Beefsteak Room talked over the play till the windows began to show their edges brightening in the coming day, that he made up his mind to the reproduction.

We were then deep in the run of *Faust*, which had passed its three hundredth representation at the Lyceum; but in the running of a London theatre it is necessary to look a long way ahead; a year at least. In this case there was need of a longer preview, for our plans had already been made for a considerable time. We were to run *Faust* through the season with some weeks at the end to prepare other plays which together with *Faust* we were to take to America in the tour already arranged for 1887-8. As we should not be back till the spring of the later year the production of a new play, together with the music and selection of the company, had all to be thought of in time. Irving had—and justifiably—great hopes of the play, and spared on it neither pains nor expense. With regard to the scenery he thought that he would get Keeley Halswelle, A.R.S.A., to make the designs. He was very fond of his work and considered that it would be exactly suitable for his purpose. The painter consented and made some lovely sketches.

He expressed a wish to paint the scenes himself,

and when the sketches and then the models in turn had been approved of, we engaged the great paint-rooms of the Covent Garden Opera House, then available, for his use. The canvas-cloths, framed pieces, borders and wings were got ready by our own carpenters and "primed" for the painting.

After a while we began to get anxious about the scenery. We kept asking, and asking and asking as to time of completion; but without result. Finally I paid a visit of inspection to Covent Garden and to my surprise and horror found the acres of white untouched even to the extent of a charcoal outline.

The superb painter of pictures, untutored in stage art and perspective, had found himself powerless before those vast solitudes. He had been unable even to begin his task!

The work was then undertaken by Hawes Craven, J. Harker, T. W. Hall, W. Hann, and Perkins and Carey, with magnificent result.

Macbeth is a play that really requires the aid of artistic completeness. Its diction is so lordly, so poetical, so searching in its introspective power that it lifts the mind to an altitude which requires and expects some corresponding elevation of the senses.

Here, by the way, a certain incident comes back to my memory. In the Queen's Theatre, Dublin, some forty years ago the tragedy was being given and when the actor who played Lennox came to the lines :

"The night has been unruly: where we lay,
Our chimney was blown down . . ."

he spoke them, in the very worst of Dublin accents, as follows :

"The night hath been rumbunctious where we slep,
Our chimbleys was blew down."

For the music incidental to the play Sir Arthur Sullivan undertook the composition. He wrote overture, preludes, incidental music and choruses one and all suitable as well as fine. Throughout there is a barbaric ring which seems to take us back and place us amongst a warlike and undeveloped age. Wherever required he altered it during the progress of rehearsals.

It was a lesson in collaboration to see the way in which these two men, each great in his own craft, worked together. Arthur Sullivan knew that with Irving lay the responsibility of the *ensemble*, and was quite willing to subordinate himself to the end which the other had in view. Small-minded men are unwilling, or perhaps unable, to accept this position. If their susceptibilities are in any way wounded by even a non-recognition of the superiority of their work they are apt to sulk; and when an artist sulks those who have to work with him are apt to encounter a paralysing dead-weight. In any form *vis inertia* is cramping to artistic effort. But these men were both too big for chagrin or jealousy. As example of the harmony of their working and of the absolute necessity in such matters for absolute candour let me instance one scene. Here the music had all been written and rehearsed and Sir Arthur sat in the conductor's chair. In a pause of the rehearsal of action on the stage he said :

"We are ready now, Irving, if you can listen."

"All right, old man; go ahead!" When the

numbers of that particular piece of incidental music had been gone through the composer asked :

"Do you like that? Will it do?" Irving replied at once with kindly seriousness :

"Oh, as music it's very fine ; but for our purpose it is no good at all. Not in the least like it!"

Sullivan was not offended by the frankness. He was only anxious to get some idea of what the other wanted. He asked him if he could give any hint or clue as to what idea he had. Irving, even whilst saying in words that he did not know himself exactly what he wanted, managed by sway of body and movement of arms and hands, by changing times and undulating tones, and by vowel sounds without words to convey his inchoate thought, instinctive rather than of reason. Sullivan grasped the idea and the anxious puzzlement of his face changed to gladness.

"All right!" he said heartily, "I think I understand. If you will go on with the rehearsal I shall have something ready by-and-by." Sitting where he was, he began scoring, the band waiting. When some of the scenes had been rehearsed there was some movement in the orchestra—the crowding of heads together, little chirpy sounds from some of the instruments and then in a pause of the rehearsal :

"Now, Mr. Ball!"—John Meredith Ball was the Musical Director of the Lyceum. "If you are ready now, Irving, we can give you an idea. It is only the theme. If you think it will do I will work it out to-night."

The band struck up the music and Irving's face kindled as he heard.

"Splendid!" he said. "Splendid! That is all I could wish for. It is fine!"

I could not help feeling that such recognition and praise from a fellow artist was one of the rewards which has real value to the creator of good work.

II

It was necessary that *Henry VIII.* should be very carefully done; for its period is well recorded in architecture, stone-carving, goldsmith work, tapestry, stuffs, embroideries, costumes and paintings. Indeed many historical lessons may be taken from this play. Shakespeare, if he did not actually know or intend this, had an intuition of it. *Henry VIII.* marks one of the most important epochs in history, and as it was by the very luxury and extravagance of the nobles of the time that the power of the old feudalism was lowered, such naturally becomes a pivotal point of the play. It was a part of the subtle policy of Cardinal Wolsey to bring the great nobles to London, instead of holding local courts of their own, and surrounding themselves with vast retinues of armed retainers. Combination amongst a few such might shake even the throne. When round the Court of the King they were encouraged and incited to vie with each other in the splendour of their dress and equipment; and soon their capacity for revolt was curbed by the quick wasting of their estates. The wonderful pageant of the Field of the Cloth of Gold had its political use and bearing which the student of the future will do well to investigate. In his play Shakespeare bore all this in mind and took care to lay down in exact detail the order of his processions and rituals. It can be therefore seen that in this renaissance of art with a political meaning—and therefore a structural part of a historical play—it was advisable, if not necessary, to be exact in the *décor* of the play. To this end the greatest care was taken, with of course the added managerial intention of making the piece as attractive as possible. Seymour Lucas (then A.R.A. now R.A.), who undertook to superintend the production, went to and fro examining the buildings and pictures and art work of the period wherever to be found. For months he had assistants working in the South Kensington Museum making coloured drawings of the many stuffs used at that time; reproducing for the guidance of the weavers who were to make up their part of the work in turn, both texture and pattern and colour. Further months were occupied with the looms before the antique stuffs thus reproduced were ready for the costumier.

Irving's own dress—his robe as Cardiual—was, after months of experiment, exactly reproduced from a genuine robe of the period kindly lent to him by Rudolph Lehmann, the painter.

Many lessons in stage values and effects were to be learned from this magnificent production. Let me give a couple of instances. As the period was that of the Field of the Cloth of Gold naturally there was a good deal of cloth of gold used in the English Court; and such, or the effect of it, had to be set forth in the play. A day was fixed when Seymour Lucas was to choose the texture, make and colour of the various patterns of gold cloth submitted. For this purpose the curtain was taken up and the footlights were turned on. A row of chairs, back out, were placed along the front of the stage, and on each was hung a sample of cloth of gold. Lucas and Irving, with Loveday and myself, sat in the stalls; and with us the various artists and workpeople employed in the production of the play—property master, wardrobe mistress, costumiers, &c. Something like the following took place as the painter's eye ranged along the glittering line of fabrics:

"That first one—well, fair. Let it remain! The next, take it away. No use at all! Third and fourth—put them on one side—We may want them for variety. Fifth—Oh! that is perfect! Just what we want!"

When the examination was finished we all went on the stage to look at the specimens accepted and discarded. There we found the second so peremptorily rejected was real cloth of gold at ten guineas a foot; whilst the fifth whose excellence for the purpose we had so enthusiastically accepted was Bolton sheeting stencilled in our own property-room, and costing as it stood about eighteen pence a yard.

Again, very fine jewellery—stage jewellery—had been prepared to go with the various dresses. In especial in the procession at the beginning of the fourth act the collars of the Knights of the Garter were of great magnificence. One of the actors, however, was anxious to have everything as real as possible, and not being content with the splendour of the diamond collars provided, borrowed a real one from one of the Dukes, whose Collar of the Garter was of a magnificence rare even amongst such jewels. He expected it to stand out amongst the other jewelled collars seen in the procession. But strange to say, amongst them all it was the only one that did not look well. It did not even look real. Stage jewels are large and are backed with foil which throws back the fierce light of the " floats " and the " standards " and the " ground rows" and all those aids to illusion which have been perfected by workmen competent to their purpose.

III

The play ends with the christening of the Infant Princess Elizabeth, in which of course a dummy baby was used. This gave a chance to the voices clamant for realism on the stage. When the play had run some forty nights Irving got a letter from which I quote:

"The complete success of *Henry VIII.* was marred when the King kissed the china doll. The whole house tittered. . . . Herewith I offer the hire of our real baby for the purpose of personating the offspring. . . ." To this I replied:

"Mr. Irving fears that there might be some difficulty in making the changes which you suggest with regard to the infant Princess Elizabeth in the play. If reality is to be achieved it should of necessity be real reality and not seeming reality; the latter we have already on the stage. A series of difficulties then arises, any of which you and your family might find insuperable: If your real baby were provided it might be difficult, or even impossible, for the actor who impersonates King Henry VIII. to feel the real feelings of a father towards it. This would necessitate your playing the part of the King; and further would require that your wife should play the part of Queen Anne Boleyn. This might not suit either of you—especially as in reality Henry VIII. had afterwards his wife's head cut off. To this your wife might naturally object; but even if she were willing to accept this form of reality and you were willing to accept the responsibility on your own part, Mr. Irving would, for his own sake, have to object. By law, if you had your wife decapitated you would be tried for murder; but as Mr. Irving would also be tried as an accessory before the fact, he too would stand in danger of his life. To this he distinctly objects, as he considers that the end aimed at is not worth the risk involved.

"Again, as the play will probably run for a considerable time, your baby would grow. It might, therefore, be necessary to provide another baby. To this you and your wife might object—at short notice.

"There are other reasons—many of them—militating against your proposal; but you will probably deem those given as sufficient."

Henry VIII. was produced on the night of Tuesday, January 5, 1892, and ran at the Lyceum for two hundred and three performances, ending on November 5. Its receipts were over sixty-six thousand pounds.

XII

SHAKESPEARE PLAYS—IV

"King Lear"—Illness of Irving—A Performance at sight—"Richard III."—A splendid First Night—A sudden check

I

In the Edinburgh theatre during his three years' engagement there, 1856-9, Irving had played the part of Curan in *King Lear*. This was, I think, the only part which he had ever played in the great tragedy; and it is certainly not one commending itself to an ambitious young actor. It is not what actors call a "fat" part; it is only ten lines in all, and none of those of the slightest importance. But the ambitious young actor had his eye on the play very early, and had thought out the doing of it in his own way. The play was not produced till the end of 1892, but nearly ten years before he had talked it over with me. I find this note rough in my diary for January 5, 1883:

> "Theatre 7 till 2. H. and I supper alone. He told me of intention to play Lear on return from America. Gave rough idea of play—domestic—gives away kingdom round a wood fire, &c."

On the night of the 9th he spoke again of it

Henry Irving as King Lear.
from the Drawing by J. Bernard Partridge.

AN EMERGENCY LEAR

under similar circumstances. And on April 10 he returned to the subject."

King Lear, in the production of which Ford Madox Brown advised, was produced on November 10, 1892, and ran in all seventy-six nights. My diary of November 10 says:

> "First night; *King Lear*. Great enthusiasm between acts. Whilst scenes on, stillness like the grave. An ideal audience. Thunders of applause and cheers at end."

II

On the morning of January 19, after *King Lear* had run for sixty nights, I received a hurried note, written with pencil, from Irving, asking me to call and see him as soon as possible. I hurried to his rooms and found him ill and speechless with "grippe." This was one of the early epidemics of influenza and its manifestations were very sudden. He could not raise his head from his pillow. He wrote on a slip of paper:

"Can't play to-night. Better close the theatre."

"No!" I said, "I'll not close unless you order me to. I'll *never* close!" He smiled feebly and then wrote:

"What will you do?"

"I don't know," I said; "I'll go down to the theatre at once. Fortunately this is a rehearsal day and everybody will be there." He wrote again:

"Try Vezin."

"All right," I said. Just then Ellen Terry, to whom he had sent word, came in. When she knew how bad he was she said to me:

"Of course you'll close, Bram" (we use Christian names a good deal on the stage).

"No!" said I again.

"Then what will you do?"

"I don't know. But we'll play—unless of course *you* won't play!"

"Don't you know that I'll do anything!"

"Of course I do! It will be all right." This was a wild presumption, for at the time Loveday the Stage Manager, was away ill.

All the time Irving was hearing every word, and smiled a little through his pain and illness. He never liked to hear of any one giving up, and I think it cheered him a little to know that things were going on. I went to Mr. Vezin's rooms at once but he was out of town. When I got to the theatre all the company were there. I asked Terriss if he could play Lear. He said no, that he had not studied the part at all—adding in regret: "I only wish to goodness that I had. It will be a lesson to me in the future." I then asked the company in general if any of them had ever played Lear—or could play it; but there was no affirmative reply.

In the company was Mr. W. J. Holloway, who played the part of Kent. He was an old actor—that is, the *actor* was old though the *man* was in active middle age. He had, I knew, played in what is called "leading business" with his own company in Australia, where he had made much success. I asked him if he could read the part that night. If so, I should before the play ask the favour of the audience in the emergency; and that he would then play it "without the book" on the next night. He answered that he would

READING OR PLAYING

rather wait till the next night, by which time he would be ready to play. To this I replied that if we closed for the night we should not re-open until Mr. Irving was able to resume work. After thinking a moment he said:

"Of course any one can *read* a part."

"Then," said I, "will you read it to-night and play to-morrow?"

He answered that he would. So I said to him:

"Now, Mr. Holloway, consider that from this moment till the curtain goes up you own the theatre. If there is anything you want for help or convenience, order it; you have *carte blanche*. Mr. Irving's dresser will make you up, and the Wardrobe Mistress will alter any dress to suit you. We will have a rehearsal if you wish, now or in the evening before the play; or all day, if you like."

"I think," he said after a pause, "I had better get home and try to get hold of the words. I know the business pretty well as I have been at all the rehearsals. I am usually a quick study and it will be so much better if I can do without the book—for part of the time at any rate."

In this he was quite wise; his experience as an old actor stood to him here. Kent is all through the play close to Lear, either in his own person or in disguise. The actor, therefore, who played the part, which in stage parlance is a "feeder," had been at all the rehearsals of Lear's scenes when the "business" of the play is being fixed and when endless repetitions of speech and movement make all familiar with both text and action. Also for sixty nights he had gone through the play till every part of it was burned into his brain. Still, knowledge of a thing is not doing it; and it was a very considerable responsibility to undertake to play such a tremendous part as Lear at short notice.

When he came down at night he seemed easier in his mind than I expected; his wife, who was present though without his knowing it lest it might upset him, told me privately that he was letter perfect—in at least the two first acts. "I have been going over it with him all day," she said, "so I am confident he will be all right."

And he was all right. From first to last he never needed a word of prompting. Of course we had prepared for all emergencies. Not only had the prompter and the call-boy each a prompt book ready at every wing, but all his fellow actors were primed and ready to help.

I shall never forget that performance; it really stirred me to look at it as I did all through from the wings in something of the same state of mind as a hen who sees her foster ducklings toddling into the ditch. I had known that good actors were fine workmen of their craft, but I think I never saw it realised as then. It was like looking at a game of Rugby football when one is running with the ball for a touch-down behind goal with all the on-side men of his team close behind him. *He could not fall or fail if he wanted to.* They backed him up in every possible way. The cues came quick and sharp and there was not time to falter or forget. If any of the younger folk, upset by the gravity of the occasion, forgot or delayed in their speeches some one else spoke them for them. The play went with a rush right through; the only difference from the sixty previous performances being that though the *entr'actes* were of the usual length the play was shorter by some twenty minutes. When the call came at the end the audience showed their approval of Mr. Holloway's plucky effort by hearty applause. When the curtain had finally fallen the actor received that most dear reward of all. His comrades of all ranks closed round him and gave him a hearty cheer. Then the audience beyond the curtain, recognising the rare honour, joined in the cheer till from wall to wall the whole theatre rang.

It was a moving occasion to us all and I am right sure that it bore two lessons to all the actors present, young and old alike: to be ready for chances that *may* come; and to accept the responsibility of greatness in their work when such may present itself.

Of acting in especial, of all crafts the motto might be:

" The readiness is all ! "

III

One other incident of the run of *King Lear* is, I think, worthy of record, inasmuch as it bears on the character and feeling of that great Englishman, Mr. Gladstone. In the second week of the run he came to see the play, occupying his usual seat on the stage on the O.P. corner. He seemed most interested in all that went on, but not entirely happy. At the end, after many compliments to Mr. Irving and Miss Terry, he commented on the unpatriotic conduct of taking aid from the French

—from any foreigners—under any circumstance of domestic stress.

IV

Saturday, December 19, 1896, was an eventful day in Irving's life. That evening, in the full tide of his artistic success and with a personal position such as no actor had ever won, he placed on the stage *Richard III.*, his acting in which just twenty years before had added so much and so justly to the great reputation which he had even then achieved.

His early fight had long been won. The public, and in especial the growing generation whose minds were free from the prejudice of ancient custom, had received his philosophic acting without cavil; the "Irving school" of acting had become a part of the nation's glory.

From the early morning of that day crowds were waiting to gain admission. Many of those in the passage to the pit door, leading in from the Strand, had camp-stools. One man had brought a regular chair so that he might sit all day with as little discomfort as possible. At four o'clock, when a great crowd had assembled, Irving had them all supplied with tea and bread-and-butter at his own expense. This was a custom which had grown up under his care and which made for a feeling of great personal kindness between the actor and his unknown friends. Most of those who waited at the pit door on first nights were young ladies and gentlemen and of course quite able to provide for themselves. But nothing would induce them to have a cup of tea till it was sent out to them by the management. That came to be a part of their cherished remembrance of such occasions, and was not to be foregone.

Many and many a time since then have I met in society persons, both ladies and gentlemen, who introduced themselves as old friends since the days when I had spoken to them, whilst waiting, through the iron rail which kept them from lateral pressure by new-comers and preserved the *queue*.

That day they were in great force, and even then, long before the house was, or could be, opened, there was no denying the hope-laden thrill of expectation with which they regarded the coming of the night's endeavour.

They were well justified, for nothing, so far as the Richard was concerned, could have gone with more marked success. The audience was simply wild with enthusiasm. That alone helps to make success in a theatre; the whole place seems charged with some kind of electric force and every one is lifted or even exalted beyond the common—the actors to do, the others to be receptive. At the close of the performance there were endless calls and cheering which made the walls ring.

In his very early youth Irving had found a certain attractiveness in *Richard III.*, though doubtless he did not then know or realise what a play was. His cousin, John Penberthy, told me in 1890 how when they were both boys " Johnny " had a book opening out into long series of scenes of plays and that he used to be fond of saying dramatically: " My horse! my horse! A kingdom for my horse! " Whether the error lay with the child's knowledge or the man's memory I know not.

Some of the scenes—not merely the painted or

built pictures, but that which took in the persons as well as the setting of the stage—were of great beauty. In especial was the first scene when the funeral procession of King Henry VI. came on. Irving had tried to realise some of the effect of the great picture by Edwin A. Abbey, R.A. Here the tide of mourners seems to sweep along in resistless mass, with an extraordinary effect of the spear-poles of royal scarlet amidst the black draperies.

Whilst the bulk of the audience were taking their reluctant way home certain invited guests from their body were beginning to fill up again the great stage which had by now been transposed into a room surrounded by supper-tables. Irving was receiving his friends after what had by then grown to be an established custom of first and last nights. From the buoyancy and joy of the guests it was easy to see how the play had gone. All were rejoicing as if each one had achieved a personal success.

V

In his own rooms that night he met with an accident which prevented his working for ten weeks. And so the run of *Richard III.* at that time was limited to one triumphant night.

On February 27 it was resumed till the coming of the time, which had long before been fixed, for the production of *Madame Sans-Gêne*.

XIII

IRVING'S METHOD

"Eugene Aram"—Sudden Change—"Richelieu"—Impersonation fixed in Age—"Louis XI."—"Up against it" in Chicago—"The Lyons Mail"—Tom Mead—Stories of his Forgetfulness—"Charles I."—Dion Boucicault on Politics in the Theatre—Irving's "make-up"—Cupid as Mephistopheles

I

THE first time I saw *Eugene Aram,* June 6, 1879, I was much struck with one fact—amongst many—which afforded a real lesson in the art of acting in all its phases—philosophy, effect, value and method. It is that of the effect, intellectual as well as emotional, of a lightning-like change in the actor's manner. In this play, the Yorkshire schoolmaster, who under the stress of violent emotion wrought by wrong to the woman he loved, has avoided the danger of discovery and has for a long time remained in outward peace in the house of Parson Meadows, the Vicar of Knaresborough. The evil genius of his early day, Richard Houseman, who alone knew of his crime, had succeeded in "tracking" him down; and now, being in desperate straits, tried to blackmail him. Knowing his man, however, he will not meet him. Such a one as Houseman is a veritable " daughter of the horseleech"; the giving is each time a firmer ground for further *chantage*. Houseman, grown desperate, threatens him that he will expose him to Meadows ; and Eugene Aram, who has long loved in secret the Vicar's daughter Ruth, seeing all his cherished hopes of happiness shattered, grows more desperate still. All the murderous potentialities which have already manifested themselves wake to new life in the "climbing" passion of the moment—the *hysterica passio* of *King Lear*. As Irving played it the hunted man at bay was transformed from his gentleness to a ravening tiger ; he looked the spirit of murder incarnate as he answered threat by threat. Just at that moment the door opened and in walked Ruth Meadows, bright and cheery as a ray of spring sunshine. In a second—less than a second, for the change was like lightning—the sentence begun in one way went on in another without a quaver or pause. The mind and powers of the remorse-haunted man who had for weary years trained himself for just such an emergency worked true. Unfailingly a sudden and marked burst of applause rewarded on each occasion this remarkable artistic *tour de force*.

II

The play of *Richelieu* had always a particular interest for those who knew that in it he made his first appearance on the stage in the small part of Gaston, Duke of Orleans.

Regarding this first appearance three names

should be borne in memory as those who helped the ambitious young clerk to an opening in the art he had chosen. The names of two of these are already known. One was William Hoskins, who at considerable self-sacrifice had helped to teach him his craft, and who had predicted good things for him. The other was E. D. Davis, an old actor, who was just entering upon the management of the Lyceum Theatre, Sunderland; and who at Mr. Hoskins' request gave him an engagement.

The third friend made his way possible, and gave him opportunity of appearing to advantage in his parts by supplying him with the sinews of war. This friend was none other than his uncle, Thomas Brodribb, the second of the four brothers of whom Irving's father, Samuel, was fourth. He was— perhaps fortunately for his nephew—a bachelor. He had but small means; but also, happily, small wants. Amongst his assets he had a policy of insurance on which many premiums had been paid; and wishing to do something for his nephew on his starting in a new life, he made over to him this policy so that he might realise on it. This his nephew did to the result of nearly one hundred pounds sterling, all of which was by degrees laid out carefully with most anxious thought on such wardrobe and personal properties as are not usually "found" by provincial managements. This kindly and timely assistance enabled the young actor to appear during his first years on the stage in many parts with something of that suitability of presence which his characters demanded. In those early days the wardrobe of country theatres was limited and the actors often chose their dresses in the sequence of importance; so that it was much to a young man to be able to supplement such costume as came to him. Could the generous, kindly-hearted Uncle Thomas have lived to see the grand consequences eventually resulting in part from his thoughtful kindness he might have indeed been proud.

There was this difference in Irving's Richelieu and the same part as played by any other actor I have seen. In the great scene of the quarrel between Baradas and the Cardinal, when the former wants, for his own purposes, to take, by the King's authority, Julie from his custody, the latter hurls at him the magnificently effective speech beginning: " Then wakes the power which in the Age of Iron."

This by the players of the old school was thundered out with the same vigour with which they fought in their sword combats; and certainly the effect was very telling. It was the act as well as the word of personal mastery.

Irving kept the full effect; but did it in such a way that he superadded to the Cardinal's character the flickering spasmodic power of an infirm old man. He too began in tones of thunder. To his full height he drew the tall form that seemed massive in the sacerdotal robes. He was manifestly inspired and borne up by the divine force of his sacred office. But at the end he collapsed, almost sinking into a swoon. Thus the effect was magnified and the sense of both reality and characterisation enhanced.

Henry Irving as Louis XI.
from a Pastel by J. Bernard Partridge.
(Copyright by Partridge.)

III

With Louis XI., a part which in France is called *le grand rôle,* Henry Irving was fairly familiar in his early years on the stage. He had played the part of both Coitier and Tristan, and as one or other of these in most of the scenes he had full experience of the acting value of the title *rôle.* It would be very unlike the method of study habitual to him even before he went on the stage if he had not all the time, both at rehearsal and performance, grasped the acting possibilities of both character and situations, and devised new and subtle means for characterisation. When in 1878 he had run the piece for some three months he had learned much, both by practice and from the opinions of his friends. In those days he did not often read criticisms of an ordinary kind. He found that some of them, written by irresponsible writers imperfectly equipped for their task, only disturbed and irritated him. And so he only read such as had filtered through the judgment of his friends; a habit which George Eliot had adopted about the same time.

Though I had not seen his performance that year I could tell, in 1879, from his anxiety about the rehearsal of certain scenes and the care bestowed on the new or altered scenery and appointments, that his new work was to be on a slightly different plane from the old.

After a few performances Louis XI. became a sort of holiday part to him. There is in it but one change of dress: that between the fourth and fifth acts. This change, though exceptionally heavy, is as nothing to the exhaustion consequent on the many changes of costume necessary in most heavy plays. These ordinarily absorb in swift and laborious work the only breathing times between the periods of action. A series of small labours may in the long run amount to more than one large one. The remark of Charles Lamb, who lived in an age when beards were unknown, may be applied:

"A man suffers as much in the aggregate of life in shaving as a woman does in child-birth!"

The limitation of violent effort in this play made him very "easy" in it. In one scene only does such occur; that at the end of the fourth act as originally played. Of late years he played it in four acts altogether, amalgamating the first and second acts with much benefit to the play.

Only once have I seen him put out at anything during the playing of *Louis XI*. It was in Chicago on the night of Saturday, February 13, 1904. For five weeks following the burning of the Iroquois Theatre in that city no theatre had been allowed to open. The official world, which had itself been gravely in fault in allowing the theatre to be opened before it had been tested, tried to show their integrity by imposing rigid perfection—after the event—on other people. The Illinois Theatre, where we were to play, was the first theatre opened, and naturally we had to stand the brunt of official over-zeal. We had been harassed beyond belief from the moment we entered the theatre. We were served with a notice that we should not be allowed to open until the whole of the scenery, &c., used on the stage had been fireproofed to the satisfaction of the City officials. When we asked what fireproofing would be considered satisfactory they would not tell us; so the only thing we could do with any reasonable chance of success was to employ the fireproofer whom they recommended. It was an expensive luxury in a small way, for we had to pay some five hundred dollars for what our own men could have done for a tenth of the money. Then they would not allow the gallery to be opened at all, and took out whole sections of seats on the floor and in the balconies. Again, the firemen kept charge of the stage, even during the day when there were in the house but the few workmen employed on the stage. One day our Master Machinist was arranging some small matter at the side of the proscenium when a fireman stepped up to him and said:

"If you touch that I'll jail you!"

On the night of *Louis XI.* all went well till the end of the bedroom scene between the King and Nemours. Here, when the Duke has escaped, the King calls for aid and his guards rush in with torches and by their master's direction search the room for his enemy. The effectiveness of the scene depends on the light thus introduced, for the scene is a dark one, lit only by the King's chamber-lamp. To Irving's dismay the cue for the lights was not answered. True, the guards came on, but in darkness. The firemen in the wings had seized from the guards the spirit torches—implements carefully made to obviate any possible danger from fire and each carried by one of our own men practised in the handling of them.

After a night or two matters got a little easier. The fire regulations, which directed that the men of that department on the stage should make requisition to the responsible manager who would see them carried out, began to be more decorously observed.

IV

The Lyons Mail is the especial title of Charles Reade's version of *Le Courier de Lyons*. The play has often been done in its older form, but in the newer only by Charles Kean and Henry Irving. Indeed when Irving took it in hand he got Reade to make some changes, especially in the second act, where Joseph Lesurques has the interview with his father, who believes him guilty, and that he saw him fire the shot by which he himself was wounded.

Irving has often told me that in playing the double part the real difficulty was not to make the two men unlike and guilt look like guilt, but the opposite. He used to adduce instances told him by experienced judges and counsel of where they had been themselves deceived by demeanour. It is indeed difficult for any one to discriminate between the shame, together with the submission to the Divine Law to which he has been bred, of the innocent, and the fear, whose expression is modified by hardihood, of the guilty. In Irving's case the points of difference were not merely overt; there were subtle differences of tone and look and bearing. Loftiness for instance, as against supreme and fearless indifference and brutality.

The Lyons Mail was always one of the most anxious and exhausting of his plays. In the first place he was always on the stage, either in the one

HENRY IRVING AS DUBOSC

From the picture by James Pryde

character of Lesurques or the other of Dubosc—except at the end of the play where he appeared to be both. All the intervals were taken up with necessary changes of dress. In the next place the *time* is all-important. In any melodrama accuracy as to time is important to success; but in this one of confused identity it is all-important. There are occasions when the delay of a single second will mar the best studied effect, and when to be a second too soon is to spoil the plot. In certain plays the actors must " overlap " in their speeches; the effect of their work must be to carry the thought of the audience from point to point without wavering. Thus they receive the necessary information without the opportunity of examining it too closely. This is a part of the high art of the stage. There can be illusions by other means than light.

Once there was a peculiar *contretemps* in the acting. Tom Mead was a fine old actor with a tall thin form and a deep voice that sounded like an organ. His part was that of Jerome Lesurques, the father of the unhappy man whose double was the villain Dubosc. He had played it for many years and very effectively. The end of the first act comes when Dubosc, the robber and murderer, is confronted by Jerome Lesurques. The old man thinks it is his son whom he sees rifling the body of the mail guard. As he speaks the words : " Good God ! my son, my son," Dubosc fires at him, wounding him on the arm, and escapes as the curtain comes down.

On this particular night—it was one of the last nights in New York, closing the tour of 1893-4—

Mead forgot his words. Dubosc stood ready with his pistol to fire; but no words came. Now, if the audience do not know that Jerome Lesurques thinks that his son is guilty the heart is taken out of the play, for it is his unconscious evidence that proves his son's guilt. The words had to be spoken at any cost *by some one*. Irving waited, but the old man's memory was gone. So he himself called out in a loud voice: "I'm not your son!" and shot him. And, strange to say, none of the audience seemed to notice the omission.

Tom Mead was famous in his later years amongst his comrades for making strange errors, and when he had any new part they always waited to see what new story he would beget. Once on a voyage to America when we were arranging the concert for the Seamen's Orphans, he said he would do a scene from *Macbeth* if Mrs. Pauncefort would do it with him. She, a fine old actress, at once consented and from thence on the members of the company were waiting to see what the slip would be. They were certain there would be one; to them there was no "might" or "if" in the matter. The scene chosen was that of the murder of Duncan, and all went well till the passage was reached:

> "And Pity, like a naked new-born babe
> Striding the blast, or heaven's cherubim, horsed
> Upon the sightless carriers of the air."

This noble passage he repeated as follows:

> "And Pity, like a naked new-born babe
> Seated on the horse. No! Horsed on the seat!
> No! What is the word?"

Once before, during the first run of *Macbeth*, he played one of the witches; when circling round the cauldron he had to say: "Cool it with a baboon's blood." This he changed to:

"Cool it with a dragoon's blood!"

As the words are spoken before Macbeth enters, Irving, standing ready in the wings, of course heard the error. Later in the evening he sent for Mead and called his attention to the error, pointing out that as the audience knew so well the words of the swinging lines they might notice an error and that it would be well to read over the part afresh. This he promised to do. Next night he got very anxious as the time drew near. He moved about restlessly behind the scenes saying over and over again to himself, " dragoon, no baboon—baboon! —dragoon!—dragoon!—baboon!"—till he got himself hopelessly mixed and his comrades were in ecstasy. When at last he came to say the word he said it wrong; and as he had a voice whose tones he could not modify this is what the audience heard:

"Cool it with dragoon's blood—No, no, baboon's. My God! I've said it again! baboon's blood."

When we did *Iolanthe*, a version by W. G. Wills of *King René's Daughter*, Mead took the part of Ebn Jaira an Eastern Wizard. At one part of the piece, where things look very black indeed for the happiness of the blind girl, he has to say: "All shall be well in that immortal land where God hath His dwelling." One night he got shaky in his words and surprised the audience with:

"In that immortal land where God hath His— Ah—um—His—apartments!"

Such mental aberrations used to be fairly common in the old days when new parts had to be learned every night, and when the prompter, in so far as the "book" was concerned, was a hard-worked official and not an anachronism, as now. Macready had an experience of it once when playing Hamlet. The actor who took the part of the Priest in the graveyard scene was inadequately prepared and in the passage:

> "for charitable prayers,
> Shards, flints, and pebbles shall be thrown on her."

he said, "shards, flints and beadles." This almost overcame the star, who was heard to murmur to himself before he went on; "Beadles! Beadles!" and at the end of the play one behind him heard him say as he walked to his dressing-room:

"He said 'beadles'!"

V

Charles I. is rather too slight and delicate a play for great popularity; and in addition its politics are too aggressive. Whenever I think of it in its political aspect I am always reminded of a pregnant saying of Dion Boucicault—I mean Dion Boucicault the Elder, for the years have run fast—spoken in the beautiful Irish brogue which was partly natural and partly cultivated:

"The rayson why historical plays so seldom succeed is because a normal audience doesn't go into the thayatre with its politics in its breeches pockets!"

This is really a philosophical truth, and the man who had then written or adapted over four hundred plays knew it. A great political situation may

HENRY IRVING AS CHARLES I.

like any other great existing force form a *milieu* for dramatic action; making or increasing difficulties or abrogating or lessening them; or bringing unexpected danger or aid to the persons of the drama. But where the political situation is supposed to be lasting or eternally analogous it is apt to create in the minds of an audience varying conditions of thought and sympathy. And where these all-powerful forces of an audience are opposed they become mutually destructive, being only united into that one form which makes for the destruction of the play.

One of the most notable things of Irving's *Charles I.* was his extraordinary reproduction of Van Dyck's pictures. The part in its scenic aspect might have been called Van Dyck in action. Each costume was an exact reproduction from one of the well-known paintings, and the reproduction of Charles's face was a marvel. In this particular case he had a fine model, for Van Dyck painted the King in almost every possible way of dignity. To aid him in his work Edwin Long made for him a tryptich of Van Dyck heads, and this used to rest before him on his dressing-table on those nights when he played Charles.

Irving was a painter of no mean degree with regard to his "make-up" of parts. He spared no pains on the work and on nights when he played parts requiring careful preparations such as Charles I., Shylock, Louis XI., Gregory Brewster (in *Waterloo*), King Lear, Richelieu and some few others he always came to his dressing-room nearly an hour earlier than at other times. It has often amazed me to see the physiognomy of Shylock gradually emerge from the actor's own generous countenance. Though I have seen it done a hundred times I could never really understand how the lips thickened, with the red of the lower lip curling out and over after the manner of the typical Hebraic countenance; how the bridge of the nose under his painting—for he used no physical building-up—rose into the Jewish aquiline; and, most wonderful of all, how the eyes became veiled and glassy with introspection—eyes which at times could and did flash like lurid fire.

But there is for an outsider no understanding what strange effects stage make-up can produce. When my son, who is Irving's godson, then about seven years old, came to see *Faust* I brought him round between acts to see Mephistopheles in his dressing-room. The little chap was exceedingly pretty—like a cupid—and a quaint fancy struck the actor. Telling the boy to stand still for a moment he took his dark pencil and with a few rapid touches made him up after the manner of Mephistopheles; the same high-arched eyebrows; the same sneer at the corners of the mouth; the same pointed moustache. I think it was the strangest and prettiest transformation I ever saw. And I think the child thought so too, for he was simply entranced with delight.

Irving loved children and I think he was as enchanted over the incident as was the child himself.

XIV

ART-SENSE

"The Bells"—Worn-out Scenery—An Actor's Judgment of a Part—"Olivia"—"Faust"—A Master Mind and Good Service—A Loyal Stage Manager and Staff—Whistler on Business—Twenty-fifth Anniversary of "The Bells"—A Presentation—A Work of Art—"The Bells" a Classic—Visit of Illustrious Frenchmen—Sarcey's Amusement

I

No successful play, perhaps, had ever had so little done for it as *The Bells* on its production. Colonel Bateman did not believe in it, and it was only the concatenation of circumstances of his own desperate financial condition and Irving's profound belief in the piece that induced him to try it at all. The occasion was in its effect somewhat analogous to Edmund Kean's first appearance at Drury Lane; the actor came to the front and top of his profession *per saltum*. The production was meagre; of this I can bear a certain witness myself. When Irving took over the management of the Lyceum into his own hands the equipment of *The Bells* was one of the assets coming to him. When he did play it he used the old dresses, scenery and properties and their use was continued as long as possible. Previous to the American tour of 1883-4, fifty-five performances in all constituted the entire wear and tear.

On our first expedition to America everything was packed in a very cumbrous manner; the amount of timber, nails and screws used was extraordinary. There were hundred-weights of extracted screws on the stage of the Star Theatre of New York whilst the unpacking was in progress. When I came down to the theatre on the first morning after the unloading of the stuff, Arnott, who was in charge of the mechanics of the stage, came to me and said:

"Would you mind coming here a moment, sir, I would like you to see something!" He brought me to the back of the stage and pointed out a long heap of rubbish some four feet high. It was just such as you would see in the waste-heap of a house-wrecker's yard.

"What on earth is that?" I asked.

"That is the sink-and-rise of the vision in *The Bells*." In effecting a vision on the stage the old method used to be to draw the back scenes or "flats" apart or else to raise the whole scene from above or take it down through a long trap on the stage. The latter was the method adopted by the scene-painter of *The Bells*.

"Did it meet with an accident?" I asked.

"No, sir. It simply shook to bits just as you see it. It was packed up secure and screwed tight like the rest!"

I examined it carefully. The whole stuff was simply rotten with age and wear; as thoroughly worn out as the deacon's wonderful one-horse shay in Oliver Wendell Holmes' poem. The canvas had been almost held together by the overlay of paint, and as for the wood it was cut and hacked and pieced to death; full of old screw-holes and nail-holes. No part of it had been of new timber or canvas when *The Bells* was produced eleven years before. With this experience I examined the whole scenery and found that almost every piece of it was in a similar condition. It had been manufactured out of all the odds and ends of old scenery in the theatre.

Under the modern conditions of Metropolitan theatres it is hard to imagine what satisfied up to the "seventies." Nowadays the scenery of good theatres is made for travel. The flats are framed in light wood, securely clamped and fortified at the joints and in folding sections like screens, each section being not more than six feet wide so as to be easily handled and placed in baggage-waggons. The scenes are often fixed on huge castors with rubber bosses so as to move easily and silently. But formerly they were made in single panels and of heavy timber and took a lot of strength to move.

II

From the time of my joining him in 1878 till his death Irving played *The Bells* in all six hundred and twenty-seven times, being one hundred and sixty-eight in London; two hundred and seventy-three in the British provinces, and one hundred and eighty-six in America. During its first run at the Lyceum in 1872–3 it ran one hundred and fifty-one nights, so that in all he played *The Bells* seven hundred and seventy-eight times besides certain occasions when he gave it in his provincial tours previous to 1878. Altogether he probably played the piece over eight hundred times.

Colonel Bateman originally leased the rights of the play from the author, Leopold Lewis. Finally, at a time of stress—sadly frequent in those days with poor old Lewis—he sold them to Samuel French, from whom Irving finally purchased them. Nothwithstanding this double purchase Irving used, after the death of Lewis, to allow his widow a weekly sum whenever he was playing—playing not merely *The Bells* but anything else—up to the time of his death.

Mathias was an exceedingly hard and exhausting part on the actor, but as years rolled on it became in ever greater demand.

III

The original choice of the play by Irving is an object-lesson of the special art-sense of an actor regarding his own work. Irving *knew* that the play would succeed. It was not guessing nor hoping nor any other manifestation of an optimistic nature. Had Bateman, in the business crisis of 1872, not allowed him to put it on, he would infallibly have put it on at some other time.

It would be difficult for an actor to explain in what this art-sense consists or how it brings conviction to those whose gift it is. Certainly any one not an actor could not attempt the task at all. In the course of a quarter of a century of intimate experience of this actor, when he has confided to me the very beginnings of his intentions and let me keep in touch with his mind when such intentions became at first fixed and then clamorous of realisation, I have known him see his way to personal success with regard to several characters. For instance:

When in 1885 he had arranged to do *Olivia* and was making up the cast he put himself down as Dr. Primrose. I had not seen the play in which Ellen Terry had appeared under John Hare's management—with enormous success for a long run—and I had no guiding light, except the text of the play, as to the excellence of the part as an acting one. But neither had Irving seen it. He too had nothing but the text to go by, but he was quite satisfied with what he could do. He knew of course from report that Ellen Terry would be fine. For myself I could not see in the Vicar a great part for so great an actor, and tried my best to dissuade him from acting it. "Get the best man in London, or out of it—at any price," I said; "but don't risk playing a part like that already played exhaustively and played well according to accounts!" Hermann Vezin had played it in the run. Irving answered me with all his considerate sweetness of manner:

"My dear fellow, it is all right! I can see my way to it thoroughly. If I can't play the Vicar to please I shall think I don't know my business as an actor; and that I really think I do!"

This was said not in any way truculently or self-assertively, but with a businesslike quietude which always convinced. When any man was sincere with Irving, he too was always both sincere and sympathetic, even to an opposing view to his own. When one was fearless as well as sincere he gained an added measure of the actor's respect.

Again, when in 1885 *Faust* was being produced I began to have certain grave doubts as to whether we were justified in the extravagant hopes which we had all formed of its success. The piece as produced was a vast and costly undertaking; and as both the *décor* and the massing and acting grew, there came that time, perhaps inevitable in all such undertakings of indeterminate bounds, as to whether reality would justify imagination. With me that feeling culminated on the night of a partial rehearsal, when the Brocken scene on which we all relied to a large extent was played, all the supers and ballet and most of the characters being in dress. It was then, as ever afterwards, a wonderful scene of imagination, of grouping, of lighting, of action, and all the rush and whirl and triumphant cataclysm of unfettered demoniacal possession. But it all looked cold and unreal—that is, unreal to what it professed. When the scene was over—it was then in the grey of the morning—I talked with Irving in his dressing-room, where we had a sandwich and something else, before going home. I expressed my feeling that we ought not to build too much on this one play. After all it *might* not catch on with the public as firmly as we had all along expected—almost taken for granted. Could we not be quietly getting something else ready, so that in case it did not turn out all that which our fancy painted we should be able to retrieve ourselves. Other such arguments of judicious theatrical management I used earnestly.

Irving listened, gravely weighing all I said; then he answered me genially:

"That is all true; but in this case I have no doubt. I *know* the play will do. To-night I think you have not been able to judge accurately. You are forming an opinion largely from the effect of the Brocken. As far as to-night goes you are quite right; but you have not seen my dress. I do not want to wear it till I get all the rest correct. Then you will see. I have studiously kept as yet all the colour to that grey-green. When my dress of flaming scarlet appears amongst it—and remember that the colour will be intensified by that very light—it will bring the whole picture together in a way you cannot dream of. Indeed I can hardly realise it myself yet, though I know it will be right. You shall see too how Ellen Terry's white dress and even that red scar across her throat will stand out in the midst of that turmoil of lightning!"

He had seen in his own inner mind and with his vast effective imagination all these pictures and these happenings from the very first; all that had been already done was but leading up to the culmination.

IV

Let me say here that Irving loved sincerity, and most of all in those around him and who had to aid him in his work—for no man can do all for himself. Alfred Gilbert the sculptor once said to me on seeing from behind the scenes how a great play was pulled through on a first night, when every soul in the place was alive with desire to aid and every nerve was instinct with thought:

" I would give anything that the world holds to be served as Irving is ! "

He was quite right. There must be a master mind for great things, and the master of that mind must learn to trust others when the time of action comes. The time for doubting, for experimenting, for teaching and weighing and testing is in the antecedent time of preparation. But when *the* hour strikes every doubt is a fetter to one's own work—a barrier between effort and success.

In artistic work this is especially so. The artist temperament is sensitive—almost super-sensitive ; and the requirements of its work necessitate that form of quietude which comes from self-oblivion. It is not possible to do any work based on individual qualities when from extrinsic cause some unrequired phase of that individuality looms large in the foreground of thought. Dickens, who was himself a sensitive man and understood both consciously and unconsciously the needs of artistic nature, was only putting the thought into humorous and exaggerated words when he made Mr. Chevy Slyme say that his friend had in his nature " infernally fine-touched chords."

This quality is of the essence of every artist, but is emphasised in the actor; for here his individuality is not merely a help to creative power but is a medium by which he expresses himself. Thus it will be found as a working rule of life that the average actor will not, if he can help it, do anything or take any responsibility which will make for the possibility of unpopularity. The reason is not to be found in vanity, or in a merely reckless desire to please; it is that unpopularity is not only harmful to his aim and detrimental to his well-being, but is a disturbing element in his work *quâ* actor. In another place we shall have to consider the matter of " dual consciousness " which Irving considered to be of the intellectual mechanism of acting. Here we must take it that if to a double consciousness required for work a third—self-consciousness—is added, they are apt to get mixed; and fine purpose will be thwarted or overborne.

Thus it is that an actor has to keep himself, in certain ways at least, for his work. When in addition he has the cares and worries and responsibilities and labours and distractions of management to encounter daily and hourly, it is vitally necessary that he has trutsworthy and, to him, sufficing assistance. Oliver Wendell Holmes has a shrewd remark in one of his breakfast-table books; that "genius should wed with character." This has perhaps a wider application than the author intended, and the business side of art work is a fair example of its width. It is quite sufficient for one man to originate the scope and ultimate effect of a play; to bring all the workers of different crafts employed in its production; to select the various actors each for special qualities, to rehearse them and the less skilled labourers employed in effect; in fact to bring the whole play into harmonious completeness. All beyond this is added labour, exhausting to the individual and ineffective with regard to the work in hand. When, therefore, an actor-manager has such trusty and efficient assistance as is here suggested many things become possible to him with regard to the finesse of his art, which he dared not otherwise attempt. *Somebody* must stand the stress of irritating matters; there must be *some* barrier to the rush of mordant distractions. Irving could do much and would have in the long run done at least the bulk of what he intended; but he never could have done *all* he did without the assistance of his friend and trusty stage-lieutenant, H. J. Loveday, who through the whole of his management stood beside him in all his creative work and shaped into permanent form his lofty ideas of stage effect. It is not sufficient in a theatre to see a thing properly done and then leave it to take care of itself for the future. Stage perfection needs constant and never-ending vigilance. No matter how perfectly a piece may be played, from the highest to the least important actor, in a certain time things will begin to get "sloppy" and fresh rehearsals are required to bring all up again to the standard of excellence fixed. To Loveday and the able staff under him, whose devotion and zeal were above all praise, the continued excellence of the Lyceum plays had to be mainly trusted.

Let it be clearly understood here, however, that I say this not to belittle Irving, but to add to his honour. In addition to other grand qualities he had the greatness to trust where trust was due. With him lay all the great conception and imagination and originality of all his accomplishments. He was quite content that others should have their share of honour.

When one considers the amazing labour and expense concerned in the "production" of a play, he is better able to estimate the value of devoted and trusted assistance.

V

Even the thousand and one details of the business of a theatre need endless work and care—work which would in the long run shatter entirely the sensitive nervous system of an artist. In fact it may be taken for granted that no artist can properly attend to his own business. As an instance I may point to Whistler, who, long after he had made money and lost it again and had begun to build up his fortune afresh, came to me for some personal advice before going to America to deliver his "Five o'clock" discourse. In the course of our conversation he said:

"Bram, I wish I could get some one to take me up and attend to my business for me—I can't do it myself; and I really think it would be worth a good man's while—some man like yourself," he courteously added. "I would give half of all I earned to such a man, and would be grateful to him also for a life without care!"

I think myself he was quite right. He was before his time—long before it. He did fine work and created a new public taste . . . and he became bankrupt. His house and all he had were sold; and the whole sum he owed would, I think, have been covered by the proper sale of a few of the pictures which were bought almost *en bloc* by a picture-dealer who sold them for almost any price offered. He had a mass of them in his gallery several feet thick as they were piled against the wall. One of them he sold to Irving for either £20 or £40, I forget which.

This was the great picture of Irving as King Philip in Tennyson's drama *Queen Mary*. It was sold at Christie's amongst Irving's other effects after his death and fetched over five thousand pounds sterling.

VI

During the run of *Cymbeline* a pause of one night was made for a special occasion. November 25, 1896, was the twenty-fifth anniversary of the first performance of *The Bells*, and on that memorable birth-night the performance was repeated to an immense house euthusiastic to the last degree.

After the curtain had finally fallen the whole of the company and all the employees of the theatre gathered on the stage for a presentation to Irving to commemorate the remarkable occasion. One and all without exception had contributed in proportion to their means. Most of all, Alfred Gilbert, R.A., who had given his splendid genius and much labour as his contribution. Of course on this occasion it was only the model which was formally conveyed. The form of the trophy was a great silver bell standing some two feet high, exquisite in

THE VOICE OF THE BELL

design and with the grace and beauty of the work of a Cellini; a form to be remembered in after centuries. I had the honour of writing the destined legend to be wrought in a single line in raised letters on a band of crinkly gold on the curve of the bell. Gilbert had made a point of my writing it, and be sure I was proud to do so. It ran:

HONOUR TO IRVING. THROUGH THE LOVE OF HIS COMRADES. I RING THROUGH THE AGES.

Gilbert was enthusiastic about it, for he said it fulfilled all the conditions of the legend on a bell. In the first place, according to the ancient idea a bell is a person with a soul and a thought and a voice of its own; it is supposed to speak on its own initiative. In the second place, the particular inscription was short and easily wrought and would just go all round the bell. Moreover from its peculiar form the reading of it could begin anywhere. I felt really proud when he explained all this to me and I realised that I had so well carried out the idea.

VII

It may perhaps be here noted that according to the tradition of the Comédie-Française a play becomes a classic work when it has held the boards for a quarter of a century. The director, M. Jules Claretie asked Irving if they might play it in the House of Molière. Of course he was pleased and sent to Claretie a copy of the prompt-book and drawings of the scenes and appointments.

Jules Claretie was by now an old friend. In 1879, when the Comédie-Française came to London and played at the Gaiety Theatre, he came over as one of the men of letters interested in their success. It was not till afterwards that he was selected as Director. I remember well one night when he came to supper with Irving in the Lyceum. This was before the Old Beefsteak Room was reappointed to its old use; and we supped in the room next to his own dressing-room, occasionally used in those days for purposes of hospitality. There came also three other Frenchmen of literary note: Jules Clery, Jacques Normand and the great critic Francisque Sarcey. There was a marked scarcity of language between us as none of the Frenchmen spoke in those days a word of English, and neither Irving nor I knew more than a smattering of French. We got on well, however, and managed to exchange ideas in the manner usual to people who *want* to talk with each other. It was quite late, and we had all begun to forget that we did not know each other's language, when we missed Sarcey. I went out to look for him, fearing lest he might come to grief through some of the steps or awkward places in the almost dark theatre. In those days of gas lighting we always kept alight the "pilot" light in the great chandelier of bronze and glass which hung down into the very centre of the auditorium—just above the sight-line from the gallery. This pilot was a matter of safety, and I rather think that we were compelled to see it attended to, either by the civic authorities or the superior landlord. The gas remaining in the pipes of the theatre was just sufficient to keep it going for four and twenty hours. If it went out there must be a leak somewhere; and that leak had to be discovered and attended to without delay.

I could not find Sarcey on the dim stage or in the front of the house. In a theatre the rule is to take up the curtain when the audience have passed out so that there may be as much time and opportunity as possible for ventilating the house. I began to get a little uneasy about the missing guest; but when I came near the corner of the stage whence the private staircase led to Irving's rooms I heard a queer kind of thumping sound. I followed it out into the passage leading from the private door in Burleigh Street to the Royal box. This was shut off from the theatre by an iron door—not locked, but falling gently into the jambs by its own weight. When I pushed open the door I found Sarcey all by himself, dancing a queer sort of dance something after the manner of the "Gillie Callum." It was positively weird. I never afterwards could think of Sarcey without there rising before me the vision of that lively, silent, thickset, agile figure moving springily in the semi-darkness.

Jules Claretie was many times at the Lyceum after that first visit, and in his *régime* the Theâtre Français was the home of courtesy to strangers. Once when my wife was in Paris he asked her what play she would like particularly to see; and on her saying that she much wanted to see some time Mounet-Sully in *Hamlet* he had the piece put up a few nights after and sent her his box.

XV

STAGE EFFECTS

"The Lady of Lyons"—A Great Stage Army—Supers: their work and pay—"The Corsican Brothers"— Some great "Sets"—A Royal Visitor behind scenes— —Seizing an Opportunity—A Triton amongst minnows —Gladstone as an Actor—Beaconsfield and Coryphées —A Double—A cure for haste

I

The Lady of Lyons was produced on April 17, 1879. It kept in the bill for a portion of each week for the remainder of the first and the whole of the second season; in all forty-five times—no inconsiderable run of such an old and hackneyed play.

The production was a very beautiful one. There was a specially attractive feature in it: the French army. At the end of the fourth act Claude, all his hopes shattered and being consumed with remorse, accepts Colonel Damas' offer to go with him to the war in that fine melodramatic outburst:

"Place me wherever a foe is most dreaded— wherever France most needs a life!"

As Irving stage-managed it the army, already on its way, was tramping along the road outside.

A STAGE ARMY

Through window and open door the endless columns were seen, officers and men in due order and the flags in proper place. It seemed as if the line would stretch out till the crack of doom! A very large number of soldiers had been employed as supers and were of course especially suitable for the work. In those days the supers of London theatres were largely supplied from the Brigade of Guards. The men liked it, for it provided easy beer-money, and the officers liked them to have the opportunity as it kept them out of mischief. We had always on our staff as an additional super-master a Sergeant of Guards who used to provide the men and was of course in a position to keep them in order.

The men entered thoroughly into the spirit of the thing, and it was really wonderful how, availing themselves of their professional training, they were able to seemingly multiply their forces. Often have I admired the dexterity, ease and rapidity with which that moving army was kept going with a hundred and fifty men. Four abreast they marched across the stage at the back. The back cloth of the landscape outside the cottage was set far up the stage so that there was but a narrow space left between it and the back wall, scarcely room for one person to pass; and it was interesting to see the perfection of drill which enabled those soldiers to meet the difficulties of keeping up the constant stream of the troops. They would march into the wings with set pace, but the instant they passed out of sight of the audience they would break into a run; in perfect order they would rush in single file round the back of the scene and arrive at the other side just in time to fall into line and step again. And so the endless stream went on. When Claude ran out with Damas the ranks opened and a cheer rose; he fell into line with the rest and on the army marched.

That marching army never stopped. No matter how often the curtain went up on the scene—and sometimes there were seven or eight calls, for the scene was one specially exciting to the more demonstrative parts of the house—it always rose on that martial array, always moving on with the resistless time and energy of an overwhelming force.

It was only fair that Irving should always get good service from supers for they never had such a friend. When their standard pay was sixpence per night he gave a shilling. When that sum became standard he gave one and sixpence. And when that was reached he paid two shillings—an increase of 300 per cent. in his own time.

If the smallness of the pay, even now, should strike any reader, let me remind such that supers are not supposed to live on their pay. There are a few special people who generally dress with them, but such are in reality minor actors and get larger pay. The super proper is engaged during the day—porters, workmen, gasmen, &c., and simply add to their living wage by work at night. At the Lyceum if a man only worked as a super; we took it for granted that he was in reality a loafer, and did not keep him.

II

The Corsican Brothers is one of the pieces which requires picturesque setting. The story is so weird that it obtains a new credibility from unfamiliar *entourage*. Corsica has always been accepted as a land of strange happenings and stormy passions. Things are accepted under such circumstances which would ordinarily be passed by as bizarre. The production was certainly a magnificent one. There are two scenes in it which allow of any amount of artistic effort, although their juxtaposition in the sequence of the play makes an enormous difficulty. The first is the scene of the Masked Ball in the Opera House in Paris; the other the Forest of Fontainebleau, where takes place the duel between Fabian and de Château-Rénaud. Each of these scenes took up the whole stage, right away from the footlights to the back wall; thus the task of changing from one to the other, with only the interval of the supper at Baron de Montgiron's to do it in, was one of extraordinary difficulty. The scene of the Masked Ball represented the interior of the Opera House, the scenic auditorium being furthest from the footlights. In fact it was as though the audience sitting in the Lyceum auditorium saw the scene as though looking in a gigantic mirror placed in the auditorium arch. The scene was in reality a vast one and of great brilliance. The Opera House was draped with crimson silk, the boxes were practical and contained a whole audience, all being in perspective. The men and women in the boxes near to the footlights were real;

those far back were children dressed like their elders. Promenading and dancing were hundreds of persons in striking costumes. It must be remembered that in those days there were no electric lights, and as there were literally thousands of lights in the scene it was a difficult one to fit. Thousands of feet of gas-piping, the joining hose being flexible, were used and the whole resources of supply were brought into requisition. We had before that brought the use of gas-supply to the greatest perfection attainable. There were two sources of supply, each from a different main, and these were connected with a great " pass " pipe workable with great rapidity, so that if through any external accident one of the mains should be disabled we could turn the supply afforded by the other into all the pipes used throughout the house. This great scene came to an end by lowering the " cut " cloth which formed the background of Montgiron's salon, the door leading into the supper-room being in the centre at back. Whilst the guests were engaged in their more or less rapid banquet, the covered scene was being obliterated and the Forest of Fontainebleau was coming down from the rigging-loft, ascending from the cellar and being pushed on right and left from the wings. Montgiron's salon was concealed by the descent of great tableau curtains. These remained down from thirty-five to forty *seconds* and went up again on a forest as real as anything can be on the stage. Trees stood out separately over a large area so that those entering from side or back could be seen passing behind or amongst them. All over the stage was a deep blanket of snow, white and glistening in the winter sunrise. Snow that lay so thick that when the duellists, stripped and armed, stood face to face, they each secured a firmer foothold by kicking it away. Of many wonderful effects this snow was perhaps the strongest and most impressive of reality. The public could never imagine how it was done. It was *salt*, common coarse salt which was white in the appointed light and glistened like real snow. There were tons of it. A crowd of men stood ready in the wings with little baggage-trucks such as are now used in the corridors of great hotels; silent with rubber wheels. On them were great wide-mouthed sacks full of salt. When the signal came they rushed in on all sides each to his appointed spot and tumbled out his load, spreading it evenly with great wide-bladed wooden shovels.

III

One night—it was October 18—the Prince of Wales came behind the scenes as he was interested in the working of the play. It was known he was coming, and though the stage hands had been told that they were not supposed to know that he was present they all had their Sunday clothes on. It was the first time his Royal Highness had been " behind " in Irving's management and he seemed very interested in all he saw. King Edward VII. has and has always had a wonderful memory. He told how Charles Kean had set the scenes, the rights and lefts being different from the present setting; how Kean had rested on a log in a particular place, and so forth. Some of our older stage men who had been at the Princess's in Kean's time bore it out afterwards that he was correct in each detail.

That night the men worked as never before; they were determined to let the Prince see what could, under the stimulating influence of his presence, be done at the Lyceum, of which they were all very proud. That night the tableau curtains remained down only *thirty seconds*—the record time.

The Corsican Brothers was produced on September 18, 1880, and ran for one hundred and ninety performances in that season, *The Cup* being played along with it ninety-two times. The special reason for *The Corsican Brothers* being played during that season was that Ellen Terry had long before promised to go on an Autumn tour in 1880 with her husband, Charles Kelly. It was therefore necessary that a piece should be chosen which did not require her services, and there was no part suitable to her in *The Corsican Brothers*. This was the only time that she had a tour except with Irving until when during his illness in 1899 she went out by herself to play *Madame Sans-Gêne* and certain other plays. When she returned to the Lyceum at the close of her tour *The Cup* was added to the bill.

IV

In the course of the run of *The Corsican Brothers* there were a good many incidents, interesting or amusing. Amongst the latter was one repeated nightly during the run of the piece. In the first scene, which is the house of the Dei Franchi in Corsica, opportunity had been taken of the peculiarity of the old Lyceum stage to make the entrance of Fabian dei Franchi—the one of the twins remaining at home—as effective as possible. The old stage of the Lyceum had a "scene-dock" at the back extending for some thirty feet beyond the squaring of the stage. As this opening was at the centre, the perspective could by its means be enlarged considerably. At the back of the Dei Franchi "interior" ran a vine-trellised way to a wicket gate. As there was no side entrance to the scene-dock it was necessary, in order to reach the back, to go into the cellarage and ascend by a stepladder as generously sloped as the head room would allow. But when the oncomer did make an appearance he was some seventy feet back from the footlights and in the very back centre of the stage, the most effective spot for making entry as it enabled the entire audience to see him a long way off and to emphasise his coming should they so desire. In that scene Irving wore a Corsican dress of light green velvet and was from the moment of his appearance a conspicuous object. When therefore he was seen to ascend the mountain slope and appear at the wicket the audience used to begin to applaud and cheer, so that his entrance was very effective.

But in the arrangement the fact had been lost sight of that another character entered the same way just before the time of his oncoming. This was Alfred Meynard, Louis's friend from Paris, a somewhat insignificant part in the play. Somehow at rehearsal the appearance of the latter did not seem in any way to clash with that of Fabian, and be sure that the astute young actor who played Alfred did not call attention to it by giving himself any undue prominence. The result was that on the first night—and ever afterwards during the run—when Alfred Meynard appeared the audience, who expected Irving, burst into wild applause. The gentleman who played the visitor had not then achieved the distinction which later on became his and so there was no reason, as yet, why he should receive such an ovation. From the great stage talent and finesse which he afterwards displayed I am right sure that he saw at the time what others had missed—the extraordinary opportunity for a satisfactory entrance so dear to the heart of an actor. It was a very legitimate chance in his favour, and nightly he carried his honours well. That first night a play of his own, his second play, was produced as the *lever de rideau*. The young actor was A. W. Pinero, and the play was *Bygones*. Pinero's first play, *Daisy's Escape*, had been played at the Lyceum in 1879.

V

The Masked Ball was a scene which allowed of any amount of fun, and it was so vast that it was an added gain to have as many persons as possible in it. To this end we kept a whole rack in the office during the run full of dominoes, masks and slouched hats, so that any one who had nothing else to do could in an instant make a suitable appearance on the scene and not be recognised. As the masculine dress of the time, the forties, was very much the same as now, a simple domino passed muster. I shall never forget my own appearance in the scene a few nights after the opening. We had amongst others engaged a whole group of clowns. There were eight of them, the best in England; the pantomime season being still far off, they could thus employ their enforced leisure—they were of course changed as their services were required elsewhere according to their previously made agreements. These men had a special dance of their own which was always a feature of the scene, and in addition they used to play what pranks they would, rushing about, making fun of others, climbing into boxes and then hauling others in, or dropping them out—such pranks and *intrigué* funniments as give life to a scene of the kind. When I ventured amongst them they recognised me and made a ring round me, dancing like demons. Then they seized me and spun me round, and literally played ball with me, throwing me from one to the other backwards and forwards. Sometimes they would rush me right down to the footlights and then whirl me back again breathless. But all the time they never let me fall or gave me away. I could not but admire their physical power as well as their agility and dexterity in their own craft.

The second time I went on I rather avoided them and kept up at the back of the stage. But even here I was not safe from another cause of mirth. I was lurking at the back when Irving, his face as set as flint with the passion of the insult and the challenge in the play, came hurriedly up the stage on his way to R.U.E. (right upper entrance). When he saw me the passion and grimness of his face relaxed in an instant and his laughter came explosively, fortunately unnoticed by the audience as his back was towards them. I went after him and asked him what was wrong, for I couldn't myself see anything of a mirthful nature.

"My dear fellow!" he said, "it was you!" Then in answer to my look he explained:

"Don't you remember how we arranged when the scene was being elaborated that in order to increase the effect of size we were to dress the shorter extras and then boys and girls and then little children in similar clothes to the others and to keep in their own section. You were up amongst the small children and with your height"—I am six feet two in my stockings—"with that voluminous domino and that great black feathered hat and in the painted perspective you looked fifty feet high!" And he laughed again uproariously.

VI

The Corsican Brothers was, so far as my knowledge goes, the first play—under Irving's management—which Mr. Gladstone came to see. The occasion was January 3, 1881—the first night when *The Cup* was played. He sat with his family in the box which we called in the familiar slang of the theatre "The Governor's Box"—the manager of a theatre is always the Governor to his colleagues of all kinds and grades. This box was the stage

GLADSTONE ON THE STAGE

box on the stall level, next to the proscenium. It was shut off by a special door which opened with the pass key and thus, as it was approachable from the stage through the iron door and from the auditorum by the box door, it was easy of access and quite private. After *The Cup* Mr. Gladstone wished to come on the stage and tell Irving and Ellen Terry how delighted he was with the performance. Irving fixed as the most convenient time the scene of the masked ball, as during it he had perhaps the only " wait " of the evening—a double part does not leave much margin to an actor. Mr. Gladstone was exceedingly interested in everything and went all round the vast scene. Seeing during the progress of the scene that people in costume were going in and out of queer little alcoves at the back of the scene he asked Irving what these were. He explained that they were the private boxes of the imitation theatre; and added that if the Premier would care to sit in one he could see the movement of the scene at close hand, and if he was careful to keep behind the little silk curtain he could not be seen. The statesman took his seat and seemed for a while to enjoy the life and movement going on in front of him. He could hear now and again the applause of the audience, and by peeping out through the chink behind the curtain, see them. At last in the excitement of the scene he forgot his situation and, hearing a more than usually vigorous burst of applause, leaned out to get a better view of the audience. The instant he did so he was recognised—there was no mistaking that eagle face—and then came a quick and sudden roar that seemed to shake the building. We could hear the "Bravo Gladstone!" coming through the detonation of hand-claps.

VII

One night, Wednesday, November 17, 1880, the sixty-first performance of the play, Lord Beaconsfield came to a box with some friends. I saw him coming up the stairs to the vestibule of the theatre. This was the only time I ever saw him, except on the floor of the House of Commons. He was then a good deal bent and walked feebly, leaning on the arm of his friend. He stayed to the end of the play and I believe expressed himself very pleased with it. His friend, "Monty" Corry, who was with him, told Irving afterwards that it seemed to revive to him old memories. As an instance, when he was coming away he asked:

"Do you think we could have supper somewhere, and ask some of the *coryphées* to join us, as we used to do in Paris in the fifties?"

The poor dear man little imagined how such a suggestion would have fluttered the theatrical dovecote. These *coryphées*, minor parts of course in the play, were supposed to be very "fast" young persons, and the difficulty of getting them properly played seemed for a long time insurmountable. The young ladies to whom the parts were allotted were all charming-looking young ladies of naturally bright appearance and manner. But they would *not* act as was required of them. One and all they seemed to set their faces against the histrionic levity demanded of them. It almost seemed that they felt that their personal characters were at stake. Did they act with their usual charm and brightness and verve somebody *might* to their detriment mix up the real and the simulated characters. The result was that never in the history of choregraphic art was there so fine an example of the natural demureness of the *corps de ballet*. They would have set an example to a confirmation class.

VIII

For the tableau curtains in *The Corsican Brothers*, Irving had had manufactured perhaps the most magnificent curtains of the kind ever seen. They were of fine crimson velvet and took more than a thousand yards of stuff. The width and height of the Lyceum proscenium were so great that the curtains had to be fastened all over on canvas, fortified with strong webbing where the drag of movement came. Otherwise the velvet would with the vast weight have torn like paper. They were drawn back and up at the same time, so as to leave the full stage visible, whilst picturesquely draping the opening. Material, colour and form of these curtains—which were a full 50 per cent. wider than the opening which they covered— brought both honour and much profit to the manufacturers, who received many orders for repetitions on a smaller scale. When John Hollingshead burlesqued *The Corsican Brothers* at the Gaiety Theatre this curtain was made a feature. It was represented by an enormous flimsy patchwork quilt which tumbled down all at once in the form of a tight-drawn curtain covering the whole proscenium arch.

In this burlesque too there was a notable incident when J. D. Stoyle—an actor with the power and skill of an acrobat—who personated Irving, walked up a staircase in *one step*.

IX

Another feature was the " double." In a play where one actor plays two parts there is usually at least one time when the two have to be seen together. For this a double has to be provided. In *The Corsican Brothers*, where one of the two *sees the other seeing his brother* more than one double is required. At the Lyceum, Irving's chief double was the late Arthur Matthison, who though a much smaller man than Irving resembled him faintly in his facial aspect. He had a firm belief that he *was* Irving's double and that no one could tell them apart. This belief was a source of endless jokes. There was hardly a person in the theatre who did not at one time or another take part in one. It was a never-ending amusement to Irving to watch and even to foment such jokes. Even Irving's sons, then little children, having been carefully coached, used to go up to him and take his hand and call him " Papa." On the Gaiety stage they had about twenty doubles of all sizes and conditions —giants, dwarfs, skinny, fat—of all kinds. At the end of the scene they took a call—all together. It was certainly very funny.

One more funny matter there was in the doing of

STAGE CHAMPAGNE

the play. The supper-party at Baron Montgiron's house was supposed to be a very "toney" affair, the male guests being the *crême de la crême* of Parisian society, the ladies being of the *demi-monde;* all of both classes being persons to whom a "square" meal was no rarity. As, however, the majority of the guests were "extras" or "supers" it was hard to curb their zeal in matters of alimentation. When the servants used to throw open the doors of the supper-room and announce "*Monsieur est servi!*" they would make one wild rush and surround the table like hyenas. For their delectation bread and sponge-cake—media which lend themselves to sculptural efforts—and *gâteaux* of alluring aspect were provided. The champagne flowed in profusion—indeed in such profusion and of so realistic an appearance that all over the house the opera-glasses used to be levelled and speculations as to the brand and *cuvée* arose. Indeed a rumour went round the press that the nightly wine bill was of colossal dimensions. In reality the champagne provided was lemonade put up specially in champagne bottles and foiled with exactness. It certainly *looked* like champagne and foamed out as the corks popped. The orgy grew nightly in violence till at the end of a couple of weeks the noblesse of France manifested a hunger and thirst libellous to the Faubourg St. Germain. Irving pondered over the matter, and one day gave orders that special food should be provided, wrought partly of plaster-o'-Paris and partly of *papier-mâché*. He told the Property Master to keep the matter secret. There was hardly any need for the admonition. In a theatre a joke is a very sacred thing, and there is no one from highest to lowest that will not go out of his way to further it. That night when the emaciated noblesse of France dashed at their quarry one and all received a sudden check. There were many unintentional ejaculations of surprise and disappointment from the guests, and much suppressed laughter from the stage hands who were by this time all in the secret and watching from the wings.

After that night there was a notable improvement in the table manners of the guests. One and all they took their food leisurely and examined it critically. And so the succulent sponge-cake in due time reappeared; there was no need for a second lesson against greed.

XVI

THE VALUE OF EXPERIMENT

"*Robert Macaire*"—*A Great Benefit*—"*Our Genial friend Mr. Edwards*—"*Faust*"—*Application of Science*—*Division of stage labour*—*The Emperor Fritz*—*Accidental Effects*—*A "top angel"*—*Educational value of the Stage*—"*Faust*" *in America*—*Irving's Fiftieth Birthday*

I

IN 1883 the Prince of Wales was very much interested in the creation and organisation of the new College of Music, and as funds had to be forthcoming very general efforts were made by the many who loved music and who loved the Prince. On one occasion the Prince hinted to Irving that it would show the interest of another and allied branch of art in the undertaking if the dramatic artists would give a benefit for the new College. He even suggested that *Robert Macaire* would do excellently for the occasion and could have an "all-star" cast. Of course Irving was delighted and got together a committee of actors to arrange the matter. By a process of natural selection Irving and Toole were appointed to Macaire and Jacques Strop.

The Prince and Princess of Wales attended at

the performance. The house was packed from floor to ceiling, and the result to the College of Music was £1002 8s. 6d.—the entire receipts, Irving himself having paid all the expenses.

An odd mistake was made by Irving later on with regard to this affair. In the first year of its working, when the class for dramatic study was organised, he was asked by the directorate to examine. This he was of course very pleased to do. In due season he made his examination and sent in his report. Then in sequence came a letter of thanks for his services. It was, though quite formal, a most genial and friendly letter, and to the signature was appended " Chairman." In acknowledging it to Sir George Grove, the Director of the College, Irving said what a pleasure it had been to him to examine and how pleased he would be at all times to hold his services at the disposal of the College and so forth. He added by way of postscript:

" By the way, who is our genial friend Mr. Edwards ? I do not think I have met him!"

He got a horrified letter sent by messenger from Sir George explaining that the signature was that of " Albert Edward "—now His Most Gracious Majesty Edward VII., R. et I. In his modest estimate of his own worth Irving had not even thought that the Prince of Wales would himself write. But the gracious act was like all the kindness and sweet courtesy which both as Prince and King he always extended to his loyal subject the player—Henry Irving.

II

Faust was produced on December 19, 1885. The occasion was graced by the presence of the Prince and Princess of Wales. It ran till the end of that season, the tenth of Irving's management; the whole of the next season, except a few odd nights; again the latter part of the short season of 1888; and for a fourth time in the season of 1894. The production was burned with the other plays in storage in 1898, but the play was reproduced again in 1902.

Altogether it was performed in London five hundred and seventy-seven times; in the provinces one hundred and twenty-eight times; and in America eighty-seven times. In all seven hundred and ninety-two times, to a total amount of receipts of over a quarter of a million pounds sterling.

Irving had a profound belief in *Faust* as a "drawing" play. He was so sure of it that he would not allow of its being presented until it was in his estimation ready for the public to see. This scrupulosity was a trait in his artistic character, and therefore noticeable in his management. When he was with Miss Herbert at the St. James's Theatre he was cast for the part of Ferment in *The School of Reform* at short notice; he insisted on delaying the piece for three days as he would not play without proper rehearsal. This he told me himself one night when we were supping together at the theatre, December 7, 1880. As *Faust* was an exceedingly heavy production there was much opportunity for delay. It had been Irving's intention to produce the play very early in the season which opened on September 5, but as the new play grew into shape he found need for more and more care. Many of the effects were experimental and had to be tested; and all this caused delay. As an instance of how scientific progress can be marked even on the stage, the use of electricity might be given. The fight between Faust and Valentine—with Mephistopheles in his supposed invisible quality interfering—was the first time when electric flashes were used in a play. This effect was arranged by Colonel Gouraud, Edison's partner, who kindly interested himself in the matter. Twenty years ago electric energy, in its playful aspect, was in its infancy; and the way in which the electricity was carried so as to produce the full effects without the possibility of danger to the combatants was then considered very ingenious. Two iron plates were screwed upon the stage at a given distance so that at the time of fighting each of the swordsmen would have his right boot on one of the plates, which represented an end of the interrupted current. A wire was passed up the clothing of each from the shoe to the outside of the indiarubber glove, in the palm of which was a piece of steel. Thus when each held his sword a flash came whenever the swords crossed.

The arrangement of the fire which burst from the table and from the ground at command of Mephistopheles required very careful arrangement so as to ensure accuracy at each repetition and be at the same time free from the possibility of danger. Altogether the effects of light and flame in *Faust* are of necessity somewhat startling and require the greatest care. The stage and the methods of producing flame of such rapidity of growth and exhaustion as to render it safe to use are well known to property masters. By powdered resin, properly and carefully used, or by lycopodium great effects can be achieved.

There was also another difficulty to be overcome. Steam and mist are elements of the weird and supernatural effects of an eerie play. Steam can be produced in any quantity, given the proper appliances. But these need care and attention, and on a stage, and below and above it, space is so limited that it is necessary to keep the tally of hands as low as possible. In the years that have elapsed, inspecting authorities have become extra careful with regard to such appliances; nowadays they require that even the steam kettle be kept outside the curtilage of the building.

In addition to all these things—perhaps partly on account of them—Mr. Loveday, the stage-manager, became ill and Irving had to superintend much of the doing of things himself in an unwonted way. The piece we were then running, *Olivia*, however, was comparatively light work for Irving, and as it was doing really fine business the time could partially be spared. I say "partially" because prolonged rehearsals mean a fearful addition to expense, and when rehearsals come after another play has been given the expense mounts up in arithmetical progression. For instance, the working day of a stage hand is eight working hours. If he be employed for longer the next four hours is counted as a day, and the next two hours beyond that again as a third day. All this time the real work done by the stage hands is very little. Whilst actors or supers or ballet or chorus, or some or all of them, are being rehearsed the men have to stand idle most of the time. Moreover they are now and again idle *inter se.* Stage work is divided into departments, and the mechanical things are under several masters, each controlling his own set of men. There is the Master Machinist—commonly called Master Carpenter—the Property Master, the Gas Engineer and the Electric Engineer, the Limelight Master. In certain ways the work of these departments impinge on each other in a way to puzzle an outsider. Thus, when a stage has to be covered it is the work of one set of men or the other, but not of both. Anything in the nature of a painted cloth, such as tessellated flooring, is scenery, and therefore the work of the carpenters; but a carpet is a " property " and as such to be laid down by the property staff. A gas light or an electric light is to be arranged by the engineer of that cult, whilst an oil lamp or a candle belongs to properties. The traditional laws which govern these things are deep seated in trade rights and customs and are grave matters to interfere with. In the production of *Faust* much of the scenery was what is called " built out "; that is, there are many individual pieces—each a completed and separate item, such as a wall, a house, steps, &c. So that in this particular play the property department had a great deal to do with the working of what might be broadly considered scenery.

When Irving was about to do the play he made a trip to Nuremberg to see for himself what would be most picturesque as well as suitable. When he had seen Nuremberg and that wonderful old town near it, Rothenberg, which was even better suited to his purpose, he sent for Hawes Craven. That the latter benefited by his experience was shown in the wonderful scenes which he painted for *Faust*. He seemed to give the very essence of the place.

III

When the Emperor Frederick—then Crown Prince of Germany—came to the Lyceum to see *Faust*, I was much struck by the way he spoke of the great city of the Guttenburgs and Hans Sachs. He had come alone, quite informally, from Windsor, where he was staying with Queen Victoria. As he modestly put it in his own way when speaking to me: "The Queen was gracious enough to let me come!" He was delighted and almost fascinated with the play and its production and acting. I had good opportunity of hearing his views. It was of course my duty to wait upon him, as ceremonial custom demanded, between the acts. In each "wait" he went into the Royal room to smoke his cigarette, and on each occasion was gracious enough to ask me to join him. Several times he spoke of Nuremberg with love and delight, and it seemed as if the faithful and picturesque reproduction of it had warmed his heart. Once he said:

"I love Nuremberg. Indeed I always ask the Emperor to let me have the autumn manœuvres in such a place that I can stay there during part of the time they last!"

IV

As a good instance of how on the stage things may change on trial I think we may take the last scene of *Faust*—that where the scene of Margaret's prison fades away—after the exit of Faust in answer to the imperious summons of Mephistopheles: " Hither to me." Then is the vision of Margaret's lying dead at the foot of the Cross with a long line of descending angels. For this tableau a magnificent and elaborate scene had been prepared by William Telbin—a rainbow scene suggestive of Hope and Heavenly beauty. In it had been employed the whole resources of scenic art. Indeed a new idea and mechanism had been used. The edges of the great rainbow which circled the scene were made of a series of stuffs so fine as to be actually almost invisible, beginning with linen, then skrim, and finally ending up with a tissue like gold-beaters' skin; all these substances painted or stained with the colours of the prism in due order. I believe Telbin would have put in the " extra violet ray " if it had been then discovered.

When, however, the scene was set, which was on the night before the presentation of the play, Irving seemed to be dissatisfied with it. Not with its beauty or its mechanism; but somehow it seemed to him to lack simplicity. Still he waited till it was lit in all possible ways before giving it over. The lighting of scenes was always Irving's special province; later on I shall have something to say about it. To do it properly and create the best effect he spared neither time nor pains. Many and many and many a night did we sit for four or five hours, when the play of the night had been put aside and the new scene made ready, experimenting.

On this occasion Irving said suddenly:

"Strike the scene altogether, leaving only the wings!"

This was done and the "ladder" of Angels was left stark on the empty stage. For such a vision a capable piece of machinery has to be provided, for it has to bear the full weight of at least a dozen women or girls. The backbone of it is a section of steel rail which is hung from the flies with a steel rope, to this are attached the iron arms made safe and comfortable for the angels to be strapped each in her own "iron." The lower end of the ladder rests on the stage and is fastened there securely with stage screws. The angels are all fixed in their places before the scene begins, and when the lights are turned on they seem to float ethereally. This ladder was of course complete with its living burden when the lighting was being essayed, for as it is the centre figures are pure white—the strongest colour known on the stage—it would not be possible to judge of effect without it. Again Irving spoke:

"Now put down a dark blue sky border as a backing; two if necessary to get height enough." This was done. He went on:

"Put sapphire mediums on the limelights from both sides so as to make the whole back cloth a dark night blue. Now turn all the white limelights on the angels!"

Then we saw the nobly simple effect which the actor had had in his imagination. Never was seen so complete, so subtle, so divine a vision on the stage. It was simply perfect, and all who saw it at once began to applaud impulsively. After a minute Irving, turning to Telbin who stood beside him, said :

"I think, Telbin, if you will put in some stars —proper ones you know—in the back cloth when you have primed it—it had better be of cobalt !"—a very expensive paint by the way—" it will be all right. They can get a cloth ready for you by morning."

The device of the "ladder of angels" was of course an old one ; it was its suitable perfection in this instance that made it remarkable. For this ladder it is advisable to get the prettiest and daintiest young women and children possible, the point of honour being the apex. A year before a box was occupied by a friend of Irving's who had three lovely children, little girls. The children were so beautiful that between the acts the people on the stage kept peeping out at them. Then the Master Carpenter asked Ellen Terry to look out from the prompt entrance. As she did so Mather whispered to her :

"Oh, miss ! Wouldn't that middle one make a lovely 'top angel' ? "

Even children as well as grown-ups have their vanities. It became a nightly duty of the Wardrobe Mistress to inspect the "ladder" when arranged. She had to make each of the angels in turn show their hands so that they should not wear the little rings to which they were prone.

V

The educational effect of *Faust* was very great. Every edition of the play in England was soon sold out. Important heavy volumes, such as Anster's, which had grown dusty on the publisher's shelves were cleared off in no time. New editions were published and could hardly be printed quick enough. We knew of more than a hundred thousand copies of Goethe's dramatic poem which were sold in the first season of its run.

One night early in the run of the play there was a mishap which might have been very serious indeed. In the scene where Mephistopheles takes Faust away with him after the latter had signed the contract, the two ascended a rising slope. On this particular occasion the machinery took Irving's clothing and lifted him up a little. He narrowly escaped falling into the cellar through the open trap—a fall of some fifteen feet on to a concrete floor.

VI

When we played *Faust* in America, it was curious to note the different reception accorded to it undoubtedly arising from traditional belief.

In Boston, where the old puritanical belief of a real devil still holds, we took in one evening four thousand five hundred and eighty-two dollars—$4582—the largest dramatic house up to then known in America. Strangely the night was that of Irving's fiftieth birthday. For the rest the lowest receipts out of thirteen performances was two thousand and ten dollars. Seven were over three thousand, and three over four thousand.

In Philadelphia, where are the descendants of the pious Quakers who followed Penn into the wilderness, the average receipts were even greater. Indeed at the *matinée* on Saturday, the crowd was so vast that the doors were carried by storm. All the seats had been sold, but in America it was usual to sell admissions to stand at one dollar each. The crowd of "standees," almost entirely women, began to assemble whilst the treasurer, who in an American theatre sells the tickets, was at his dinner. His assistant, being without definite instructions, went on selling till the whole seven hundred left with him were exhausted. It was vain to try to stem the rush of these enthusiastic ladies. They carried the outer door and the checktaker with it; and broke down by sheer weight of numbers the great inner doors of heavy mahogany and glass standing some eight feet high. It was impossible for the seat-holders to get in till a whole posse of police appeared on the scene and cleared them all out, only re-admitting them when the seats had been filled.

But in Chicago, which as a city neither fears the devil nor troubles its head about him or all his works, the receipts were not much more than half the other places. Not so good as for the other plays of the *répertoire* presented.

In New York the business with the play was steady and enormous. New York was founded by the Bible-loving righteous-living Dutch.

XVII

THE PULSE OF THE PUBLIC

"Ravenswood" — Delayed Presentation — The Public Pulse—"Nance Oldfield"—Ellen Terry as a Dramatist

I

In 1882 Irving purchased from Herman Merivale the entire acting rights in his play *Edgar and Lucy*, founded on Scott's novel *The Bride of Lammermoor*, but it was not till eight years later that he was able to produce it.

This delay is a fair instance of the difficulties and intricacies of theatrical management. So many things have to be considered in the high policy of the undertaking; so many accidental circumstances or continuations of causes necessitate the deviation of intention; so many new matters come over the horizon that from a long way ahead to undertake to produce a play at a given time is almost always attended with great risk.

Ravenswood is a thoroughly sad, indeed lugubrious play, as any play must be which adheres fairly to the lines of Scott's tragic novel. By the way this novel was written at Rokeby, the home of the Morritt family, in Yorkshire. The members of that family tell a strange circumstance relating to it. Sir Walter Scott was a close friend of the family and often stayed there; he wrote two of his novels whilst a guest. Whilst at Rokeby on this occasion he was in very bad health; but all the time he worked hard and wrote the novel. When he had finished he was laid up for a while; and when he was well he could not remember any detail at all of his story. He could hardly believe that he had written it.

For seven years after Irving had possession of Merivale's play he had thought it over. He had in his own quiet way made up his mind about it, arranging length and way of doing the play and excogitating his own part till he had possession of it in every way. Then one evening—November 25, 1889—he broached the subject of its definite production. The note which I find in my diary is succinct and explanatory and comprehensive:

> "Theatre 7 (P.M.) till 5 (A.M.). H. I. read for Loveday and me *Edgar and Lucy*, Merivale's dramatisation to his order of *The Bride of Lammermoor*. It was delightful. Play very fine. Literature noble. H. I. had cut quite one-half out."

I can supplement this brief note from memory. Irving read the play with quite extraordinary effect. He had quite an added gift for this sort of work. I heard him read through a good many plays in the course of a quarter of a century of work together and it was always enlightening. He had a way of conveying the *cachet* of each character by inflection or trick of voice or manner; and his face was always, consciously or unconsciously, expressive. So long before as 1859,

when he had read *The Lady of Lyons* at Crosby
Hall, the *Daily Telegraph* had praised, amongst
other matters, his versatility in this respect.
I have heard him read in public in a large
hall both *Hamlet* and *Macbeth*, and his characterisation was so marked that after he had
read the entries of the various characters he
did not require to refer to them again by name.
On this occasion he seemed familiar with every
character, and, I doubt not, could have played
any of them, so far as his equipment fitted him
for the work, within a short time. Naturally
the most effective part was that of Edgar of
Ravenswood. Not only is it the most prominent
part in the cast, but it was that which he was to
play himself and to which he had given most special
attention. In it he brought out all the note of
destiny which rules in both novel and play.
Manifestly Edgar is a man foredoomed, but not
till the text sounded the note of doom in the weird
and deathly utterances of Ailsie Gourlay could
one tell that all must end awfully. Throughout,
the tragic note was paramount. Well Edgar
knew it; the gloom that wrapped him even in
the moment of triumphant love was a birth-gift.
As Irving read it that night, and as he acted it
afterwards, there was throughout an infinite and
touching pathos. But not this character alone,
but all the rest were given with great and convincing power. The very excellence of the rendering made each to help the other; variety
and juxtaposition brought the full effect. The
prophecies, because of their multiplication, became of added import on Edgar's gloom, and

toned the high spirit of Hayston of Bucklaw. Lucy's sweetness was intensified by the harsh domination of Lady Ashton. The sufferings of the faithful Caleb under the lash of Ailsie's prophecy only increased its force.

We who listened were delighted. For myself I seemed to see the play a great success and one to be accomplished at little cost. We had now, since 1885, produced in succession three great plays, *Faust*, *Macbeth* and *The Dead Heart*, and had in contemplation another, *Henry VIII.*, which would exceed them all in possibilities of expense both of production and of working. These great plays were and always must be hugely expensive. As I was chancellor of the exchequer I was greatly delighted to see a chance of great success combined with a reasonable cost and modest accessories. From the quiet effectiveness of Irving's reading I was satisfied that the play would hold good under the less grand conditions. This opinion I still hold. I must not, however, be taken as finding fault with Irving's view, which was quite otherwise. He looked on the play as one needing all the help it could get; and I am bound to say that his views were justified by success, for the play as he did it was an enormous success. The production account was not large in comparison with that of some other great plays, being a little under five thousand pounds. There were no author's fees, as the play had long ago been bought outright and paid for, so that expense had been incurred and was chargeable against estate whether the play was produced or not. But the running expenses were very heavy, between £180 and

£200 a performance. As it was the play was a heavy one for Ellen Terry; we could only play it six times a week. To the management there is always an added advantage in a *matinée* or any extra performance.

Ravenswood was presented on September 20, 1890, and altogether was given during the season one hundred and two times.

II

During its run we had a strange opportunity of experiencing the extraordinary way in which a play fluctuates with the public pulse. From the first night it was a great success, and the booking became so great that we were obliged to enlarge the time for the advance purchase of seats. Our usual time was four weeks, and as a working rule it was found well to keep to this. Where booking is not under great pressure too long a time means extra particularity in choice of seats, and a *de facto* curtailment of receipts. For *Ravenswood* we had to advance, first one week and then a second; so that about the end of the first month we were booking six weeks ahead. I may say that we were *booked* that long, for as each day's advance sheet was opened it became quickly filled. The agents, too, were hard at work and we were not able to allot to any of them the full number of seats for which they asked. I have a special reason for mentioning this, as will appear. Now at the Lyceum from the time of my taking charge of the business we did not ever "pencil" to agents

—that is, we did not let them have seats after the customary fashion "on sale or return." We had, be sure, good reason for this. Whatever seats they had they took at their own risk by week or month, a sort of running agreement terminable at fixed notice. When we arrived at the fiftieth performance the play was going as strong as ever, the receipts being on or about two thousand pounds per week. Within the end of the year, theatre receipts generally began to drop a little; Christmas is coming, and many things occupy family attention. The autumn visit visitors have all departed, and the fogs of November are bad for business. We did not therefore give it a second thought that the door receipts got a little less, for all the bookable seats were already secure. On Thursday, November 20, I had an experience which set me thinking. During that day I had visits from three of the theatre agents having businesses in the West End and the City. They came separately and with an unwonted secrecy. Each wished to see me alone, and being secured from interruption, stated the reason. Each had the same request and spoke in almost identical terms, so that the conversation of one will illustrate all. The first one asked me:

"Will you tell me frankly—if you don't mind—are you really doing good business with *Ravenswood?*"

"Certainly," I answered. "All we can do. Why you know that we can only let you have for six weeks ahead a part of the seats you have asked for." After some odd nervousness he said again:

"I suppose I may take it that that applies to every one you deal with? I know I can trust you, for you always treat me frankly; and this is a matter I am exceedingly anxious about." For answer I rang the bell for the commissionaire in waiting on the office and sent him round to the box office to bring me the booking sheets for six weeks ahead. These I duly placed before the agent--Librarian they called them in those days as they were the survivors of the old lending libraries who used to secure theatre tickets for their customers.

"See for yourself!" I said; and he turned over the sheets, every seat on which was marked as sold.

"It is very extraordinary!" he said after a pause. By this time my own curiosity was piqued and I asked him to tell me what it all meant.

"It means this," he said. "Things can't go on at this rate. We have not sold a single ticket this week for any theatre in London!"

I opened a drawer and took out what we called the "Ushers' Returns" for each night that week. We used to have, as means of checking the receipts of the house in addition to the tickets, a set of returns made by the ushers. Each usher had a sectional chart of the seats under his charge and he had to show which was occupied during the evening and which, if any, were unoccupied. I had not gone over these as all the seats having been sold it did not much matter to us whether they were occupied or not. To my surprise I found that on each night, growing as the week went on, were quite a number of seats unoccupied. On reference to the full plan I found that most of these were seats sold to the libraries, but that a good proportion of them had been booked at our own office. Neither of us could account for such a thing in any way. When the next, and then the third agent came there was a strong sense over me that *something* was happening in the great world. As a rule when there is pressure in a theatre the seats belonging to agents remaining unsold can always be disposed of in the theatre box office.

That night Irving had a little supper-party of intimate friends in the Beefsteak Room ; amongst them one man, Major Ricarde-Seaver, well skilled in the world of *haute finance*. In the course of conversation I asked him :

" What is up ? There is something going to happen ! What is it ? " He asked me why I thought so and I told him.

" That is certainly strange ! " was his comment. " Then you don't know ? "

" Know what ? " I asked. " What is going to happen ? " His answer came after a pause.

" You will know soon. Possibly to-morrow; certainly the next day ! " The mystery was thickening. Again I asked :

" What is it ? " The answer came with a shock :

" Baring's ! They've gone under ! "

Now any one of a speculative tendency in London, or out of it, could have that day made a fortune by selling " bears "—and there is no lack of sportsmen willing to make money on a "sure thing." And yet for three days at least there must have been in business circles some uneasiness of so pronounced a character that it for the time obliterated social life with many people. Had they knowledge where the public pulse lay, and how to time its beats, they might have plucked fortune from disaster.

In the Lyceum we became wide awake to the situation. In a time of panic and disaster there is no need for mimetic tragedy; the real thing crowds it out. The very next day we arranged to change the bill on the earliest day possible. As we were booked for six weeks we arranged to change the tragic *Ravenswood* for *Much Ado About Nothing*—the brighest and cheeriest comedy in our *répertoire*—on Monday, January 3.

This we did with excellent result. From the day of the failure of Baring's the receipts began to dwindle. The nightly return dropped from three hundred pounds odd to two hundred pounds odd, and finally to one hundred pounds odd. With the change to Comedy they jumped up again at once to the tune of an extra hundred pounds a performance.

Except for some performances in the provinces in the autumn that was the last of *Ravenswood*. There was never a chance for its revival, though from that we might have expected much; it was burned in the fire at our storage in 1898—of which more anon.

III

Nance Oldfield, as Ellen Terry plays it, is the concentration of a five-act comedy into one act and one scene. It is a play that allows an inexhaustible opportunity of the gifts of the great actress. For Ellen Terry's gifts are of so wide a range that the mere variety of them is in itself a gift; and the congruity of them in such a play allows them to help each other and each to shine out all the stronger for the contrast.

Ellen Terry had long had in her mind Reade's play as one to be given in a single act. And now that its opportunity came over the horizon she began to prepare it. This she did herself, I having the honour of assisting her. That preparation was a fine lesson in dramatic construction. Ellen Terry has not only a divine instinct for the truth in stage art, but she is a conscious artist to her finger-tips. No one on the stage in our time—or at any other time—has seen more clearly the direct force of sympathy and understanding between the actor and the audience. At the same time she was not herself an experienced dramatist. She knew in a general way what it was that was wanting and what she aimed at, but she could not always give it words. During rehearsal or during the play she would in a pause of her own stage work come dancing into my office to ask for help. Ellen Terry's movements, when she was not playing a sad part, always gave one the idea of a graceful dance. Looking back now to twenty-seven years of artistic companionship and eternal community of ideas, I cannot realise that she did not always actually dance. She would point to some mark which she had made in the altered script and say :

"I want two lines there, please!"

"What kind of lines? What about?" I would ask. She would laugh as she answered :

"I don't know. I haven't the least idea. You must write them!" When she would dance back again I would read her the lines. She would laugh again and say :

"All wrong, absolutely wrong. They are too serious," or "they are too light; I should like something to convey the idea of——" and she would in some subtle way—just as Irving did—convey the sentiment, or purpose, or emotion which she wished conveyed. She would know without my saying it when I had got hold of the idea and would rush off to her work quite satisfied. And so the little play would grow and then be cut again and grow again; till at last it was nearly complete. The last bit of it puzzled us both for a long time. At last she conveyed her idea to me that Alexander must not be left with a serious personal passion for Mrs. Oldfield and that yet she should not sink in his esteem. Finally I wrote a line which had the reward of her approbation. The actress was explaining to Mr. Alworthy how his son did not really love her :

"It was the actress he loved and not the woman!"

In this little play, which is typical of her marvellous range of varied excellences, she runs the whole gamut of human emotion. The part where the great actress, wishing to disenchant her boy lover, exemplifies her art and then turns it into ridicule could not be adequately played by any one not great in both tragedy and comedy. Her rendering here of Juliet's great speech before taking the potion: " My dismal scene I needs must act alone," is given with the full tragic force with which she played the real part—when she swept the whole audience, and yet, without the delay of a second, she says to the emotional poet: " Now, that's worth one and ninepence to me! " It is such moments as these that put an actor into history. Records are not troubled with mere excellence.

Happy, I say, should be the real dramatist who has the co-operation of Ellen Terry in a play she is to appear in—of a part she is to act.

XVIII

TENNYSON AND HIS PLAYS—I

Irving on Tennyson — Frankness — Irving's Knowledge of Character—The "Fighting" Quality—Tennyson on Irving's Hamlet—Tennyson's Alterations of his Work—As a Dramatist—"First Run"—Experts on Greek Art

I

IRVING had been a friend of Tennyson before I had first met him in 1876. When during the Bateman rule *Queen Mary* had been produced, he had naturally much to do with the author, and the friendship thus begun lasted during the poet's life. In my own young days Tennyson was a name of something more than reverence. Not only was his work on our tongue-tips, but the extraordinary isolation of his personal life threw a halo of mystery over him. It is a strange thing how few of the people of his own time—and all through his long life of such amazing worth and popularity, had ever seen him. Naturally a man who knew him was envied if only from this source alone. Whenever we met in early days Irving, knowing my love and reverence for the poet, used to talk about him—always with admiration. More than once when speaking of his personality as distinguished from his work he said:

"Tennyson is like a great Newfoundland dog. He is like an incarnate truth. A great creature!"

From some persons comparison with a dog might not have seemed flattery, but to Irving a dog was the embodiment of all the virtues. Often and often he compared the abstract dog to the abstract man, very much to the detriment of the latter. And certainly Tennyson had all that noble simplicity which is hard to find in sophisticated man—that simplicity which lies in the wide field of demarcation between naked brutal truth and an unconsciousness of self. That simplicity it is which puts man on an altitude where lesser as well as greater natures respect him. To him truth was a simple thing; it was to be exact. Irving told me of an incident illustrating this which happened to himself. He had heard a story that not long before Tennyson had been lunching with friends of his in his own neighbourhood not far from Haslemere. His hostess, who was a most gracious and charming woman whom later I had the honour to know, said to him as they went into the dining-room:

"I have made a dish specially for you myself; I hope you will try it and tell me exactly what you think of it."

"Of course I shall," he answered. After lunch she asked him what he thought of it and he answered at once:

"If you really wish to know, I thought it was like an old shoe!"

When they met Irving asked him if the story were true.

"No!" he answered at once, "I didn't say

IRVING'S KNOWLEDGE OF CHARACTER

that. I said something ; but it wasn't that it was like an old shoe!"

"What did you say?"

"I said it was like an old boot!"

With him ethical truth was not enough ; exactness was a part of the whole. I had myself an instance of his mental craving for truth on the very last day I saw him.

Irving had a wonderful knowledge of character. I have never in my own experience known him to err in this respect ; though many and many a time has he acted as though he trusted when he knew right well that a basis was wanting. This was of the generosity of his nature ; but be it never so great, generosity could not obscure his reason. This was shown, even at the time, by the bounds set to his trust ; he never trusted beyond recall, or to an amount of serious import. He had, in the course of a lifetime spent in the exercise of his craft, which was to know men from within, given too much thought to it not to be able from internal knowledge to fathom the motives of others. In philosophy analysis precedes synthesis. On one occasion there was a man with whom we had some business dealings and who, to say the least of it, did not impress any of us favourably. Irving was very outspoken about him, so much so that I remonstrated, fearing lest he might let himself in for an action for libel. I also put it that we had not sufficient data before us to justify so harsh a view. Irving listened to me patiently and then said :

"My dear fellow, that man is a crook. I *know* it. I have studied too many villains not to understand!"

In another matter also Tennyson had the quality of a well-bred dog: he was a fighter. I do not mean that he was quarrelsome or that he ever even fought in any form. I simply mean that he had the quality of fighting—quite a different thing from determination. In a whole group of men of his own time Tennyson would have, to any physiognomist, stood as a fighter. A glance at his mouth would at once enlighten any one who had the "seeing eye." In the group might be placed a good many men, each prominent in his own way, and some of whom might not *prima facie* be suspected of the quality. In the group, all of whom I have known or met, might be placed Archbishop Temple, John Bright, Gladstone, Sir Richard Burton, Sir Henry Stanley, Lord Beaconsfield, Jules Bastien Le Page, Henry Ward Beecher, Professor Blackie, Walt Whitman, Edmund Yates. I have selected a few from the many, leaving out altogether all classes of warriors in whom the fighting quality might be suspected.

Tennyson had at times that lifting of the upper lip which shows the canine tooth, and which is so marked an indication of militant instinct. Of all the men I have met the one who had this indication most marked was Sir Richard Burton. Tennyson's, though notable, was not nearly so marked.

Amongst other things which Irving told me of Tennyson in those early days was regarding the author's own ideas of casting *Queen Mary*. He wanted Irving to play Cardinal Pole, a part not in the play at all as acted. One night years afterwards, January 25, 1893, at supper in the Garrick Club with Toole and two others, he told us the same thing. I think the circumstance was recalled to him by the necessary excision of another character in *Becket*.

It was my good fortune to meet Tennyson personally soon after my coming to live in London. On the night of March 20, 1879, he being then in London for a short stay, he came to the Lyceum to see *Hamlet*. It was the sixty-ninth night of the run. James Knowles was with him and introduced me. After the third act they both came round to Irving's dressing-room. In the course of our conversation when I saw him again at the end of the play he said to me:

"I did not think Irving could have improved his Hamlet of five years ago; but now he has improved it five degrees. And those five degrees have lifted it to Heaven!"

Small wonder that I was proud to hear such an opinion from such a source.

I remember also another thing he said:

"I am seventy, and yet I don't feel old—I wonder how it is!" I quoted as a reason his own lines from the *Golden Year*:

> "Unto him that works, and feels he works,
> The same grand year is ever at the doors."

He seemed mightily pleased and said:
"Good!"

After this meeting I had a good many opportunities of seeing Tennyson again. Whenever he made a trip for a few days to London it was usually my good fortune to meet him and Lady Tennyson. My wife and I lunched with them; and their sons, Hallam and Lionel, spent Sunday evenings in our house in Cheyne Walk. Meeting with Tennyson and his family has given us many many happy hours in our lives, and I had the pleasure of being the guest of the great poet both at Farringford and Aldworth. I am proud to be able to call the present Lord Tennyson my friend. My wife and I were lunching with the Tennysons during their stay in London when the first copy arrived from Hubert Herkomer—now Von Herkomer—R.A., of his fine portrait etching of the Poet Laureate. It is a fine portrait; but there is a look in the eye which did not altogether please the subject.

II

Just before the end of the season 1879-80, Irving completed with Tennyson an agreement to play *The Cup*. This play, which he had not long before finished, he had offered to Irving. It had not yet been seen by any one, and he was willing that it should not be published till after it had been played. The play required some small alterations for stage purposes—little things cut out here and there, and a few explanatory words inserted at other places. Tennyson assented without demur to any change suggested. As it has been said that Tennyson was absolutely set as to not altering a line for the stage, let me say here, after an experience of his two most successful plays, that any such statement was absurd. Of course he was careful of his rights. Every one ought to be careful in such a matter, and to him there was special need. His manuscript was so valuable that it was never safe; and in other ways he had to be suspicious. Years afterwards he told me that one of his poems had been sold by a critic in America with errors in it which had been corrected.

"I hate the creature! He said he was owner of the proof!"

Perhaps it was for this reason he was so careful when a play was being printed for stage use. He always wished his own copy returned with the proof.

In his agreements he had a clause that the licensee should not without his consent make any alteration in the play. This was absolutely right and wise; it is the protection of the author. The time for arranging changes is *before* the agreement; then both parties to the contract know what they are doing. In no case did Tennyson hesitate to give Irving permission to make changes. Like the good workman that he was he was only too anxious to have his work at its best and its highest suitability.

Tennyson had in him all the elements of a great dramatist; but unhappily he had little if any technical knowledge of the stage. Each art and each branch of art has its own technique. Though a play, like any other poem, has its birth, the means of its expression is different. A poem for reading conveys thoughts by words alone. A poem for the stage requires suitable opportunity for action and movement—both of individuals and numbers. Sound and light and scene; music, colour and form; the vibration of passion, the winning sweetness of tremulous desire, and the overwhelming obliteration that follows in the wake of fear have all their purpose and effect on the stage. Inasmuch as on the one hand there is only thought, whilst on the other there is a superadded mechanism, the two fields of poetry may be fairly taken to deal in different media. In his later years when Tennyson began to realise in his own work the power of glamour and stress and difficulty of the stage he was willing to enlist into his service the skill and experience of others. Had he begun practical play-writing younger, or had he had any kind of apprenticeship to or experience of stage use, he would have had no second as a dramatist.

In the draft agreement was an interesting clause which Mr. (afterwards Sir) Arnold White, Tennyson's solicitor, and I worked out very carefully, having regard to the rights of both parties. This was concerning the definition of the "first run" of a play. We were quite at one in intention and only wished to make the purpose textually correct. Finally we made it to read as thus:

". . . first run of the said play (that is to say) during such time as the said play shall remain in the Bills of the Theatre where it is first produced announcing its continuance either nightly or at fixed periods without a break in such announcements."

III

Irving was determined to do all in his power to put *The Cup* worthily on the stage. Accordingly much study and research in the matter began. Galatia has ceased to exist on the map, and the period of the play is semi-mythical. The tragedy

HYPERCRITICISM

stands midway between East and West; when the belief in the old Gods was a vital force. For the work which Tennyson and Irving undertook, learning and experience lent their aid. James Knowles reconstructed a Temple of Artemis on the ground plan of the great Temple of Diana. The late Alexander Murray, then Assistant Keeper —afterwards Keeper—of the Greek section of the British Museum, made researches amongst the older Etruscan designs. Capable artists made drawings from vases, which were reproduced on the great amphoræ used in the Temple service. The existing base and drum of a column from Ephesus was remodelled for use, and lent its sculptured beauty to the scene. William Telbin painted some scenes worthy of Turner; and Hawes Craven and Cuthbert made such an interior scene of the Great Temple as was surely never seen on any stage.

By the way, there was regarding this another experience of super-criticism. In judging the scene, and with considerable admiration *The Architect*, I think, found fault with the proportions of the columns supporting the Temple roof. They should have been of so many diameters more than were given. The critic quite overlooked the difficulty —in extremes the impossibility—of adhering to fact in fiction. For the mechanism of the stage and for purposes of lighting it is necessary that every stage interior have a roof of some sort. Now in this case there was a dilemma. If the columns were of exact proportion they would have looked skimpy in that vast edifice; and the general architecture would have been blamed instead of the detail.

As it was the stage perspective allowed of the massive columns close to the proscenium appearing to tower aloft in unimaginable strength, and at once conveyed the spirit of the scene. Just as the colossal figure of Artemis far up the stage—an image of fierce majesty wrought in green bronze—was intended to impress all with the relentless power of the Goddess.

But it was to Irving that the scene owed most of its beauty and grandeur. Hitherto, in all pagan ceremonials on the stage—and, indeed, in art generally—priestesses and votaries were clothed in white. But he, not finding that there was any authority for the belief, used colours and embroideries—Indian, Persian, Greek—all that might add conviction and picturesque effect. Something like a hundred beautiful young women were chosen for Vestals; and as the number of persons already employed in *The Corsican Brothers* was very great, the stage force available for scenic display was immense. Irving himself devised the processions and the ceremonies; in fact he invented a ritual. One of the strange things about the audience all through the run of the play was the large number of High Church clergy who attended. The effect of the entry into the Temple of the gorgeously armoured Roman officers was peculiarly strong.

IV

It is not given to man, however, to achieve full perfection. When *The Cup* had been running for a considerable time, Dr. Alexander Murray, whom at first we had in vain tried to persuade, came to see it. We were all anxious to know how the Greek-Eastern effect impressed him, and I made it a point to see him at the end of the play. When I asked him how he liked it he said :

"Oh, I liked it well enough at first; but when the Temple scene came it was different. At the beginning two girls came on bearing a great amphora; but you will hardly believe me when I tell you it had red figures on a black ground, instead of black figures on a red ground. I need not say that after that I could enjoy nothing!"

Both forms of using the colours were practised in the history of Etruscan art, and our people, since the time of the play was somewhat indeterminate, used the older one.

The dress of Ellen Terry as Camma in this scene was a difficult matter. It had for stage purposes to be one which would stand out distinct and apart from the rest. Dress after dress was tried, stuff after stuff was chosen; but all without satisfaction. At length, as the opening night drew near, she began to get seriously anxious. Finally, as a last resource, she asked me to try to find her something. I had been peculiarly lucky in coming across just such stuffs for dresses as she had seemed to want. Now I went off, hot-foot, and was fortunate enough to find, through turning over a whole stock of old material at Liberty's, an Indian tissue of a sort of loosely woven cloth of gold, the *wrong* side of which produced the exact effect sought for. I may here say that a good many of the special effects on the Lyceum stage were got by using the inside instead of the outside of stuffs.

Amongst them was the basis of Irving's dress as Shylock.

The Cup was produced on the evening of January 3, 1881. It was an immense success, and was played one hundred and twenty-seven times that season. It was burned in the great scenery fire in 1898.

Tennyson came himself to see it for the first time on February 26, 1881.

XIX

TENNYSON AND HIS PLAYS—II

Before "Becket"—Irving's Preparation of the Play—Re "Robin Hood"—Visit to Tennyson at Aldworth—Tennyson's Humour—His Onomatopœia—Scoffing—Tennyson's Belief—He reads his new Poem—Voice and Phonograph—Irving sees his Way to Playing "Becket"

I

IN their conversations after *Queen Mary* and before *The Cup* Irving and Tennyson had talked of the possibility of putting on the stage some other play of the Laureate's. After the success of *The Cup* had been assured Irving was more fixed on the matter; and later on, in 1884, when *Becket* had been published, he considered it then and thereafter as a possibility. He was anxious to do it if he could see his way to it. Like Tennyson, he had a conviction that there was a play in it; but he could not see its outline. In fact *Becket* was not written for the stage; and, that being so, it was for stage purposes much in the position of a block of Carrara marble from which the statue has to be patiently hewn. As it was first given to the world it was entirely too long for the stage. For instance, *Hamlet* is a play so long that it must be cut for acting, but *Becket* is longer still. For many reasons he was anxious to do another play of Tennyson's. The first had added much to his reputation, and now the second was a huge success. He loved Tennyson— really loved the man as well as his work—and if for this reason alone exerted all his power to please him. Moreover as a manager he saw the wisdom of such a move. Tennyson's was a great name and there had been a lot of foolish argument in journals and magazines regarding "literature" in plays, and also concerning the national need of encouraging contemporary dramatic literature. Rightly or wrongly the public interest has to be considered, and Tennyson's name was one to conjure with. Moreover he had come to depend on the picturesque possibilities of Tennyson's work. *The Cup* had allowed of a splendid setting, and in *Becket* its picturesque aspect of the struggle between Court and Church might be very attractive. Beyond this again there were two episodes of the period which so belonged to the history of the nation that every school child had them in memory: the martyrdom of Becket and the romantic story of Fair Rosamund and her secret bower.

Irving took the main idea of the play into his heart and tried to work it out. He kept it by him for more than a year. He took it with him to America in the tour of 1884-5. And in the long hours of loneliness, consequent on such work as his, made it a part of his mental labour. But it was all without avail; he could not see his way to a successful issue. Again he took it in hand

A PLAY ON DANTE

when going to America in 1887-8, for the conviction was still with him that the play he wanted was there, if he could only unearth it. Again long months of effort; and again failure. This time he practically gave up hope. He had often tried to get Tennyson to think of other subjects; but without avail. Tennyson would not take any subject in hand unless he felt it and could see his way to it. Now Irving tried to interest him afresh in some of his other themes. He wished him to undertake a play on the subject of Dante. Tennyson considered the matter a while and then made a memorable reply:

"A fine subject! But where is the Dante to write it?"

Again Irving asked him to do Enoch Arden; but he said that having written the poem he would rather not deal with the same subject a second time in a different way.

Then he tried King Arthur; but again Tennyson applied the same reasoning with the same result.

At last he suggested as a subject, Robin Hood. Tennyson did not acquiesce, but he said he would think it over. I remember that Irving, hoping to interest him further in the matter, got all the books treating of the subject; all the romances and plays which he could hear of. He had hopes that the romantic side of the outlaw's life would touch the poet. In fact Tennyson did write a play, *The Foresters*, which has been successful in America. I shall have something to say later on about the London production for the purposes of copyright.

II

In the spring of 1890, in response to a kindly invitation, Irving visited Aldworth, the lovely home which Tennyson made for himself under the brow of Blackdown. It was nine years since the two men had had opportunity for a real talk. Sunday, October 19, was fixed for the visit. I was invited to lunch also, and needless to say I looked forward to the visit, for it was to be the first opportunity I should have of seeing Tennyson in his own home.

On the Sunday morning Irving and I made an early start, leaving Victoria Station by the train at 8.45 and arriving at Haslemere a little after half-past ten. Blackdown is just under mountain height—one thousand feet; but it is high enough and steep enough to test the lungs and muscles of man or beast. It was a typically fine day in autumn. The air was dry and cold and bracing, after a slight frost whose traces the bright sun had not yet obliterated. All was bright and clear around us, but the hills in the distance were misty.

Aldworth is a wonderful spot. Tennyson chose it himself with a rare discretion. It is, I suppose, the most naturally isolated place within a hundred miles of London. Doubtless this was an element in his choice, for he is said to have had a sickening of publicity at his other home, "Farringford," at Freshwater in the Isle of Wight. The house lies just under the brow of the hill to the east and faces south. This side of the hill is very steep, and now that the trees which he planted have grown tall the house cannot be seen from anywhere above. It is necessary to go miles away to get a glimpse of it from below. When he bought the ground it was all mountain moorland and he had to make his own roads. The house is of stone with fine mullioned windows and the spaces everywhere are gracious. In front, which faces south, is a small lawn bounded by a stone parapet with a quickset hedge below and just showing above the top of the stonework. From here you look over Surrey and Sussex right away to Goodwood and the bare Downs above Brighton. A glorious expanse of country articulated with river and wood and field of seeming toy dimensions. It would, I think, be impossible to find a more ideal place for quiet work. From it the howling, pushing, strenuous world is absolutely shut out, and the mind can work untrammelled, fancy free. To the west lies a beautiful garden fashioned into pleasant nooks and winding alleys, with flower-starred walks, and bowers of roses, and spreading shrubs. Behind it rise some fine forest trees. The garden trends some way down the hillside, opening to seas of bracken and the dim shelter of pine woods. In the fringes these woods in due season are filled with a natural growth of purple foxglove, the finest I have ever seen. Just below where the garden ends is a level nook, a corner between shelving lines of tree-clad hill where a tiny stream flows from a vigorous bubbling well. Just such a nook as Old Crome or Nasmyth would have loved to paint.

Hallam Tennyson met us at the door. When we entered the wide hall, one of the noticeable things was quite a number of the picturesque wide-brimmed felt hats which Tennyson always wore. I could not but notice them, for a certain similarity struck me. In the house of Walt Whitman at Camden, New Jersey, was just such a collection of hats; except that Walt Whitman's hats—he being paralysed and not naturally careful of his appearance at that time of his life—were worn out. Walt only got a new hat when the old one was badly worn. But he did not part with the old ones even then.

After a short visit to Lady Tennyson in the drawing-room we were brought upstairs to Tennyson's study, a great room over the drawing-room, with mullioned windows facing south and west. We entered from behind a great eight-fold screen some seven or eight feet high. Tennyson was sitting at a table in the western window writing in a book of copy-book size with black cover. His writing was very firm. He had on a black skull-cap. As we entered he held up his hand saying:

"Just one minute if you don't mind. I am almost finished!" When he had done he threw down his pen and rising quickly came towards us with open-handed welcome. In the room were many tall bookcases. The mullioned windows let in a flood of light.

I went with Hallam to his own study, leaving Irving alone with Tennyson. Half an hour later we joined them and we all went out for a walk. The medical nurse who had been attending

Tennyson, who had lately had a long illness, came with us. Strangely enough she had been one of my brother George's nurses in the Zulu War, where he had been Stafford House Commissioner. In the garden Tennyson pointed out to us some blue flowering pea which had been reared from seed found in the hand of a mummy. Tennyson stooped a little as he walked—he was then aged, eighty-two—but seemed strong and was very cheerful—sometimes even merry. With us came his great Russian wolf-hound which seemed devoted to him. We walked through the grounds and woods for some three miles altogether, Hallam and Irving walking in front. As I walked with Tennyson we had much conversation, every word of which comes back to me. I was so fond of Tennyson and admired him so much that I could not, I think, forget if I tried anything which he said. Amongst other things he mentioned a little incident at Farringford, when in his own grounds an effusive lady, a stranger, said at rather than to him, of course alluding to the berries of the wild rose, then in profusion :

"What beautiful hips!"

"I'm so glad you admire 'em ma'am!" he had answered, and he laughed heartily at the memory. I mention this as an instance of his love of humour. He had intense enjoyment of it.

He also mentioned an error made by the writer of *Tennyson Land* of a dog which in Demet Vale saved the child of an old local farmer.

"It's a lie," he said, "I invented it all; though there was such a character when I was a boy. When he was dying he said :

"'Th' A'mighty couldn't be so hard. An' Squire would be so mad an' a'!'" He said it in broad Lincolnshire dialect such as he used in *The Northern Farmer*. Tennyson was a natural character-actor; when he read or spoke as such in the first person he conveyed in voice and manner a distinct impression of an individual other than himself.

Then he told me some Irish anecdotes generally bearing on that quality in the Irish nature which renders them unsatisfied. He suggested a parody of a double row of shillelaghs working automatically on each side "and then they would be unsatisfied!" At another time he spoke to me in the same vein.

Then I told him some Irish dialect stories which were new to him and which really seemed to give him pleasure. I told him also some of the extravagant Orange toasts of former days whereat he laughed much. Then turning to me he said:

"When we go in I want to read you something which I have just finished; but you must not say anything about it yet!"

"All right!" I said, "of course I shall not. But why, may I ask, do you wish it so?"

"Well, you see," he said, "I have to be careful. If it is known that I am writing on a particular subject I get a dozen poems on it the next day. And then when mine comes out they say I plagiarised them!"

In the course of our conversation something cropped up which suggested a line of one of his poems, *The Golden Year*, and I quoted it. "Go on!" said Tennyson, who seemed to like to know that any one quoting him knew more than the bare quotation. I happened to know that poem and went on to the end of the lyrical portion. There I stopped:

"Go on!" he said again; so I spoke the narrative bit at the end, supposed to be spoken by the writer:

> "He spoke; and, high above, I heard them blast
> The steep slate-quarry, and the great echo flap
> And buffet round the hills, from bluff to bluff."

Tennyson listened attentively. When I spoke the last line he shook his head and said:

"No!"

"Surely that is correct?" I said.

"No!" There was in this something which I did not understand, for I was certain that I had given the words correctly. So I ventured to say:

"Of course one must not contradict an author about his own work; but I am certain those are the words in my edition of the poem." He answered quickly:

"Oh, the words are all right—quite correct!"

"Then what is wrong?" For answer he said:

"Have you ever been on a Welsh mountain?"

"Yes! on Snowdon!"

"Did you hear them blast a slate-quarry?"

"Yes. In Wales, and also on Coniston in Cumberland."

"And did you notice the sound?" I was altogether at fault and said:

"Won't you tell me—explain to me. I really want to understand?" He spoke the last line, and further explanation was unnecessary. The whole gist was in his pronunciation of the word "bluff" twice repeated. He spoke the word with a sort of quick propulsive effort as though throwing the word from his mouth.

"I thought any one would understand that!" he added.

It was the exact muffled sound which the exploding charge makes in the curves of the steep valleys.

This is a good instance of Tennyson's wonderful power of onomatopœia. To him the sound had a sense of its own. I had another instance of it before the day was over.

That talk was full of very interesting memories. Perhaps it was apropos of the peas grown from the seed in the mummy hand, but Lazarus in his tomb came on the *tapis*. This stanza of *In Memoriam* had always been a favourite of mine, and when I said so, he said:

"Repeat it!" I did so, again feeling as if I were being weighed up. When I had finished

"He told it not; or something seal'd
The lips of that Evangelist:"

he turned to me and said:

"Do you know that when that was published they said I was scoffing. But"—here both face and voice grew very very grave—"I did not mean to scoff!"

When I told him of my wonder as to how any sane person could have taken such an idea from such a faithful, tender, understanding poem he went on to speak of faith and the need of faith. There was nothing strange or original to rest in my mind. But his finishing sentence I shall never forget. Indeed had I forgotten for the time I should have remembered it from what he said the last interview I had with him just before his death:

"You know I don't believe in an eternal hell, with an All-merciful God. I believe in the All-merciful God! It would be better otherwise that men should believe they are only ephemera!"

When we returned to the house we lunched, Lady Tennyson and Mrs. Hallam Tennyson having joined us. Then we went up again to the study, and Tennyson, taking from the table the book in which he had been writing, read us the last poem, *The Churchwarden and the Curate*. He read it in the Lincolnshire dialect, which is much simpler when heard than read. The broadness of the vowels and their rustic prolongation rather than drawl adds force and also humour. I shall never forget the intense effect of the last lines of the tenth stanza. The shrewd worldly wisdom—which was plain sincerity of understanding without cynicism:

"But niver not speäk plaain out, if tha wants to git forrards a bit,
But creeäp along the hedge-bottoms, an' thou'll be a Bishop yit."

Tennyson was a strangely good reader. His voice was powerful and vibrant, and had that quality of individualism which is so convincing. You could not possibly mistake it for the voice of any one else. It was a potent part of the man's identity. In his reading there was a wonderful sense of time. The lines seemed to swing with an elastic step—like a regiment marching.

In a little time after came his hour for midday rest; so we said good-bye and left him. Irving and I went for a smoke to Hallam's study, where he produced his phonograph and adjusted a cylinder containing a reading of his father's. Colonel Gouraud had taken special pains to have for the reception of Tennyson's voice the most perfect appliance possible, and the phonograph was one of peculiar excellence, without any of that tinny sharpness which so often changes the intentioned sound.

The reading was that of Tennyson's own poem, *The Charge of the Heavy Brigade*. It was strange to hear the mechanical repetition whilst the sound of the real voice, which we had so lately heard, was still ringing in our ears. It was hard to believe that we were not listening to the poet once again. The poem of Scarlett's charge is one of special excellence for both phonographic recital and as an illustration of Tennyson's remarkable sense of time. One seems to hear the rhythmic thunder of the horses' hoofs as they ride to the attack. The ground seems to shake, and the virile voice of the reader conveys in added volume the desperate valour of the charge.

With Hallam we sat awhile and talked. Then we came away and drove to Godalming, there to catch our train for London. The afternoon sun was bright and warm, though the air was bracing; and even as we drove through the beautiful scene Irving's eyes closed and he took his afternoon doze after his usual fashion.

I think this visit fanned afresh Irving's wish to play *Becket*. I do not know what he and

Tennyson spoke of—he never happened to mention it to me; but he began from thence to speak again of the play at odd times.

III

That season was a busy one, as we had taken off *Ravenswood* and played *répertoire.* That autumn there was a provincial tour. The 1891 season saw *Henry VIII.* run from the beginning of the year. The long run, with only six performances a week, gave some leisure for study; and Irving once more took *Becket* in hand. I think that again the character he was playing had its influence on him. He was tuned to sacerdotalism; and the robes of a churchman sat easy on him. There was a sufficient difference between Wolsey—the chancellor who happened to be a cleric—and Becket—who was cleric before all things—to obviate the danger of too exact a repetition of character and situation. At all events Irving reasoned it out in his usual quiet way, and did not speak till he was ready. It was during the customary holiday at Holy Week in 1892 that he finally made up his mind. I had been spending the vacation in Cornwall at Boscastle, a lovely spot which I had hit upon by accident. Incidentally I so fell in love with the place and gave such a glowing account of it that Irving, later on, spent two vacations at it. I came up to London on the night of Good Friday in a blinding snowstorm, the ground white from the Cornish sea to London. Irving had evidently been waiting, for as soon as we met in the theatre about noon on Saturday he asked me if I could stop and take supper in the theatre. I said I could, and he made the same request to Loveday. After the play we had supper in the Beefsteak Room; and when we had lit our cigars, he opened a great packet of foolscap and took out *Becket* as he had arranged it. He had taken two copies of the book, and when he had marked the cuts in duplicate he had cut out neatly all the deleted scenes and passages. He had used two copies as he had to paste down the leaves on the sheets of foolscap. He had cut the play in this way so that any one reading it would not see as he went along what had been cut out. Thus such a reader would be better able to follow the action as it had been arranged, unprejudiced by obvious alteration, and with a mind single of thought—for it would not be following the deleted matter as well as that remaining. He knew also that it would be more pleasant to Tennyson to read what he had written without seeing a great mass cut out. *Becket* as written is enormously long; the adapted play is only five-sevenths of the original length. Before he began to read he said:

"I think I have got it at last!"

His reading was of its usual fine and enlightening quality; as he read it the story became a fascination. There was no doubting how the part of Becket appealed to him. He was greatly moved at some of the passages, especially in the last act.

Loveday and I were delighted with the play. And when the reading was finished, we, then and there, agreed that it should be the next play produced after *King Lear*, which was then in hand, and which had been arranged to come on in the autumn of that year.

We sat that night until four o'clock, talking over the play and the music for it. Irving thought that Charles Villiers Stanford would be the best man to do it. We quite agreed with him. When he saw that we were taken with it, equally as himself, he became more expansive regarding the play. He said it was a true " miracle " play—a holy theme ; and that he had felt already in studying it that it made him feel a better man.

Before we parted I had by his wish written to Hallam Tennyson at Freshwater asking him if he could see me on business if I came down to the Isle of Wight. I mentioned also Irving's wish that it might be as soon as possible.

Hallam Tennyson telegraphed up on Monday, after he had received my letter, saying that I would be expected the next day, April 19—Easter Tuesday, 1892.

In the meantime, I had read both the original play and the acting version, and was fairly familiar with the latter.

XX

TENNYSON AND HIS PLAYS—III

"Becket" for the stage—My visit to Farringford—"In the Roar of the Sea"—Tennyson on "interviewers"—Relic hunters—"God the Virgin"—The hundred best stories—Message to John Fiske—Walter Map—Last Visit to Tennyson—Tennyson on Homer and Shakespeare—His own reminiscences—Good-bye

I

I WENT down by the 10.30 train from Victoria and got to Freshwater about four o'clock. Hallam was attending a meeting of the County Council but came in about five. He and I went carefully over the suggested changes, in whose wisdom he seemed to acquiesce. We arranged provisionally royalties and such matters, as Irving had wished to acquire for a term of years the whole rights of the play for both Britain and America. We were absolutely at one on all points.

At a little before six he took me to see his father, who was lying on a sofa in his study. The study was a fine room with big windows. Tennyson was a little fretful at first, as he was ill with a really bad cold; but he was very interested in my message and cheered up at once. At the beginning I asked if he would allow Irving to alter *Becket*, so far as cutting it as he thought necessary. He answered at once :

"Irving may do whatever he pleases with it!"

"In that case, Lord Tennyson," said I, "Irving will do the play within a year!"

He seemed greatly gratified, and for a long time we sat chatting over the suggested changes, he turning the manuscript over and making a running commentary as he went along. He knew well where the cuts were ; he knew every word of the play, and needed no reference to the fuller text.

When he came to the end of the scene in Northampton Castle, I put before him Irving's suggestion that he should, if he thought well of it, introduce a speech—or rather amplify the idea conveyed in the shout of the kneeling crowd : "Blessed is he that cometh in the name of the Lord!" In our discussion of the play on the night of the reading we had all agreed that something was here wanting. Something which would, from a dramatic point of view, strengthen Becket's position. If he could have the heart of the people behind him it would manifestly give him a firmer foothold in his struggle with the King. Naturally there was an opening for an impassioned voicing of the old cry, "*Vox populi, vox Dei.*" When I ventured to suggest this he said in a doubting way :

"But where am I to get such a speech ?"

As we sat we were sheltered by the Downs from the sea which thunders night and day under one of the highest cliffs in England. I pointed out towards the Downs and said :

"There it is! In the roar of the sea!" The idea was evidently already in his mind, and when he sent up to Irving a few days later the new material the mighty sound of the surge and the blast were in his words:

"*Hubert.* The voice of the people blesses thee.
"*Becket.*   And I bless
The people, love them, live for them—and yet
Not me, not me! they bless the Church in me.
The Voice of the people goes against the King,
The Voice of the Lord is in the Voice of the People!
The Voice of the Lord is in the warring floods,
And He will lead his people into Peace!
The Voice of the Lord will shake the wilderness
The barren wilderness of unbelief!
The Voice of the Lord will break the cedar-trees—
The Kings and Rulers that have closed their ears
Against the Voice—and at their hour of doom
The Voice of the Lord will hush the hounds of Hell
That ever yelp and snarl at Holy Church
In everlasting silence!"

Any one who studies this fine passage in connection with the difference between the play as written and as adapted can see the extraordinary mental subtlety with which the dramatist reconciled two ideas of opposing purpose. In *Becket*, Tennyson takes as his main purpose—as the dramatic "tug" of the play—the opposition of Church and State as spoken of in Henry's speech:

"Sceptre and crozier clashing, and the mitre
Grappling the Crown."

Becket was, except in the prologue, all churchman when interests clashed. When, however, the dramatist knew that stage exigency required the appearance of opposition between King and people, he did it in such a way, whilst fulfilling all requirements both of the character and the drama, that Becket used the very circumstance to the advantage of his own cause. This is real dramatic instinct, and may be taken as a good illustration of Tennyson's natural capacity for the drama. It is all the more illustrative in that he was not only creating, but creating within very narrow bounds.

II

When Tennyson had run roughly through the altered play, he seemed much better and brighter. He put the play aside and talked of other things. In the course of conversation he mentioned the subject of anonymous letters from which he had suffered. He said that one man had been writing such to him for forty-two years. He also spoke of the unscrupulous or careless way in which some writers for the press had treated him. That even Sir Edwin Arnold had written an interview without his knowledge or consent, and that it was full of lies—Tennyson never hesitated to use the word when he felt it—such as: "'Here I parted from General Gordon!' And that I had 'sent a man on horseback after him.' General Gordon was never in the place!" This subject both in general and special he alluded to at our last meeting; it seemed to have taken a hold on his memory.

He also said:

"Irving paid me a great compliment when he said that I would have made a fine actor!"

That evening the younger members of the family went to a political meeting, at which the local member, Sir Richard Webster, then Attorney-

General, was addressing his constituents, and I went with them.

In the morning, Hallam and I walked in the garden before breakfast. Farringford is an old Feudal farm, and some of the trees are magnificent —ilex, pine, cedar. Primrose and wild parsley everywhere, and underneath a great cedar a wilderness of trailing ivy. The garden gave me the idea that all the wild growth had been protected by a loving hand.

After breakfast Hallam and I walked in the beautiful wood behind the house, where beyond the hedgerows and the little wood rose the great bare rolling Down, at the back of which is a great sheer cliff five hundred feet high. We sat in the summer-house where Tennyson had written nearly all of *Enoch Arden*. It had been lined with wood, which Alfred Tennyson himself had carved; but now the bare bricks were visible in places. The egregious relic-hunters had whittled away piecemeal the carved wood. They had also smashed the windows, which Tennyson had painted with seaplants and dragons; and had carried off the pieces! When we returned I was brought up to Tennyson's room.

He was not feeling well. He sat in a great chair with the cut play on his knee, one finger between the pages as though to mark a place. He had been studying the alterations; and as he did not look happy, I feared that there might be something not satisfactory with regard to some of the cuts. Presently he said to me suddenly:

" Who is God, the Virgin ? "

" Who is *what* ? " I asked, bewildered as to

his meaning. I feared I could not have heard aright.

"God, the Virgin! That is what I want to know too. Here it is!"

As he spoke he opened the play where his finger marked it. He handed it to me and there to my astonishment I read:

" I do commend my soul to God, the Virgin."

When Irving had been cutting the speech he had omitted to draw his pencil through the last two words. The speech as written ran thus:

> "I do commend my soul to God, the Virgin,
> St. Denis of France, and St. Alphege of England,
> And all the tutelary saints of Canterbury."

In doing the scissors-work, he had been guided by the pencil-marks, and so had made the error.

The incident amused Tennyson very much, and put him in better spirits. We went downstairs into what in the house is called the "ballroom"—a great sunny room with the wall away from the light covered with a great painting by Lear of a tropical scene intended for *Enoch Arden*. Here we walked up and down for a long time, the old man leaning on my arm. He told me that he had often thought of making a collection of the hundred best stories.

"Tell me some of them?" I asked softly. Whereupon he told me quite a number, all excellent. Such as the following:

> " A noble at the Court of Louis XIV. was extremely like the King, who, on it being pointed out to him, sent for him and asked him:
>
> "'Was your mother ever at Court?' Bowing low he replied:
>
> "'No, sire! But my father was!'"

Again :

"Colonel Jack Towers was a great crony of the Prince Regent. He was with his regiment at Portsmouth on one occasion; and was in Command of the Guard of Honour when the Prince was crossing to the Isle of Wight. The Prince had not thought of his being there, and was surprised when he saw him. After his usual manner he began to banter :

"'Why, Jack, they tell me you are the biggest blackguard in Portsmouth!' To which the other replied, bowing low :

"'I trust that your Royal Highness has not come down here to take away my character!'"

Again :

"Silly Billy—the sobriquet of the Duke of Gloucester—said to a friend :

"'You are near a fool as you can be!' He too bowed as he answered :

"'Far be it from me to contradict your Royal Highness!'"

III

That evening at dinner Tennyson was, though far from well in health, exceedingly bright in his talk. To me he seemed to love an argument and supported his side with an intellectual vigour and quickness which were delightful. He was full of insight into Irish character. He asked me if I had read his poem, *The Voyage of Maeldune;* and when I told him I had not yet read it he described it and repeated verses. How the Irish ship sailed to island after island, finding in turn all they had longed for, from fighting to luscious fruit, but were never satisfied and came back, fewer in numbers, to their own island. In the drawing-room he said to me, as if the idea had struck him, I daresay from something I said :

"Are you Irish?" When I told him I was he said very sweetly :

"You must forgive me. If I had known that I would not have said anything that seemed to belittle Ireland."

He went to bed early after his usual custom.

That evening in the course of conversation the name of John Fiske the historian, and sometime a professor of Yale University, came up. To my great pleasure, for Fiske had been a close friend of mine for nearly ten years, Tennyson spoke of him in the most enthusiastic way. He asked me if I knew his work. And when I replied that I knew well not only the work but the man, he answered :

"You know him! Then when you next meet him will you tell John Fiske from me that I thank him—thank him most heartily and truly—for all the pleasure and profit his work has been to me!"

"I shall write to him to-morrow!" I said. "I know it will be a delight to him to have such a message from you!"

"No!" said Tennyson, "Don't write! Wait till you see him, and then tell him—direct from me through you, how much I feel indebted to him!"

I did not meet John Fiske till 1895. When the message was delivered it was from the dead.

IV

On the next morning I saw Tennyson again in his bedroom after early breakfast. He looked very unwell, and was in low spirits. Indeed he seemed too dispirited to light his pipe, which he held ready in his hand. He said that he had not yet got the lines he wanted: " The Voice of the People is the Voice of God"—or: "The Voice of the People is the Voice of England!" I think that he had been over the altered text again and that some of the cutting had worried him. Before I came away after saying good-bye he said suddenly, as if he had all at once made up his mind to speak :

" I suppose he couldn't spare me Walter Map ? "

Walter Map was a favourite character of his in the original *Becket*. He it is who represents scholarly humour in the play.

When I told Irving about this he was much touched, and said that he would go over the play again, and would, if he possibly could see his way to it, retain the character. He spent many days over it ; but at last came to the conclusion that it would not do.

At this last meeting—at that visit—when I asked Tennyson what composer he would wish to do the music for his play he said :

" Villiers Stanford ! " He and Irving had independently chosen the same man. How this belief was justified is known to all who have heard the fine *Becket* music.

V

On September 25 the same year, 1892, my wife and I spent the day with Lord and Lady Tennyson at Aldworth. We were to have gone a week earlier, but as Tennyson was not well the visit was postponed. We left Waterloo by the 8.45 train. At the station we were joined by Walter Leaf, the Homer scholar, who had been at Cambridge with Hallam. We had met him at Lionel Tennyson's years before. The day was dull but the country looked very lovely, still full of green though the leaves were here and there beginning to turn. The Indian vines were scarlet. A carriage was waiting and we drove to Aldworth, meeting Mrs. Tennyson on her way to church. On Blackdown Common the leaves were browner than in the valley, and there was a sense of autumn in the air; but round the house, where it was sheltered, green still reigned alone. Far below us the plain was a sea of green, with dark lines of trees and hedgerows like waves. In the distance the fields were wreathed with a dark film—a sapphire mystery.

We all sat awhile with Lady Tennyson, who was in the drawing-room on a sofa away from the light. She had long been an invalid. She was perhaps the most sweet and saintly woman I ever met, and had a wonderful memory. She had been helper and secretary to her husband in early days, trying to save him all the labour she could; and she told us of the enormous correspondence of even that early time. Presently Hallam took us all up to his father, who was in his study overhead.

The room was well guarded against cold, for we had to pass from the door all along one side of it through a laneway made between the bookcases and the high manifold screen. Tennyson was sitting on a sofa with his back to the big mullioned window which looked out to the south. He had on a black skull-cap, his long thin dark hair falling from under it. He seemed very feeble, a good deal changed in that way during the five months that had elapsed since I had seen him. His fine brown nervous hands lay on his lap. Irving had the finest and most expressive hands I have ever seen; Tennyson's were something like them, only bigger. When he began to talk he brightened up. Amongst other things he spoke of the error in the alteration of *Becket*, "God the Virgin." We did not stay very long, as manifestly quietude was best for him, and no one else but ourselves was allowed to see him that day. Presently we all went for a walk, Mrs. Allingham, the painter, who was an old and close friend of the Tennysons, joining us. As we went out we had a glimpse from the terrace of Tennyson reading; part of his book and the top of his head were visible. At that time the lawn presented a peculiar appearance. There had come a sort of visitation of slugs, and the grass was all brown in patches where paraffin had been poured on it.

VI

After lunch Hallam brought Walter Leaf and me up to the study again. Tennyson had changed his place and now sat on another sofa placed in the north-west corner of the room. He was much brighter and stronger and full of intellectual fire. He talked of Homer with Walter Leaf, and in a fine deep voice recited, in the Greek, whole passages —of the sea and the dawn rising from it. He

spoke of Homeric song as "the grandest sounds that can be of the human voice." He spoke very warmly of Leaf's book, and said he would have been proud to have been quoted in it. He ridiculed the idea of any one holding that there had been no such person as Homer. He thought Ilium was a "fancy" town—the invention of Homer's own imagination. Doubts of Homer brought up doubts as to Shakespeare, and the Bacon and Shakespeare controversy which was then raging. He ridiculed the idea. From the Shakespeare side he was indignant at a doubt. From the Bacon side he was scornful :
"What ridiculous stuff!" he said. "Fancy that greatest of all love-poems, *Romeo and Juliet*, written by a man who wrote: 'Great spirits and great business do keep out this weak passion!'" (From Bacon's Essay on *Love*.)

I told him the story which I had heard General Horace Porter—the Ambassador of the United States to France—tell long before. It may be an old story but I venture to tell it again :

> "In a hotel 'out West' a lot of men in the barroom were discussing the Shakespeare and Bacon question. They got greatly excited and presently a lot of them had their guns out. Some one interfered and suggested that the matter should be left to arbitration. The arbitrator selected was an Irishman, who had all the time sat quiet smoking and not saying a word—which circumstance probably suggested his suitability for the office. When he had heard the arguments on both sides formally stated, he gave his decision :
> "'Well, Gintlemin, me decision is this : Thim plays was not wrote be Shakespeare ! But they was wrote be a man iv the saame naame !'"

Tennyson seemed delighted with the story.

Then he spoke of Shakespeare, commenting on *Henry VIII.*, which had been running all the year at the Lyceum. He mentioned Wolsey's speech, speaking the lines :

"Cromwell, I charge thee, fling away ambition."

Then he added in a very pronounced way :

"Shakespeare never wrote that! I know it! I know it! I know it!" As he spoke he smote hard upon the table beside him.

After a long chat we left Tennyson to have his afternoon nap, and smoked in the summer-house. Then we walked to the south-west edge of Blackdown. The afternoon was very clear and we could see the hills of the Isle of Wight, which Hallam said he had never before seen from there.

VII

After tea Hallam took Leaf and me again to his father. After a while we were joined there by Mrs. Tennyson and my wife. Tennyson was then very feeble, but cheerful. He told us a lot of stories and incidents—his humour and memory were quick in him that evening.

One was of the landlord of a hotel at Stirling. He had, during a trip in Scotland, telegraphed to the hotel to have rooms kept. When he arrived he was delighted with them. They were on the first floor, airy and spacious, and in all ways desirable. He felt pleased at being treated with such consideration. After dinner he was sitting by the open window smoking his pipe when he heard a conversation going on below. One of the speakers was the landlord, the other a stranger. Said the latter:

"I hear you have Tennyson staying with you to-night?"

"Aye! That's the man's name. He telegraphed the day for rooms. Do ye ken him?"

"Know him! Why that's Alfred Tennyson, the poet!"

"The poet! I'm wishin' I had kent that!"

"Why?" asked the stranger. After a pause the answer came:

"He a poet! I'd ha' seen him dommed before I had gied him ma best rooms!"

As he was reminiscent that night his anecdotes were mostly personal. Another was of a man of the lower class in the Isle of Wight, who spoke of him in early days:

"He, a great man! Why 'e only keeps one man-servant—an' e' don't sleep in th' ouse!"

Another was of a workman who was heard to say:

"Shakespeare an' Tennyson! Well, I don't think nothin' of neither on 'em!"

Another was of a Grimsby fishmonger, who said when asked by an acquisitive autograph hunter if he happened to have any letters from Tennyson:

"No! His son writes 'em. He still keeps on the business; but he ain't a patch on his fayther!"

Tennyson was sitting on the sofa as he had been in the morning. For all his brightness and his humour, which seemed to bubble in him, he was very feeble and seemed to be suffering a good deal.

He moaned now and then with pain. Gout was flying through his knees and jaws. He had then on his black skull-cap, but he presently took it off as though it were irksome to him. In front of him was a little table with one wax candle lighted. It was of that pattern which has vertical holes through it to let the overflow of melted wax fall within, not without. When the fire of pleasant memory began to flicker, he grew feeble and low in spirits. He spoke of the coming spring and that he would not live to see it. Somehow he grew lower in spirits as the light died away and the twilight deepened, as if the whole man was tuned to nature's key. Through the window we could note the changes as evening drew nearer. The rabbits were stealing out on the lawn, and the birds picking up grubs in the grass.

Once again Tennyson seemed troubled about the press, and was bitter against certain newspaper prying. He could not get free from it. It had been found out during his illness that the beggar-man who came daily for the broken meat was getting ten shillings a week from a local reporter to come and tell him the gossip of the kitchen. Turning to me he said:

"Don't let them know how ill I am, or they'll have me buried before twenty-four hours!" Then after a while he added:

"Can't they all let me alone. What did they want digging up the graves of my father and mother and my grandfather and grandmother. I sometimes wish I had never written a line!" I said:

"Ah, don't say that! Don't think it! You have given delight to too many millions, and your words have done too much good for you to wish to take them back. And the good and the pleasure are to go on for all the future." After a moment's thought he said very softly :

"Well, perhaps you're right! But can't they leave me alone!"

We were all very still and silent for a while. The dying twilight and the moveless flame of the close-set candle showed out his noble face and splendid head in full relief. The mullioned window behind him with the darkening sky and the fading landscape made a fitting background to the dying poet. We said good-bye with full hearts.

Outside, our tears fell. We knew that we should see him no more ; we had said good-bye for ever !

XXI

TENNYSON AND HIS PLAYS—IV

"Becket" produced — Death of Tennyson — "Irving will do me justice" — "The Silent Voices" — Production of the Play — Irving reads it at Canterbury Cathedral — And at the King Alfred Millenary, Winchester

I

TENNYSON died on Thursday, October 6, eleven days after we had seen him. Two others only saw him after we did—with of course the exception of his own family — Mr. Craik, of Messrs. Macmillan, his publishers, and Dr. Dabbs, of the Isle of Wight, his physician.

Before he died he spoke of May—the spring seemed to be for him a time which the Lords of Life and Death would not allow him to pass. It had too some connection in his mind with his play, *The Promise of May.* He said to Dr. Dabbs, who wrote to me about it afterwards:

"I suppose I shall never see *Becket*?"

"I fear not!"

"Ah!" After a long pause he said again: "They did not do me justice with *The Promise of May*—but——" another long pause and then half fiercely:

"THE SILENT VOICES"

"I can trust Irving—he will do me justice!"

Tennyson was buried in the Poet's Corner of Westminster Abbey on October 12. There was a great crowd both in the Abbey and the streets without. All were still, hushed and solemn. The sense of great loss was over all. Very solemn and impressive was the service. There was gloom in the great Cathedral, and the lights were misty. Everywhere the strong odour of many flowers. A body of distinguished men of letters, science and art followed the coffin, coming behind his family. Amongst them Henry Irving, looking as usual, wherever he was, the most distinguished of all. On that sad day, Tennyson's poem, *Crossing the Bar*, was sung. Then his last poem, *The Silent Voices*. The exquisite music written for this by Lady Tennyson and arranged by Sir John Frederick Bridge was heard for the first time. The noble words ringing through the great Cathedral seemed like a solemn epitome of the teaching of the poet's life. Six years afterwards I heard Irving speak them in the crowded Senate House at Cambridge with that fervour which seemed a part of his very life. Now, from that Poet's Corner where they both rest I seem to hear the voices of the two great souls in unison, calling to the great Humanity which each in his own way loved and which was so deep in the hearts of both:

> "Call me rather, silent voices,
> Forward to the starry track
> Glimmering up the heights beyond me
> On, and always on!"

II

Becket, having been in preparation since the end of September, was ready to take its place after the run of *King Lear*. The first dress rehearsal was held on the evening of February 3, 1893, beginning at 6.30 and lasting till one o'clock. It was an excellent rehearsal and all went well. The play was produced three nights later, February 6, 1893—Irving's fifty-fifth birthday. The play was a really enormous success. The public, who had been waiting since early morning at the pit and gallery, could not contain themselves; and even the more staid portions of the house lost their reserve. It was like one huge personal triumph. No one seemed to compare the play or the character to anything seen before. Not even to *Henry VIII.* and Cardinal Wolsey, which had held the stage for eight months the previous year.

Becket was played one hundred and twelve times that season. The entire scenery was burned in the disastrous fire of 1898. There was a new production in 1904. Altogether Tennyson's play was performed three hundred and eight times, as follows:

London, 147; British Provinces, 92; America, 69.

III

In 1897 Irving gave a remarkable Reading of *Becket*. This was in the old Chapter House of Canterbury Cathedral, which had been recently restored exactly to its ancient condition. Farrar

*Henry Irving.
as Becket.
from the Painting in the Players Club, New York.*

"BECKET" AT CANTERBURY

was then Dean of Canterbury, and as Irving had promised to read *Becket* for the benefit of the Cathedral Restoration Fund, he and I had three meetings on the subject in the hall of the Athenæum Club, for which he came specially from Canterbury to London on April 21 and 28 and May 5. At our first meeting the Dean suggested that the Reading should be held in the restored Chapter House, which the Prince of Wales was to open on May 29. Thus Irving's Reading of *Becket* would be on the first occasion which the restored room should be used. I well remember my host's dismay when he met me at the doorway and apologised that there was not a single room in the club to which a member could ask a stranger; I do not know if that iron-clad rule still exists. A somewhat similar one existed at that time at the United Service Club, on the other side of Waterloo Place. There a member could ask a friend into the hall and there give him a glass of sherry. Such was the only measure of hospitality allowable at the "Senior." That rule has been since abandoned in the "Service" Club; the usual club hospitalities can now be extended to guests.

At these meetings, as I was authorised to speak for Irving on all matters, we arranged the necessary details. The Reading was to be given on Monday, May 31, at two o'clock, the tickets to be a guinea and half a guinea each. As time was then pressing and publicity with regard to the undertaking was necessary we decided at the last meeting that Dean Farrar was to write a letter to the newspapers calling attention to the coming event and its beneficent purpose. I undertook if he would send me the letter to have it facsimiled and sent to four hundred newspapers.

Of course every seat was sold long ahead of the time. A place like Canterbury cannot—and cannot be expected to—furnish such an audience as would be required on such an occasion. Most of them would have to come from London and other cities and towns. When I left the Dean I saw Mr. William Forbes, one of the powers of the London, Chatham and Dover Railway, who kindly undertook to arrange trains to and from Canterbury to suit the convenience of the audience, and especially to look after accommodation for Irving and his friends.

On the day of the Reading we went down by train from Victoria at 10 A.M., Ellen Terry being one of the party. Sir Henry's sons, Henry B. and Laurence, were with him. Another was Sir John Hassard, the Secretary of the Court of Arches, and who then was the right hand of the Archbishop of Canterbury—as he had been to several of his predecessors. At Canterbury, Irving and and I went to see the Chapter House. After a walk through the Cathedral we went to the County Hotel, where Irving rested for a while. A little before two o'clock we went to the Chapter House. At two punctually he stepped on the stage, and was introduced in the usual way by Dean Farrar. There was a fine audience. Every spot where one could stand was occupied. Irving got a great reception.

It was a remarkable occasion, and we could not but feel a certain solemnity from the place as well as from the subject. There were so many historic associations with regard to the great room that we could not dissociate them from the occasion.

Irving read magnificently. To the inspiration of the theme was to him the added force of the place and the occasion. The Reading lasted one hour and thirty-five minutes—a terrible tax on even the greatest strength. During all that time he held his audience spell-bound. At the conclusion he was, naturally, a good deal exhausted; such a *tour de force* takes all the strength one has.

We all returned to London by the 4.18 o'clock train.

The result of the Reading was an addition to the Restoration Fund of over £250.

IV

On one other historic occasion Henry Irving read *Becket*. This was at the King Alfred Millenary at Winchester in 1901. In the June of that year he had been selected by the Royal Institution to represent their body; and thinking that he might in addition give some practical aid to the cause, he told the authorities at Winchester that he would on the occasion give a Reading of *Becket* for the benefit of the Expense Fund. Wednesday, September 18, was fixed for the event. As the Autumn tour had been arranged we would be playing in Leeds; but distance nor magnitude of effort ever came between Irving and his promise. On September 17 he played *Charles I.* and left for Winchester at the close of the play. At Winchester he was the guest of the then Mayor, Mr. Alfred Bowker. The next day he gave in the Castle Hall, to a great audience, a slightly compressed Reading of *Becket*. Winchester was then thronged with strangers from all parts of the world, a large number of whom were accredited representatives of some branch or interest of the Anglo-Saxon race. Poor John Fiske was to have been one of the representatives of America. He was to have spoken, and when I had seen him last he told me that that was to be the crowning effort of his life.

At the close of the Reading Irving received an ovation and was compelled to make a speech. In it he said:

"A thousand years of the memory of a great King, who loved his country and made her loved and respected and feared, is a mighty heritage for a nation; one of which not England alone but all Christendom may well be proud. The work which King Alfred did he did for England, but the whole world benefited by it. And most of all was there benefit for that race which he adorned. In the thousand years which have elapsed since he was laid to rest in that England in whose making he had such a part, the world has grown wiser and better, and civilisation has ever marched on with mighty strides. But through all extension and all advance the land which King Alfred consolidated and the race which peopled it, have ever been to the front in freedom and enlightenment; and to-day when England and her many children, east and west and north and south, are united by one grand aspiration of human advance, it is well that we should celebrate the memory of him to whom so large a measure of that advance is due."

XXII

"WATERLOO"—"KING ARTHUR"—"DON QUIXOTE"

Acquisition and Production of "Waterloo"—The One Man in America who saw the Play—Played for Indian and Colonial Troops, 1897—"King Arthur" Plays—Burne-Jones and the Armour—"Don Quixote" Plays—A Rhadamanthine Decision

I

ONE day early in March 1892, whilst we were rehearsing Tennyson's play, *The Foresters*, Irving came into the office in a hurry. He was a little late. He, Loveday and myself always used the same office as we found it in all ways convenient for our perpetual consultations. As he came hurrying out to the stage, after putting on the brown soft broad-brimmed felt hat for which he usually exchanged his "topper" during rehearsals, he stopped beside my table where I was writing, and laying a parcel on it said:

"I wish you would throw an eye over that during rehearsal. It came this morning. You can tell me what you think of it when I come off!"

I took up the packet and unrolled a number of type-written sheets a little longer than foolscap. I read it with profound interest and was touched by its humour and pathos to my very heart's core. It was very short, and before Irving came in again from the stage I had read it a second time. When he came in he said presently in an unconcerned way:

" By the way, did you read that play ? "

" Yes ! "

" What do you think of it ? "

" I think this," I said, " that that play is never going to leave the Lyceum. You must own it—at any price. It is made for you."

" So I think, too ! " he said heartily. " You had better write to the author to-day and ask him what cheque we are to send. We had better buy the whole rights."

" Who is the author ? "

" Conan Doyle ! "

The author answered at once and the cheque was sent in due course. The play was then named *A Straggler of '15*. This Irving changed to *A Story of Waterloo*, when the play was down for production. Later this was simplified to *Waterloo*.

Irving fell in love with the character, and began to study it right away. The only change in the play he made was to get Sir Arthur—then " Dr." or " Mr."—Conan Doyle to consolidate the matter of the first few pages into a shorter space. The rest of the MS. remained exactly as written.

It was not, however, for nearly two years that he got an opportunity of playing it. It is a difficult matter to find a place for an hour-long play in a working bill. *Henry VIII.*, *King Lear*, and *Becket* held the Lyceum stage till the middle of 1893. Then came a tour in America lasting up to end of March 1894. The short London season was taken up with a prearranged reproduction of *Faust*.

Then followed a provincial tour from September to Christmas. Here was found the opportunity. *The Bells* is a short play, and for mere length allows of an addition.

In the first week of the tour at the Princes Theatre, Bristol, on September 21, 1894, *A Story of Waterloo* was given. The matter was one of considerable importance in the dramatic world; not only was Irving to play a new piece, but that piece was Conan Doyle's first attempt at the drama. The chief newspapers of London and some of the greater provincial cities wished to be represented on the occasion; the American press also wished to send its critical contingent. Accordingly we arranged for a special train to bring the critical force. Hearing that so many of his London journalistic friends were coming an old friend of Irving's then resident in Bristol, Mr. John Saunders, arranged to give a supper in the Liberal Club, to which they were all invited, together with many persons of local importance.

The play met with a success extraordinary even for Irving. The audience followed with rapt attention and manifest emotion, swaying with the varying sentiments of the scene. The brief aid to memory in my diary of that day runs:

> "New play enormous success. H. I. fine and great. All laughed and wept. Marvellous study of senility. Eight calls at end."

Unfortunately the author was not present to share the triumph, for it would have been a delightful memory for him. He was on a tour in America; "and thereby hangs a tale."

Amongst the audience who had come specially from London was Mr. H. H. Kohlsaat, owner and editor of the *Chicago Times Herald*, a close and valued friend of Irving and myself. He was booked to leave for America the next day. When the play was over and the curtain finally down, he hurried away just in time to catch the train for Southampton, whence the American Line boat started in the morning. He got on board all right. The following Saturday he arrived in New York, just in time to catch the "flyer," as they call the fast train to Chicago on the New York Central line. On Sunday night a public dinner was given to Conan Doyle to which of course Kohlsaat had been bidden. He arrived too late for the dining part; but having dressed in the train he came on to the hotel just as dinner was finished and before the speeches began. He took a chair next to Doyle and said to him:

"I am delighted to tell you that your play at Bristol was an enormous success!"

"So I am told," said Doyle modestly. "The cables are excellent."

"They are not half enough!" answered Kohlsaat, who had been reading in the train the papers for the last week.

"Indeed! I am rejoiced to hear it!" said Conan Doyle somewhat dubiously. "May I ask if you have had any special report?"

"I didn't need any report, I saw it!"

"Oh, come!" said Conan Doyle, who thought that he was in some way chaffing him. "That is impossible!"

"Not to me! But I am in all human probability the only man on the American continent who was there!" Then whilst the gratified author listened he gave him a full description of the play and the scene which followed it.

To my own mind *Waterloo* as an acting play is perfect, and Irving's playing in it was the high-water mark of histrionic art. Nothing was wanting in the whole gamut of human feeling. It was a cameo, with all the delicacy of touch of a masterhand working in the fine material of the layered shell. It seemed to touch all hearts always. When the dying veteran sprang from his chair to salute the colonel of his old regiment the whole house simultaneously burst into a wild roar of applause. This was often the effect at subsequent performances both at home and in America.

II

In 1897, when representatives of the Indian and Colonial troops were gathered in London for the "Diamond" Jubilee of Queen Victoria, Irving gave a special performance for them. It was a *matinée* on June 25. The event was a formal one, for it was given by Royal consent, and special arrangements were made by the public officials. Some two thousand troops of all kinds and classes and costumes were massed at Chelsea Barracks. The streets were cleared by the police for their passing as they marched to the Lyceum to the quickstep of the Guards' Fife and Drum Band, the public cheering them all the way. They represented every colour and ethnological variety of the human race, from coal black through yellow and brown up to the light type of the Anglo-Saxon reared afresh in new realms beyond the seas.

Their drill seemed to be perfect, and we had made complete arrangements for their seats. Section by section they marched into the theatre, all coming by the great entrance, without once stopping or even marking time in the street.

In the boxes and stalls sat the Indian Princes and the Colonial Premiers, and some few of the foreign guests. The house was crammed from wall to wall; from floor to floor; the bill was *Waterloo* and *The Bells*. No such audience could have been had for this military piece. It sounded the note of the unity of the Empire which was then in celebration; all were already tuned to it. The scene at the end was indescribable. It was a veritable ecstasy of loyal passion.

As it was impossible to furnish organised refreshment for so many men with the limited accommodation of a theatre, Irving had done the only thing possible to show hospitality to his guests. The caterer who rented the saloons had orders to throw them all open and let the audience have just what they wished at his cost. Not a single one of the strangers took too much. The only exception to the rule of absolute sobriety was the case of two drummer-boys of the band, who, seeing a unique opportunity, "lowered" brandy-and-sodas with such zeal that they were unable to stand. Their comrades, however, were strong and kind; and keeping them close amongst them they proved to the boys that they could walk. None of the public were aware of the youthful indiscretion.

This is quite possible even under more adverse conditions. My maternal grandfather, who was a subaltern in the Peninsular War, said that in his young days—they did go early into the Army a hundred years ago, and ensigns had no horses—he had walked on a forced march all night *asleep*, pushed along by the hardier veterans.

Waterloo was played by Irving seventy-eight times in London; one hundred and seventy-seven times in the provinces; and eighty-eight times in America. In all three hundred and forty-three times, the last being at Wolverhampton on February 20, 1905.

III

For a long time Irving had in view of production a play on the subject of King Arthur. He broached the subject to Tennyson, but the latter could not see his way to it. He had dealt with the subject in one way and did not wish to try it in another. Then he got W. G. Wills to write a play; this he purchased from him in 1890. As, however, he did not think it would act well, he got Comyns Carr to write another some three years later.

In 1894 the production was taken in hand. Sir Edward Burne-Jones undertook to design scenes and dresses, armour and appointments. His suggestions were new lights on stage possibilities. As he was not learned in stage technique and mechanism there were of course some seemingly insuperable difficulties; but these in the hands of artists skilled in stage work soon disappeared. To my own mind it was the first time that what must in reality be a sort of fairyland was represented as an actuality. Some of the scenes were of transcendent beauty, notably that called " The Whitethorn Wood." The scene was all green and white—the side of a hill thick with blossoming thorn through which, down a winding path, came a bevy of maidens in flowing garments of tissue which seemed to sway and undulate with every motion and every breath of air. There was a daintiness and a sense of purity about the whole scene which was very remarkable.

The armour which Burne-Jones designed was most picturesque. I fear it would hardly have done for actual combat as the adornments at shoulder and elbow were such that in the movement of the arms they took strange positions. When some virtuoso skilled in the lore of mail asked the great painter why he fixed on such a class of armour he answered:

" To puzzle the archæologists ! "

For the great Fancy Ball given by the Duchess of Devonshire in Devonshire House, the armour was lent by Irving. It furnished the men of a quadrille and was a very striking episode in a gorgeous scene.

In the preparation of the scenes we had at first some difficulty, for great scene-painters like to make their own designs. But Burne-Jones' genius together with his great reputation—to both of which all artists bow—accompanied by Irving's persuasions carried the day. When it was objected that the suggested scenes were impossible to work in accordance with stage limitations, Irving pointed out that there was in itself opportunity for the ability of the scene-painters' skill and invention. Burne-Jones suggested the effect aimed at; with them rested the carrying it out. And surely neither Hawes Craven nor Joseph Harker could have ever had any emotions except those of pleasure when the round of applause nightly welcomed each scene as the curtain went up.

The cast was a fine one; Irving as King Arthur and Johnston Forbes-Robertson as Sir Lancelot, Ellen Terry as Guinevere, and Genevieve Ward as Morgan Le Fay. Some of the parts were not easy to play. One had a difficulty all its own. In the scene where Elaine is brought in on her bier she had to remain for a considerable time stone-still in full view of the audience. All that season Miss Lena Ashwell, who played the part, never once sneezed or yielded to any other temporary convulsion.

King Arthur was produced on January 12, and ran that season for one hundred and five performances. It was played twelve times in the provinces and seventy-four times in America. In all one hundred and ninety-one performances. It was one of those plays cut short in its prime. The scenery and appointments were burned in the stage fire of 1898.

IV

The subject of Don Quixote for a play was matter that Irving had for a long time held in mind. In 1888, he had bought from W. G. Wills the entire rights of a play on the subject which he had suggested his writing. He was not, however, satisfied with it. Don Quixote is a great name and a picturesque figure to remember. He is also a great subject for a book, and Cervantes made him the hero and centre of many entertaining and amusing adventures. But he is not in reality a figure for prolonged stage use. He is too much in one note to make effective music. If any one ever succeeds in making a " full " play with him as hero the author will have to invent a story for it, or compile one out of the materials which Cervantes has in his immortal work bequeathed to mankind. The dramatic author or adapter can thus maintain the figure in its simplicity, keeping his personality always as a *deus ex machina*.

When he was satisfied that he could not do Wills' play in its entirety Irving got another enthusiast of the subject, Mr. J. I. C. Clarke of New York, to write a fresh play on the theme. Clarke made an admirable play, of which Irving bought the entire rights in 1894. There were some very fine points in this new play, especially in illustrating the gravity of the Don's high character and his deep understanding of a noble act. But the difficulty of the subject was again apparent; the character was too simple and too fixed for the necessary variety and development of character in a long, grave play. Clarke tried it a second time, but Irving could not even then see his way to it; and so he gave the author back his play to deal with it as he would. He has gone on improving it and doubtless some other player will join him in good fortune in a successful issue to his labours.

Recognising then the limitation of the subject,

Irving, being determined to essay the character, made up a one-act play from Cervantes' book, keeping as far as possible to the lines of the first act of Wills' play. There were two scenes; the first showing Don Quixote in his own house with the madness of his chivalric belief upon him. A notable figure he looked as fully armed in rusty armour and with drawn sword in hand he sat reading a great folio of *Amadis of Gaule*. His own physique—tall and lean, his fine high-bred features heightened by the resources of art to an exaggerated aquiline, all helped to the efficacy of the illusion. In his old armour, his worn leather and threadbare velvet, he was indeed the Knight of La Mancha.

When in the second scene he rode into the inn yard on his skeleton steed Rosinante the effect was heightened. The scene was beautifully lit. There was a fine, rich, soft light from the moon hung high in the semi-tropic sky. It softened everything to the possibilities of romance. One seemed to forget the unreality in the dim, quaint beauty. The very shadows seemed to be full of possibilities, and to hold a mystery of their own. No one who saw it can ever forget that spare, quaint figure marching up and down, lance on shoulder, watching his armour laid in front of the pump—a solemn, grim travesty of the vigil of a probationary knight.

V

In the preparation of *Don Quixote* there was an incident which was not without its humorous aspect—though not to some of those who had a part in it. When it was decided that Rosinante was to be a factor in the play, Irving told the Property Master, Arnott, to get a horse as thin and ragged-looking as he could.

"I think I know the very one, sir," said Arnott. "It belongs to a baker who comes down Exeter Street every day. I shall look out for him to-morrow and get him to bring the horse for you to see!"

In due course he saw the baker, and arranged that he should on the next day bring the horse. The morrow came; but neither the baker nor the horse. Inquiries having been made, it turned out that on the morning arranged, as the baker was leading the horse down Bow Street to bring it to the Lyceum, an officer of the Society for the Prevention of Cruelty to Animals saw them, and being dissatisfied with the appearance of the animal, "ran in" both man and beast. The sitting magistrate went out to the police yard and made inspection for himself. When he came back to court where the prisoner was waiting in the dock, he said that the case was one of the worst within his experience and gave his decision: He fined the owner of the horse ten pounds; sent the man who had been arrested whilst in charge of it to prison for a week without option of a fine; and ordered the horse *to be killed!*

XXIII

ART AND HAZARD

"Madame Sans-Gêne"—Size, proportions and juxtaposition—Evolution of "business"—"Peter the Great"—"Robespierre"—"Dante"—The hazard of management

I

When Irving read the report of the production of *Madame Sans-Gêne* in Paris, he bought the British rights; but it was not till April 10, 1897, that the new play could be given. This was the Saturday before Holy Week; not in itself a good time, but it would get the play into swing for Easter.

The part of Napoleon in the play is not one that could appeal to any great actor on grounds of dramatic force. Its relative position in the play is not even one that appeals to that measure of self-value which is, to some degree, in all of us. True, it is the part of a great man and such is pleasurable histrionically—if there be an opportunity of excellence. An actor of character finds his own pleasure in the study and representation of strong individuality. Irving had always been interested in Napoleon. As long as I can remember he had always in his room a print and a bust of him—both beautiful. He had many books regarding him, all of which he had studied. He was always delighted to talk of him. I had long taken it for granted that he had an idea of some day playing the character; but I hardly took it seriously. The very light of history which makes the character known to the public also has made known his stature. No two men could be further apart in matter of physique and identity. Napoleon, short and stout, full-faced, aggressive, coarse. Irving, tall, thin, ascetic; with manners of exquisite gentleness; with a face of such high, thoughtful distinction that it stood out in any assemblage of clever men. I have been with Irving in many Universities—Oxford, Cambridge, Dublin, Edinburgh, Glasgow, Manchester, Harvard, Columbia, Princeton, Chicago. I have stood by him whilst he was the host of Princes, Ambassadors, Statesmen, Soldiers, Scholars. I think I have seen him under most conditions in which man may be compared with men; but I never found his appearance, bearing or manner other than the best. How then reconcile such opposites to such beguilement of his audience that the sense of personal incongruity should not mar the effect at which he aimed. It must be by some strange *tour de force* that this could be accomplished; and a special effort of the kind, though in its own way a dangerous experiment to a reputation already won, has a charm of its own. Man always wants to climb, even if the only charms of climbing be difficulty and danger. He saw at once that a chance to essay Napoleon was in *Madame Sans-Gêne*. The play was a comedy and Napoleon's

Photo   *Window & Grove*

ELLEN TERRY AS IMOGEN, 1896

part in it was a comedy position. Matters that work against one in serious drama can be made actually to further one's purpose in comedy.

When he began to think of the part he very often spoke of it with me and took me into his confidence as to his idea of doing it.

"You see," he said to me one time, "perspective is a matter of contrast and juxtaposition. You can enlarge the appearance of anything by placing something smaller beside it, or *vice versa*. Of course you must choose for the contrasted object something which to common knowledge is of at least or at most a standard size. It would not make a man look big to put him next a doll's house—such you expect to be small and the sense of comparison does not strike one. The comparison must, on the part of the spectator, be unconscious."

Thus it was that in the play Napoleon in his study, when the scene opened and he made his first appearance, sat behind a huge writing-table piled with books; he sat on an exceedingly low chair so that he seemed dwarfed. The room was a vast one with pillars and pilasters which carried the eye upward from the floor. The attendants, the soldiers on guard, the generals and statesmen who surrounded him were all big, fine men. The ladies who played the Princesses, his sisters, were of good stature, and Ellen Terry is a tall woman. He applied here to himself the lesson of juxtaposition which in *Cymbeline* he had used for Ellen Terry's service in the previous year. She, a tall, fine woman, had to represent a timid young girl. Matters had therefore to be so arranged that size should be made a comparative and not an absolute matter. To this end Imogen was surrounded by the tallest and biggest women obtainable. The Queen looked, and Helena was, tall, and such miscellaneous ladies as are possible in a royal *entourage* even in the semi-mythical days of early England were simply giantesses. Amid her surroundings her timidity seemed natural to one so sweet and tender and almost frail. The towering height and girth of the trees and the architecture and stone-work lent themselves to the illusion. All the men too were tall and of massive build, so that the illusions of size and helplessness were perfect.

Irving was now face to face with the same difficulty, but reversed; there was still the matter of his own proportions. Long before, when we had spoken of the difficulties ahead of him in representing the part, he had said:

"I shall keep the proportions of Napoleon. After all it is only dressing a big doll instead of a little one. They have given me a big doll, whereas Napoleon had a little one. No one need notice the difference, unless the dolls are put together!"

This idea he carried out absolutely. He had made for him "fleshings" of great proportions. When these were on he looked like a Daniel Lambert for the white had no relief in variety; but this was but the doll which he had to dress. When the breeches—which were made to proportion by the best tailor in London—were drawn on, the thighs stood out as in De La Roche's picture. When the green coat was on and buttoned high up, the shoulders, especially at the back, were so wide and tight as to make him look podgy. That dress was certainly supremely artful. It was so arranged that all the lines, either actual or suggested, were horizontal. The sloping of the front of the buttoned coat was from very high on the chest and the slope very generous. The waistcoat was short and the lower line of it wide and broadly marked. The concealment of real height was further effected by the red sash and many orders which were so artfully placed as to lead the eye in the wished-for direction. All that Irving required to satisfy the audience was the *coup d'œil;* in endeavouring to convince it does not do to start off with antagonism. So long as the first glance did not militate against him, he could depend on himself to realise their preconceived idea—which was of historical truth—by acting.

And when he did act how real it all was. The little short-stepped quick run in which he moved in his restless dominance was no part of general historic record; but it fitted into the whole personality in such a way that, having seen, one cannot dissociate them. The ruthless dominance; the quick blaze of passion which recalled to our memory the whirlwind rush at Lodi; the flame-like sweep over the bridge at Arcola; the conscious acting of a part to gain his end; the typical attack on Nipperg. All these were so vivid that through the mist of their swirling memory loomed the very identity of Napoleon himself.

Strange to say the very excellence of Irving's acting, as well as his magnitude in public esteem, injured the play *quâ* play. To my mind it threw it in a measure out of perspective. The play is a comedy, and a comedy of a woman at that. Napoleon is in reality but an incidental character. It is true he and his time were chosen, because of his absolutism and his personal character; he is a glorified *deus ex machina,* whose word is law and is to be accepted as ruling life and death. So far Irving's reputation and personality helped. He was on the mimic stage what Napoleon was on the real one. Still, after all *Madame Sans-Gêne* is a comedy though the authors were a little clumsy in changing it into melodrama at the end; but when Irving was present comedy, except his comedy, had to cease. Of course in the part of the scene where he and Ellen Terry played together comedy was triumphant; but here the note of comedy was the note of the scene and nothing could be finer than the double play, each artist foiling the other, and all the time developing and explaining their respective characters. But after that Irving, as the part was written, was too big for the play. It was not in any way his fault. No modification of style or repression of action could have obviated the difficulty. It was primarily the fault of the dramatists in keeping the Emperor, who was incidental, on the stage too long.

The same reasoning applied to *Cymbeline*. Irving was too big for Iachino, and the better he played the worse the harm. Each little touch that helped to build up the individuality of the character helped—he being what he was in public esteem—to expand the sense of deliberate villainy. Iachino's purpose was not to injure; he only used wrong-doing, however base, as a means to an end: the winning of his wager.

In Ellen Terry's performance of *Madame Sans-Gêne* came an incident which I have always thought to be typically illustrative of "unconscious cerebration" in art—that "dual consciousness" which we shall by-and-by consider. The actress had steeped herself in the character; when playing the part she thought as the laundress-duchess thought. She had already played it close on a hundred times. The occasion was the first performance of the piece at Sheffield, where the audiences were enormous and the people hearty. In the scene with the dancing-master, where she is ill at ease and troubled with her unaccustomed train—"tail" she calls it—it is part of the "business" that this keeps falling or slipping from her arm. Once when she put it back its bulk seemed to attract unconsciously her troubled mind. Accordingly she began to *wring* it as she had been used to do with heavy articles in the days of her wash-tub. There was an instantaneous roar of applause. Half the women of the audience did their own washing and half the men knew the action; all throughout the house, both men and women, recognised the artistic perfection from which she utilised the impulse.

From that evening the action became an established usage.

II

In 1897 Laurence Irving completed his play on *Peter the Great* and his father purchased it from him. At that time he had in expectation a play by H. D. Traill and Robert Hichens, for which he had contracted on reading the *scenario* in July of that year. As, however, the latter play was not ready when arrangements had to be made for opening the London season early in January 1898, young Irving's play was put into preparation by his father before he went on the provincial tour. Naturally he wished to do all he possibly could for his son's play, and in the production neither pains nor expense was spared.

On July 24, the night after the closing of the season, he read the play in the Beefsteak Room to Loveday and myself and Johnston Forbes-Robertson, whom he hoped would play the part of Alexis. The reading took three hours and twenty minutes, and was a remarkably fine piece of work. Forbes-Robertson, however, did not see his way to the part, which was ultimately given to Robert Taber, a fine actor, then young and strong, who had just come from America, where he had played leading business.

Great pains were spent in the archæology of the play, so that when it was produced it was in its way a historical lesson. Irving cut off a whole week of his own work of the tour in order to come up to London to superintend the production personally. Miss Terry and the company played *Madame Sans-Gêne* at Bradford and Wolverhampton—strange to say, the last two towns he played in eight years later.

The production was certainly a very interesting one. The place and time did not allow much opportunity for beauty, but all appeared so real as to enhance the natural power of the play. The part of Peter was a terribly trying one, even to a man of Irving's "steel and whipcord" physique. I fancy it was a lesson to the dramatist—as yet not at his full skill—in saving the actor of his plays. On the seventh night the stage-manager, before the play began, asked for the consideration of the audience for Irving, who was suffering from a partial loss of voice. Laurence Irving was having a brief holiday in Paris, so we telegraphed him to return at once. On Monday night Henry Irving was unable to play and Laurence Irving took his place. It was really a wonderful effort —especially for so young a man—to play such a part on short notice. Fortunately, as author, he knew the words well; and as he had helped his father in the stage management he was familiar with the business. That night after the performance I went to see Irving and had the pleasure of telling him of his son's success.

Unfortunately the tone of the play did not suit the public taste. It was not the fault of the dramatist, but of the originals. History is history and has to be adhered to—in some measure at any rate; and the spectacle of a father hounding his son to death is one to make to shudder those whose instincts and sympathies are normal. The history of the time lent itself to horrors. On the first night in one scene where one of the conspirators who had been tortured—off the stage, but whose screams were heard—was brought in pale and bloody, the effect was too great for some of the audience, who rose quickly and left their seats. On the next night this part of the scene was taken out and other lesser horrors modified. Towards the end of the month it became necessary to prepare for a change of bill. On the last night of the piece the Prince and Princess of Wales were present as they wished to see the play again. The Prince had already seen it twice and had expressed his appreciation of it.

III

Robespierre was produced on April 15, 1899—the date on which the Lyceum was reopened under the management of the Lyceum Company. Irving's reception after his dangerous illness was exceptionally warm, even for him.

The play had been in hand for some time. In May 1896, whilst in New York, Irving and I went to see Miss Elizabeth Murbury, the agent for America of the French Dramatic Authors' Society. The purpose of the interview was regarding the writing by Sardou of a play on the subject. Irving suggested as a scene that in Robespierre's lodgings. He had read somewhere of Robespierre shaving himself whilst listening to a matter of life and death for many people and all the time turning to spit. This was a grim streak of character which fastened on his imagination. The suggestion was well received by Sardou and the following year Irving entered into a contract whereby he was, after previous acceptance of the *scenario*, to receive the play before May 1898. On his part he undertook to produce the piece in London before June 1899. In due order the *scenario* was sent and approved, and the script of the play finally delivered and translated into English by Laurence Irving.

Robespierre was played in London one hundred and five times—of which ninety-three were the first season; in the provinces forty-three times; and in America one hundred and nine times. In all two hundred and fifty-seven times.

Charles Dickens used to say that it was a perpetual wonder to him how small the world was, Here is an instance of how the same may be said to-day:

When we were playing the piece in New England a gentleman wrote to Irving to thank him for preserving in the play the honourable character of his ancestor, Benjamin Vaughan, M.P., one of the *dramatis personæ* who has an interview with Robespierre in the first act!

Robespierre was a terrific play to stage manage. There are in it no less than *sixty-nine* speaking parts. The rehearsals were endless, for there were required in the play a very large number of supers —more than a hundred. In the scene of the Convention, in which Robespierre is overthrown, much of the effect depends on the rush of the deputies across the floor of the house, and the series of fights for the tribune. It was a stormy scene, and was admirably done. Everywhere the piece was played it went with uncontrollable effect.

Irving's dressing of the part and that personal preparation which is known in the actor's craft as "make-up" afforded in themselves a lesson in stage art. In the first act, where he had to strike the true note of Robespierre's character, everything was done to create the proper effect.

Here Robespierre was shown in his true light: A doctrinaire, a self-seeking politician; vain, arrogant, remorseless; something of a poet; a little of an artist; an intriguer without scruple. Irving showed in face and form, in bearing, in speech and even in inflection of the voice the true inwardness of the man. The clear-cut face with prominent chin; the pronounced stillness of bearing except for the restless eyes; the eager suspicion of one who is watched; the gaudy colour of his well-fitting clothes. All these things had their lessons for stranger eyes. He took no chance whatever that the idea of the man's dominant qualities should not be closely and deeply marked in the minds of the audience. But after that—although the man *seemed* to be the same —he was gradually and perpetually changing. And all the changes were, in addition to the acting and the spoken words, unconsciously conveyed in dress, bearing and facial appearance. When the fatherhood woke in him in Act III., it seemed natural enough, though it would have seemed out of place in the first or second acts. In Act IV., sympathy with the mother was added to intense and over-whelming anxiety for his son—and all seemed still consistent with the original conception of the character as shown. That is, there was no jarring note as things progressed. In fact he was subtly changing in the mind of the audience the original idea of the man's nature. And all the time the face was growing refined and more marked with human kindness, till in the last act he seemed to be a saintly man full of noble and generous feelings; a patriot and martyr. In the last act all the externals were changed: wig, "make-up" of face, clothing from top to toe. The harsh colour of his first-seen coat was softened to an ineffable blue, suggestive at once of distinction, refinement and delicacy. Altogether, though the personality seemed always consistent, it was a figure of harsh and ruthless scheming that walked in at one end of the play, but a noble martyr who was carried out at the other!

IV

Irving had long wished to act the part of Dante if he could get a good play on the subject. To this end he had made several efforts, including that in the direction of Tennyson. In July 1894, when *Madame Sans-Gêne* was being played in London in French—by Rejane—after he had bought the English rights of the play Irving had a conversation regarding a play on the subject of Dante with Emile Moreau, joint author with Victorien Sardou of the French comedy. The issue of the meeting was that Sardou and Moreau were to write a play and submit it to Irving. It was not, however, till some seven years later that the idea began to materialise. There was a good deal of correspondence spread over the time, but after an interview at the end of May 1901 in London with Miss Marbury, who had just returned from paying a prolonged visit to Sardou, the matter rose over the horizon of practicability. It was agreed that Sardou was to submit a *scenario* before the end of that year. Irving felt justified after the success of *Robespierre* to venture on another play by the same author. The *scenario* was sent to him in due course, and he studied it very carefully in such pauses as were in the American tour of that autumn. When we were in Chicago in December he told me that he had practically given up hope of doing *Dante* as he could not see his way to accepting the *scenario*. By his wishes I drafted a letter for him to that effect. I considered that the matter had there ended and did not have an opportunity of reading the *scenario* which was returned.

Much to my surprise, in the following spring Irving told me that he had decided to do the play and asked me to draw out a contract on the lines of that of *Robespierre*. I asked him why he had changed his mind and reminded him that from what he had told me of the original *scenario*, we had agreed that it was not likely to make for success. He did not, however, wish to talk about it then—he could be very secretive when he wished—but said he had sent word to Sardou that he would go on with the idea of the play. I knew it would upset him to argue about anything to which he was pledged; I said no more.

MM. Sardou and Moreau delivered the completed play in August, and forthwith Irving began to use his great imagination on its production, his son Laurence having taken the translation in hand.

The production was on a gigantic scale; the arrangements for it having been made in Paris, but not through me. The labour of preparation and rehearsal was endless, the expense enormous. The curtain went up on the night of production to an incurred expense of nearly thirteen thousand pounds.

On Monday, January 12, 1903, Irving read *Dante*

to the actors and actresses of his company at his office in Bedford Street—the great room occupied for so many years by the Green Room Club. My contemporary note runs:

> "Read it wonderfully well. Adumbrated every character!"

To me this was in one way the most interesting of all his readings to the company of a new play. Hitherto I had not read the play or even the *scenario*, and I am bound to say that as it went on my heart sank. The play was not a good one. It had too many characters and covered too wide a range. Indeed had it not been for Irving's wonderful reading I should not have been able to follow the plot. When I saw the play on the first night acted by a lot of people and lacking the concentration of the whole thing passing through one skilled mind I found a real difficulty of comprehension. Strange to say this very difficulty in one way helped the play with the less cultured part of the audience. As they could not quite understand it all they took it for granted that there was some terribly subtle meaning in everything. *Omne ignotum pro magnifico.*

The play was produced at Drury Lane Theatre on April 30, 1903—the last day, by the way, allowable for production in London by the contract with Sardou and Moreau. On that night it was received with great enthusiasm. There was an immense audience, and managerial hopes ran high. Irving was certainly superb. He did not merely look like Dante—he *was* Dante; it was like a veritable re-incarnation. Naturally his features had a graet resemblance to the great poet. The high-bred " eagle " profile ; the ascetic gauntness ; the deep earnest resonant voice ; the general bearing of lofty gloom of the exile—these things one and all completed a representation which can never be forgotten by any one who saw it.

The play ran during the whole season at Drury Lane, eighty-two performances. On the provincial tour the following autumn it was given twenty-one times in only three towns. Then succeeded the American tour on which it was played thirty-four times. A total of one hundred and thirty-seven performances.

When we opened in New York the civic elections, which that term were conducted with even more than usual vigour, were on. As the receipts were not up to our normal we thought that the political " colieshangie " was the sole cause ; we found out the difference when the *répertoire* bill was put up the third week. The experience was repeated in Philadelphia, Boston, Springfield, Hartford, New Haven, Brooklyn, and Washington. The last performance in America was given at the Federal capital to a great house—the largest the piece was played to in America.

Perforce we had to accept the verdict : the public did not care for the play. Accordingly we stored it in Washington and for the rest of the tour gave the *répertoire* plays. When the tour was over we paid the expenses of sending the scenery into Canada where we gave it away. This was cheaper than paying the duty into the United States, which we should have had to do had we left it behind us.

Altogether *Dante* as a venture was a fearful hazard. Before it was done I remonstrated with Irving about the production, he being then not really able to afford such an immense loss as was possible. As Chancellor of the Exchequer to his Absolute Monarchy I had to be content with his reply :

"My dear fellow, a play like this beats Monte Carlo as a hazard. Whatever one may do about losing, you certainly can't win unless you play high!"

XXIV

VANDENHOFF

OLD Vandenhoff played his farewell engagement in Edinburgh, at the Queen's Theatre, in 1858. In the *Merchant of Venice*, Irving played Bassano to his Shylock; this was on Tuesday, February 16. In Act I., scene 3, where Shylock and Bassano enter, an odd thing occurred. I give it in Irving's words as he told me of it:

"Vandenhoff began: 'Three thousand'—there was a sort of odd click of something falling and the speech dried up. I looked up at him and saw his mouth moving, but there was no sound. At the moment my eye caught the glitter of something golden on the stage. I stooped to pick it up, and as I did so saw that it was a whole set of false teeth. This I handed to Shylock, keeping my body between him and the audience so that no one might see the transaction. He turned away for an instant, putting both hands up to his face. As he turned back to the audience his words came out quite strong and clearly: 'Three thousand ducats—well!'"

XXV

CHARLES MATHEWS

In Early Days—A Touch of character—Mathews' appreciation—Henry Russell—The Wolf and the Lamb

IRVING had always a deep regard for Charles Mathews. Not only did he look upon him as a consummate dramatic actor—which was always in itself a sure road to his heart, but he had lively recollections of his kindness to him. The first was in his youth on the stage in Edinburgh when he played the boy in one of the plays of his *répertoire*. Irving had invented for himself a little piece of business; when the lad was placed in the militant position in the play he took out his handkerchief to mop his brow. As he pulled it out there came with it an orange which rolled along the stage and which he hastily followed and recovered. Charles Mathews seemed pleased. His kindly recognition was, however, opposed a little later by another actor who played the same part as Mathews. This gentleman strongly objected to what he delicately called the "tomfoolery" which he said interfered with the gravity of his own acting. When Mathews again visited Edinburgh, Irving omitted the incident, fearing it might be out of place. But at the end of the act Mathews sent for him to his dressing-room and in a very kind manner called his attention to a piece of business of which he had made use on the last occasion, and there and then recapitulating the incident asked why he had omitted it. Irving explained that he had been held to task for it by the other actor. To his great delight Mathews spoke quite crossly of the other actor. Said he:

"He had no right to find fault! He must have been an ignorant fellow not to see that it helped his own part. The humour of the situation in the play hangs on the contrast between the boy's bellicose attitude towards the elder man whom he considers his rival, and his own extreme youthfulness. That very incident is all that is wanted to make the action complete; and since I saw you do it I have asked every other who plays the part to bring it in. I should have asked you, only that I took it of course for granted that you would repeat it. Never let any one shake you out of such an admirable piece of by-play!"

The other occasion was when he had played Doricourt at his first appearance at the St. James's Theatre in 1866. One of the first congratulations he got was from Charles Mathews, who not only sent him by hand a letter in the morning but followed it up with a visit later in the day.

Mrs. Charles Mathews was, till the day of her death, a very dear friend of Irving; and the tradition of affection was kept up till Irving's own death by the son, C. W. Mathews, the eminent barrister.

For my own part I first knew Charles Mathews in 1873, when I had the pleasure of being introduced. From that time on I met him occasionally and was always fascinated with his delightful personality. Years afterwards I was not surprised to hear an instance of its effect from the late Henry Russell, the author of the song "*Cheer boys, cheer,*" and a host of other dramatic and popular songs. It was after supper one night in the Beefsteak Room. Russell told his story thus:

"I was at that time tenant of the Lyceum, and had let it for a short season to Charles Mathews. He did not pay my rent and, as I suppose you know, the freeholder, Arnold, was not one to let *me* off my rent on that account. The debt ran on till it grew to be quite a big one. I wrote to Mathews, but I never could get any settlement. He was always most suave and cheery; *but* no cash! At last I made up my mind that *I would* have that money; and finding that letters were of no avail, I called on him one forenoon. He was having his breakfast and asked me to join him in a cup of chocolate. I said no! that I had come on business—and pretty stern business at that; and that I would not mix it up with pleasure. I had come for cash—cash! cash! He was very pleasant, quite undisturbed by my tirade; so that presently I got a little ashamed of myself and sat down. I stayed with him an hour."

"And did you get your money?" asked Irving quietly. Russell smiled:

"Get my money! I came away leaving him a cheque for three hundred pounds which he had borrowed from me; and I never asked him for rent again!" Then after a pause he added:

"He was certainly a great artist; and a most delightful fellow!"

XXVI

CHARLES DICKENS AND HENRY IRVING

IRVING often spoke with pride of the fact that Charles Dickens had thought well of his acting, when he had seen him play at the St. James's Theatre in 1866 and the Queen's Theatre in 1868. Unhappily the two men never met, for Dickens died in 1870. In later years he had the pleasure of the friendship of several of Dickens' children, and of his sister-in-law, Miss Georgina Hogarth, to whom he was so much attached. Charles Dickens the younger was an intimate friend and was often in the Beefsteak Room and elsewhere when Irving entertained his friends; Kate Dickens, the present Mrs. Perugini, was also a friend. But the youngest son, Henry Fielding Dickens, was the closest friend of all. Both he and his wife and their large family —who were all children, such of them as were then born, when I knew them first—were devoted to Irving. In all the years of his management no suitable gathering at the Lyceum was complete without them. Whenever Irving would leave London for any long spell some of them were sure to be on the platform to see him off; when he returned their welcome was amongst the first to greet him. Indeed he held close in his heart that whole united group, Harry Dickens and his sweet family and the dear old lady whom happily they are still able to cherish and as of old call " Aunty."

Lately I asked Henry Dickens if he remembered the occasion of his father speaking of Irving. The occasion of my asking was a gathering at which he had many social duties to fulfil, so that there was no opportunity of explaining fully. But next day he wrote me the following letter:

" 2 Egerton Place, S.W.
" *May* 29, 1906.

" MY DEAR BRAM

" I do not remember the exact year in which *Hunted Down* was played at the St. James's.

" It must have been somewhere about 1866. But I have a vivid recollection of the fact owing to the impression which Irving's performance made upon my father.

" He was greatly struck by it. It seemed to appeal at once to his artistic and dramatic sense.

" ' Mark my words : that man will be a great actor.'

" I should not like to pledge myself to the exact words, but that is the substance of what he said after the performance.

" He also saw Irving in *The Lancashire Lass*, when he had been much impressed by his acting though not to the same extent.

" I do not suppose any man was more competent to give an opinion than my father.

" He was himself, as you know, a great actor. The fever of the footlights was always with him.

" He had a large number of friends in the dramatic profession, amongst them Macready and Fechter, the two greatest actors of his time.

" What a pity he did not live long enough to add Irving's name to that brilliant list !

"Irving was certainly one of the most striking personalities I ever met, besides being, beyond all question, the most loyal and delightful of friends as I and those who are dear to me have good reason to know.

"We shall always hold his name in loving remembrance.

"Yours very sincerely,
"HENRY F. DICKENS."

XXVII

MR. J. M. LEVY

AMONGST many loving, true friends Irving had none more loving or more helpful than the late J. M. Levy, the owner and editor of the *Daily Telegraph*. From the first he was a warm and consistent friend, and his great paper, which in the early days of Irving's success was devoting to the drama care and space unwonted in those days, did much—very much—to familiarise the public with his work and to spread his fame. As a personal friend his hospitality was unsurpassed. His house was always open, and nothing pleased him better than when Irving would drop in unasked. Up to the time of Mr. Levy's death there were many delightful evenings spent with him. These were always on Sundays, for during working days we of the theatre had no opportunity for such pleasures. But even after his death the same hospitality was extended by his children. Some are gone, but those who happily remain, Lord Burnham, Miss Matilda Levy, Lady Faudel-Phillips, Lady Campbell Clarke, were friends up to the hour of his death; and with them all his memory is and shall be green. Lord Burnham truly held as a part of his great inheritance this friendship; and he always extended to the actor the helpfulness which had been his father's. In a thousand delicate ways he always tried to show his love and friendship. Whenever, for instance, he had the honour of entertaining at his beautiful place, Hall Barn, Edward VII., either as Prince of Wales or King, he always included Irving in his house-party.

Such a friendship is a powerful help to any artist —and to like and cherish artists is a tradition in that family.

HENRY IRVING BETWEEN ENGLAND AND AMERICA

From a drawing by Fred Barnard, 1883, after the picture by Sir Joshua Reynolds "Garrick between Tragedy and Comedy"

XXVIII

VISITS TO AMERICA

*Farewell at the Lyceum—Welcome in New York, 1883
—A Journalistic " scoop"—Farewell*

I

IRVING'S first visit to America, in 1883, was a matter of considerable importance, not only to him, but to all of his craft and to all by whom he was held in regard. At that time the body of British people did not know much about America, and perhaps—strange as it may seem—did not care a great deal. Irving had played nearly five years continuously at the Lyceum, and his theatre had grown to be looked upon as an established institution. The great *clientèle* which had gathered round it, now numbering many thousands, looked on the venture with at least as much concern as he did himself. Thus the last night of the season, July 28, 1883, was a remarkable occasion. The house was jammed to suffocation and seemingly not one present but was a friend. When the curtain fell at the end of *The Belle's Stratagem*, there began a series of calls which seemed as though it would never end. Hand-clapping and stamping of feet seemed lost in the roar, for all over the house the audience were shouting—

shouting with that detonating effect which is only to be found from a multitude animated with a common feeling. The sight and sound were moving. Wherever one looked were tears; and not from women or the young alone.

At the last, after a pause a little longer than usual—from which the audience evidently took it that the dramatic moment had arrived—came a marvellous silence. The curtain went up, showing on the stage the entire *personnel* of the company and staff.

Then that audience simply went crazy. All the cheers that had been for the play seemed merely a preparation for those of the parting. The air wherever one looked was a mass of waving hands and handkerchiefs, through which came wave after wave of that wild, heart-stirring detonating sound. All were overcome, before and behind the floats alike. When the curtain fell, it did so on two thousand people swept with emotion.

II

Something of the same kind was enacted across the Atlantic. When on the evening of Monday, October 29, the curtain rose on the first scene of *The Bells*, there was the hush of expectation, prolonged till the moment when the door of the inn parlour was thrown open and Irving seemed swept in by the rushing snowstorm. The tempest of cheers seemed just as though the prolongation of that last moment in London; and for six or seven minutes—an incredibly long

A JOURNALISTIC "SCOOP"

time for such a matter on the stage—the cheering went on.

III

For my own part, I had a curious experience of that reception. Mr. Levy had asked me to send a cable to the *Daily Telegraph* describing Irving's reception. He knew, and I knew too, that it was a close shave for such a message to reach London in time for press. For in those days printing had not reached the extreme excellence of to-day, and the multiplication of stereos in the present form had not been accomplished. The difference of longitude seemed almost an insuperable difficulty. As I had to wait till Irving had actually appeared, I arranged with the manager of the Direct United States Cable Company to keep the wire for me. He was himself anxious to make a record, and had all in readiness. I had a man on a fleet horse waiting at the door of the theatre, and when Irving's welcome had *begun*, I ran out filling up the last words of my cable at the door. The horseman went off at once *ventre à terre*.

But my cable did not arrive in time. Another did, however, that sent to the *Daily News* by its correspondent, J. B. Bishop. I could not imagine how it was done, for the account cabled was a true one, manifestly written after the event.

Years afterwards, one night at supper with two men, J. B. Bishop and George Ward, then manager of the newly established Mackey–Bennett cable, it was explained to me. They had come to know that I was cabling and in order not to be outdone

Ward had had a wire brought all the way up from the Battery, and actually over the roof of the theatre and in by a side window.

Whilst my man was galloping to Lower Broadway, Bishop was quietly wording the despatch which his friend was telegraphing to his local office as he wrote!

IV

The welcome which Irving received on that night of October 29, 1883, lasted for more than twenty years—until that night of March 25, 1904, when at the Harlem Opera House he said "Goodbye" to his American friends—for ever! Go where he would, from Maine to Louisiana, from the Eastern to the Western Sea, there was always the same story of loving greeting; of appreciative and encouraging understanding; of heartfelt *au revoirs*, in which gratitude had no little part. As Americans of the United States have no princes of their own, they make princes of whom they love. And after eight long winters spent with Henry Irving amongst them, I can say that no more golden hospitality or affectionate belief, no greater understanding of purpose or enthusiasm regarding personality or work has ever been the lot of any artist—any visitor—in any nation. Irving was only putting into fervent words the feeling of his own true heart, when in his parting he said:

> "I go with only one feeling on my lips and one thought in my heart—God bless America!"

HENRY IRVING ON SHIPBOARD, 1899

ON SS. "MENOMINEE," MAY 1900

XXIX

WILLIAM WINTER

AMONGST the many journalists who were Irving's friends, none was closer than William Winter, the dramatic critic of the New York *Tribune*, whose work is known all over America. Winter is not only a critic, but a writer of books of especial charm and excellence, and a poet of high order. One of his little poems which he spoke at a dinner of welcome to Irving on his first arrival at New York in 1883 is so delightful that I venture to give it—especially as it had a prophetic instinct as to the love and welcome which for more than twenty years was extended to the actor throughout the whole of the United States. He and Irving had been already friends for some time, and always saw a good deal of each other during Winter's visits to London. The occasion was the dinner given by Colonel E. A. Buck, to attend which many of the friends present came from Cleveland, Buffalo, West Point, Louisville, Chicago—distances varying from fifty to a thousand miles.

HENRY IRVING.
A Word of Welcome.
November 18, 1883.

I

If we could win from Shakespeare's river
    The music of its murmuring flow,
With all the wild-bird notes that quiver
    Where Avon's scarlet meadows glow,
If we could twine with joy at meeting
    Their love who lately grieved to part,
Ah, then, indeed, our word of greeting
    Might find an echo in his heart!

II

But though we cannot, in our singing,
    That music and that love combine,
At least we'll set our blue-bells ringing,
    And he shall hear our whispering pine;
And these shall breathe a welcome royal,
    In accents tender, sweet, and kind,
From lips as fond and hearts as loyal
    As any that he left behind!

WILLIAM WINTER.

XXX

PERFORMANCE AT WEST POINT

A National consent — Difficulties of travel — An Audience of steel — A startling finale — Capture of West Point by the British

THE United States Military Academy at West Point on the Hudson River had from the time of his first visit to America a great charm for Irving. One of the first private friends he met on arriving at New York was Colonel Peter Michie, Professor of Applied Mathematics at the College. During the war he had been General Grant's chief officer of Engineers. Another friend made at the same time was Colonel Bass, Professor of Mathematics. With these two charming gentlemen we had become close friends. When Irving visited West Point he told Michie that he would like to play to the cadets if it could be arranged. The matter came within hail in 1888, when he repeated the wish to Colonel Michie. The latter, as in duty bound, had the offer conveyed, through the Commandant, to the Secretary for War at Washington. To the intense astonishment of every one the War Secretary not only acquiesced at once but conveyed his appreciation of Irving's offer in most handsome and generous terms. The effect at West Point was startling. The authorities there had taken it for granted that such an exception to the iron rule of discipline which governs the Military and Naval Academies of the United States would not be permitted. The professors had a feeling that the closing his theatre in New York for a night was too great a sacrifice to make. I was made aware of this feeling by an early visit from Colonel Michie on the morning after the sanction of the War Secretary had been given. At half-past seven o'clock he came into my room at the Brunswick Hotel and was almost in a state of consternation as to what he should do. He was vastly relieved when I told him that Irving's offer had, of course, been made in earnest and that nothing would please him so much. And so it was arranged that on the evening of Monday, March 19, Irving and Ellen Terry and the whole of the company should play *The Merchant of Venice* in the Grant Hall, the cadets' mess-room.

In the meantime an obstacle arose which covered us all with concern. On the night of Sunday, March 11, the eastern seaboard was visited by the worst blizzard on record. Between one and eight in the morning some four feet deep of snow fell, and as the wind was blowing a hundred miles an hour, as recorded by the anemometer, it was piled in places in gigantic drifts. For some days New York and all around it was paralysed. The railways were blocked, the telegraph cut off. Even the cables had suffered. We were getting our news from Philadelphia *via* London—and even these had to come *via* Canada. West Point is sixty miles from New York and the two railways—the New York Central on the left hand and the West Shore line on the right—the West Point side—were simply obliterated with snowdrifts. The managers of these two lines and that of the New York, Ontario, and Western line—it having running powers over the West Shore—had most kindly arranged to place a special train at Irving's disposal for the West Point visit. Towards the end of the week the outlook of the journey, which had at first seemed unfavourable, grew a little brighter; it *might* be possible. Possible it was, for by superhuman exertions the line was cleared in time for our journey of March 19. Our train opened the line.

Of course it was not possible to use scenery in the space available for the performance; so it was arranged that the play should be given as in Shakespeare's time. To this end notices were fastened to the curtains at the proscenium: "Venice: A Public Place"; "Belmont: Portia's House"; "Shylock's House by a Bridge," &c. As it happens, the Venetian dress of the sixteenth century was almost the same as the British; so that the costumes now used in the piece were alike to those worn by the audience as well as on the stage at the Globe Theatre in Shakespeare's time. Thus the cadets of West Point saw the play almost identically as Shakespeare had himself seen it.

I think that we all in that hall felt proud when we saw over the proscenium of the little stage the flags of Britain and America draped together and united by a branch of palm. It thrilled us to our heart's core merely to see.

It was a wonderful audience. I suppose there never was another on all fours with it. I forget how many hundreds of cadets there are—I think four or five, and they were all there. As they sat in their benches they looked, at the first glance, like a solid mass of steel. Their uniforms of blue and grey with brass buttons; their bright young faces, clean-shaven; their flashing eyes—all lent force to the idea. As I looked at them I remembered with a thrill an anecdote that John Russell Young had told me after dinner the very night before. He had been with General Grant on his journey round the world and had heard the remark. At Gibraltar Grant had reviewed our troops with Lord Napier. When he saw them sweep by at the double he had turned to the great British General and said:

"Those men have the swing of conquest!"

The attention and understanding of the audience could not be surpassed. Many of these young men had never seen a play; and they were one and all chosen from every State in the Union, each one having been already trained or being on the way to it to command an army in the field. There was not a line of the play, not a point which did not pass for its full value. This alone seemed to inspire the actors, down to the least important. At the end of each act came the ringing cheers which are so inspiring to all.

When the curtain finally fell there was a pause. And then with one impulse every one of those hundreds of young men with a thunderous cheer threw up his cap; for an instant the air was darkened with them. There was a significance in this which the ordinary layman may not understand. By the American Articles of War—which govern the Military Academy—for a cadet to throw up his cap, except at the word of command given by his superior officer, is an act of insubordination punishable with expulsion. These splendid young fellows —every one of whom justified himself later on the deadly heights of Santiago or amid the jungles of the Philippines—had to find some suitable means of expressing their feelings; and they did it in a way that they and their comrades understood. Strange to say, not one of the superior officers happened to notice the fearful breach of discipline. They themselves were too much engaged in something else—possibly throwing up their own caps; for they were all old West Point men.

Right sure I am that no one who had the privilege of being present on that night can ever forget it —men, women, or children; for behind the corps of cadets sat the officers with their wives and families.

When Irving came to make the little speech inevitable on such an occasion he said at the close :

> "I cannot restrain a little patriotic pride now, and I will confess it. I believe the joy-bells are ringing in London to-night, because for the first time the British have captured West Point!"

He spoke later of that wonderful audience in terms of enthusiasm, and Ellen Terry was simply in a transport of delight. For my own part, though I have been in the theatre each of the thousand times Irving and Ellen Terry played *The Merchant of Venice*, I never knew it to go so well.

Beyond this delightful experience, which must long be a tradition in West Point, the Academy has another source of perpetual memory. In the officers' mess hangs a picture presented by Henry Irving which they hold beyond price. It is a picture of the great Napoleon done from life by Captain Marryat when he was a midshipman on the British warship *Bellerophon* which carried the Conquered Conqueror to his prison in St. Helena.

XXXI

AMERICAN REPORTERS

High testimony—Irving's care in speaking—"Not for publication"—A diatribe—Moribundity

I

I CAN bear the highest testimony to the *bona fides* of American reporters, though they do not, either individually or collectively, want any commendation from me. I have had, in the twenty years covered by our tours in America, many hundreds of "interviews" with reporters, and I never once found one that "went back" on me. I could always speak quite openly to them individually on a subject which we wished for the present to keep dark, simply telling him or them that the matter was not for present publication. Any one who knows the inner working of a newspaper, and of the keenness which exists in the competition for the acquisition of news, will know how much was implied by the silence—the scorn and contempt that would now and then be hurled at those who "couldn't get a story." I have no doubt that sometimes the engagement on the paper was imperilled, or even cancelled. Of course I always tried to let them get *something*. It was quite impossible at times that Irving should give interviews. Such take time, and time was not always available in the midst of strenuous work; sickness and weariness are bars to intellectual undertakings; and now and again the high policy of one's business demands silence. In Irving's case his utterances had to be carefully considered. He was one of the very few men who were always reported *verbatim*. With ordinary individuals there is habitual compression and "editing" which, though it may occasionally suppress some fact or step in an argument, is protective against many errors. It is an old journalistic saying that "Parliamentary reputations are made in the Gallery!" This is almost exact; were it qualified so as to admit of exceptions it would be quite exact. In ordinary speeches, or in any form of *ex tempore* and unpremeditated utterance, there are evidences of changement during the process of thought—uncompleted sentences, confused metaphors, words ill chosen or slightly misapplied. In addition, as in almost every case Irving spoke or was interviewed on professional subjects or matters closely allied to his own work or ideas, there was always a possibility of creating a wrong impression somewhere. Also, he stood so high amongst his own craft that an omission would now and again be treated as an affront. I have known him to receive, after some speech or interview or recorded conversation where he had given a few names of actors as illustrating some part, a dozen letters asking if there was any reason why the writer's name was omitted in that connection. Irving was always most loyal to all those of his own calling and considerate of their needs and wishes. And so in all matters where he was by common consent or by general repute vested with the respon-

ACCURACY IN SPEAKING

sibilities of judgment he tried to hold the scales of justice balanced. In order, therefore, to see that his real views were properly set out—and incidentally for self-protection—he always took precautions with regard to speeches and interviews. The former, he always wrote out. On occasions where he had to speak *quasi-impromptu*—such as on the stage after the performance on first or last nights; any time when mere pleasant commonplaces were insufficient—he learned the speech by heart. When he could have anything before him, such as at dinners, he would have ready his speech carefully corrected, printed in very large type on small pages printed on one side only and not fastened together—so that they could be moved easily and separately. This he would place before him on the table. He would not seem to read it, and of course he would be familiar with the general idea. But he read it all the same; with a glance he would take in a whole sentence of the big type and would use his acting power not only in its delivery but in the disguising of his effort. If there were not time to get the speech printed he would write it out himself in a big hand with thick strokes of a soft pen. With regard to interviews he always required that the proof should be submitted to him and that his changes, either by excisions or additions, should be respected. He would sign the proof if such were thought desirable. I never knew a case where the interviewer or the newspaper did not loyally hold to the undertaking. I am anxious to put this on record; for I have often heard and read diatribes by the inexperienced against not only the system of interviewing but the interviewers. Let me give an instance of the chagrin which must be felt by men, skilled in the work and with responsibilities to their newspapers, who are baffled in their undertakings by reasons which they do not understand or agree with.

In the winter of 1886 I went across to arrange a tour of *Faust* for the coming year. We especially wished the matter kept dark, for we had alternative plans in view. Therefore I went quietly and without telling any one. When I landed in New York my coming was some way known—I suppose I had been missed at the Lyceum and some one had guessed the purpose of my absence and had cabled, and I was met by a whole cloud of interviewers, nearly all of whom I had known for some years. When we were all together in my hotel I told them frankly that I would talk to them about anything they wished except the purpose of my visit. This being *their* purpose, they were naturally not satisfied. I saw this and said:

"Now, look here, boys, you know I have always tried to help you in your work in any way I was free to do. I want for a few days to keep my present purpose secret. When what I want to do is through, I shall tell you all about it. It will be only a few days at most. Won't you trust me about the wisdom of this? All I want is silence for a while; and if you will tell me that you will say nothing till I let you go ahead, I shall tell you everything—right here and now!"

One of them said at once:

"No! Don't tell us yet. If you are silent the difficulty will be only between you and us. But if you tell us we shall each have to fight his own crowd for not telling them what we know!" The general silence vouched this as accepted by all. We sat still for perhaps a minute, no one wishing to begin. Before us was the whisky of hospitality. At last one of my guests said:

"By the way, how do you like American as compared with Irish whisky?—*of course, not for publication!*"

There was a roar of laughter. I felt that my reticence was forgiven, and we had a pleasant chat through a delightful half-hour. Out of that they made a "story" of some kind to suit their mission.

II

In a few instances the reporter who writes from his own side without consultation has said funny things. Two cases I remember. The first was when more than twenty years ago we made a night journey from Chicago to Detroit. When we boarded our special train I found one strange young man with a gripsack who said he was coming with us. To this I demurred, telling him that we never took any stranger with us and explaining that, as all our company was divided into little family groups they would not feel so comfortable with a stranger as when, as usual, they were among friends and comrades only. He said he was a reporter, and that he was going to write a story about the incidents of the night. I did not know what kind of incidents he expected! However, I was firm and would not let him come.

When we arrived in Detroit in the morning a

messenger came on board with a large letter directed to me. It contained a copy of a local paper in which was marked an article on how the Irving company travelled—a long article of over a column. It described various matters, and even made mention of the appearance *en déshabille* of some members of the company. At the end was appended a note in small type to say that the paper could not vouch for the accuracy of the report as their representative had not been allowed to travel on the train. I give the whole matter from memory; but the way in which the writer dealt with myself was most amusing. It took up, perhaps, the first quarter of the article. It spoke of " an individual who *called himself* Bram Stoker." He was thus described:

> ". . . who seems to occupy some anomalous position between secretary and valet. Whose manifest duties are to see that there is mustard in the sandwiches and to take the dogs out for a run; and who unites in his own person every vulgarity of the English-speaking race."

I forgave him on the spot for the whole thing on account of the last sub-sentence.

The second instance was as follows:

When on our Western tour in 1899–1900 we visited Kansas City for three nights, playing in the Opera House afterwards destroyed by fire. At that time limelight for purposes of stage effect had been largely superseded by electric light, which was beginning to be properly harnessed for the purpose. It was much easier to work with and cheaper, as every theatre had its own plant. Irving, however, preferred the limelight or calcium light, which gives softer and more varied effects, and as it was not possible to get the necessary gas-tanks in many places we took with us a whole railway waggon-load of them. These would be brought to the theatre with the other paraphernalia of our work. As we had so much stuff that it was not always possible to find room for it, we had to leave some of the less perishable goods on the sidewalk. This was easy in Kansas City, as the theatre occupied a block and its sidewalks were wide and not much used except on the main street. Accordingly the bulk of our gas-tanks were piled up outside. The scarlet colour of the oxygen tanks evidently arrested the attention of a local reporter and gave him ideas. On the morning after the first performance his paper came out with a sensational article to the effect that at last the treasured secret was out: Henry Irving was in reality a dying man, and was only kept alive by using great quantities of oxygen, of which a waggon-load of tanks had to be carried for the purpose. The reporter went on to explain how, in order to investigate the matter properly, he had managed to get into the theatre as a stage hand and had seen the tanks scattered about the stage. Further, he went on to tell how difficult it was to get near Irving's dressing-room as rude servants ordered away any one seen standing close to the door. But he was not to be baffled. He had seen at the end of the act Irving hurry into his room to be re-invigorated. He added, with an inconceivable *naïveté*, that precautions were taken to prevent the escape of the life-giving oxygen—*for even the keyhole was stopped up.*

XXXII

TOURS-DE-FORCE

A " Hamlet " Reading—A vast " Bill "

I

PERHAPS the greatest *tour-de-force* of Irving's life was made on the night of February 23, 1887, when at the Birkbeck Hall he read the play of *Hamlet* before a large audience for the benefit of the Institute. He had, of course, cut the play, just as he did for acting; indeed his cutting for the reading was a further slight curtailment, as on such an occasion there has to be a limit of time. But the cutting is in itself at once a tribute to his immense knowledge of the play and a lesson to students.

He read the play in two sections, with an interval of perhaps ten minutes between. The sustained effort must have been a frightful strain; for in such an undertaking there is not an instant's pause. Character follows character, each necessitating an instant change of personality; of voice; of method of speech and bearing and action. Irving was a great believer in the value of time in acting. He used to say that on certain occasions the time in which things were taken increased or marred the attention, emotion and eagerness of the audience. A play like *Hamlet* has as many and as varying times as an opera; thus the first knowledge and intention of the reader must have been complete. Strong as he was, it was a wonder how he got through that evening. When I went round to him at the end of the first part I found him sitting down and almost gasping. He had a wonderful recuperative power, however, and like a good fighter he was up at the call of "time." With unimpaired vitality, strength and passion he went on with his work right to the very end. For my own part I have never had so illuminative an experience of *Hamlet*. Irving's own performance of the title *rôle* I had of course seen, and with even greater effect than then; for dress and picturesque surroundings, in addition to the significance of movement and action, can intensify speech even when aided by the expression conveyed by face and hands. But the play as a whole came into riper prominence. Imagine the play with *every part* in it done by a great actor! It was never to be forgotten. The passionate scenes were triumphant. Knowing that he had the whole thing in his own hands and that he had not to trust to others, howsoever good they might be, he could give the reins to passion. The effect was enthralling. We of the audience sat spell-bound, hardly able to breathe.

When he ceased, almost fainting with the prolonged effort and excess of emotion, the pent-up enthusiasm burst forth like a storm.

In his dressing-room he had to sit for a while to recover himself—a rare thing indeed for him in those days. The note in my diary of that night has the following:

"Immense enthusiasm—remarkable—magnificent—every character given in masterly manner—consider it greatest *tour-de-force* of his life—even *he* exhausted!"

II

Eight years before, on July 25, 1879, the night of his "Benefit," as it was called after the old-time custom, he had given another wonderful example of his power. On that occasion he had taken the great and strenuous act out of each of five plays and finished up with a comedy character. The bill was:

Richard III.	Act I.
Richelieu	Act IV.
Charles I.	Act IV.
Louis XI.	Act III.
Hamlet	Act III. (to end of Play Scene).

Raising the Wind.

The strain of such a bill was very great. Not only the playing and the changing to so many complete identities each in moments of wild passion, but even the dressing and preparation for each part. Throughout the whole of that evening there was not a single minute—or a portion of a minute—to spare. Such a strain of mind and body and psychic faculties all at once and so prolonged does not come into the working life of any other art or calling. Small wonder is it if the wear and tear of life to great actors is exceptionally great.

But Irving up to his sixtieth year was compact of steel and whipcord. His energy and nervous power were such as only came from a great brain; and the muscular force of that lean, lithe body must have been extraordinary. The standard of animal mechanics is "foot-pounds"—the force and heart effort necessary to raise a pound weight a foot high. An actor playing a heavy part judged by this rule does about as much work in an evening as a hod-man carrying bricks up a ladder. For more than forty years this man did such work almost every night of his life; with the added strain and stress of high emotion—no negligible quantity in itself. I know of no other man who could have done such work in such a way and with such astounding passion as Henry Irving on great occasions.

XXXIII

CHRISTMAS

*Christmas geese—Punch in the Green Room—
A dinner in the Theatre—Gambling without risk—
Christmas at Pittsburg*

I

ALL through Irving's management of the Lyceum Christmas was, with regard to the working staff and supers, kept in a patriarchal way. Every man and woman had on Christmas Eve or the night before it a basket containing a goose with "trimmings" —sage and onions and apples, and a bottle of gin. The children had each a goose, and a cake instead of the gin. There were some four or five hundred of them, and as they trailed away you could trace them through distant streets by their scent. On most Christmas Eves there was in the Green Room punch and cake for the company. The punch-bowl was a vast one, and was refilled as often as required. We would sometimes use a five-gallon keg of old whisky in that bowl, for a liberal supply was always left over for the stage hands.

II

On one Christmas Eve—1882—Irving had a dinner-party in the old Beefsteak Room. These were all close friends—Ellen Terry's family and my own and Loveday's, and a few others—twenty in all. We had a real Christmas dinner. Spiced beef, roast beef, turkey, plum pudding *et hoc genus omne*. All was perfect and after dinner a roulette table was placed before us. Then came the notable surprise.

Before each person was placed a canvas bag containing new silver of different denominations to the value of five pounds. Each and all could play with a good conscience as the hazard was not eating into accumulated fortune!

III

Two years later we were all at Pittsburg, Pennsylvania. Irving arranged an " off " night Christmas and had the whole company, over a hundred persons, to dinner at the Monhongaheela House, where he was staying. We drank all the loyal and usual toasts and finished with a sing-song, wherein various members of the company and the staff exhibited hitherto unknown powers of song and dance. They did amongst them a nigger entertainment which would have passed muster anywhere. There was much punch consumed that night. The whisky for it was brought in great pitchers the size of those used in a wash-basin. I brewed the punch so I know.

XXXIV

IRVING AS A SOCIAL FORCE

THE history of the Lyceum Theatre was for a quarter of a century a part of the social history of London. A mere list of Irving's hospitalities would be instructive. The range of his guests was impossible to any but an artist. As he never forgot or neglected his old friends there were generally at his table some present who represented the commonplace or the unsuccessful as well as the famous or the successful sides of life. The old days and the new came together cheerily under the influence of the host's winning personality, which no amount of success had been able to spoil.

Sometimes the Beefsteak Room, which could only seat at most thirty-six people, was too small; and at such times we migrated to the stage. These occasions were interesting, sometimes even in detail. On the hundredth night of *The Merchant of Venice*, February 14, 1880, there was a supper for three hundred and fifty guests. On March 25, 1882, ninety-two guests sat down to dinner to celebrate the hundredth night of *Romeo and Juliet*.

The Prince of Wales dined there in a party of fifty on May 7, 1883. The table was a round one, and in the centre was a glorious mass of yellow flowers with sufficient green leaves to add to its

A ROYAL BIRTHDAY-PARTY

beauty. This bouquet was thirty feet across, and was in the centre only nine inches in height, so that it allowed an uninterrupted view all round the table. I remember the Prince saying that he had never seen a more lovely table. On this as on other occasions there was overhead a great tent-roof covering the entire stage. Through this hung chandeliers. On three sides were great curtains of crimson plush and painted satin ordinarily used for tableaux curtains; and on the proscenium side a forest of high palms and flowers, behind which a fine quartette band played soft music.

One charming night I remember in the Beefsteak Room when the Duke of Teck and Princess Mary and their three sons and Princess May Victoria, whose birthday it was, came to supper. In honour of the occasion the whole decorations of room and table were of pink and white May, with the birthday cake to suit. Before the Princess was an exquisite little set of *Shakespeare* specially bound in white vellum by Zaehnsdorf, with markers of blush-rose silk.

The ordinary hospitalities of the Beefsteak Room were simply endless. A list of the names of those who have supped with Irving there would alone fill chapters of this book. They were of all kinds and degrees. The whole social scale has been represented from the Prince to the humblest of commoners. Statesmen, travellers, explorers, ambassadors, foreign princes and potentates, poets, novelists, historians—writers of every style, shade and quality. Representatives of all the learned professions; of all the official worlds; of all the great industries. Sportsmen, landlords, agriculturists. Men and women of leisure and fashion. Scientists, thinkers, inventors, philanthropists, divines. Egotists, ranging from harmless esteemers of their own worthiness to the very ranks of Nihilism. Philosophers. Artists of all kinds. In very truth the list was endless and kaleidoscopic.

Irving never knew how many personal friends he had, for all who ever met him claimed acquaintance for ever more—and always to his great delight. Let me give an instance: In the late "eighties" when he took a house with an enormous garden in Brook Green, Hammersmith, he had the house rebuilt and beautifully furnished; but he never lived in it. However, in the summer he thought it would be a good opportunity of giving a garden-party at which he might see all his friends together. He explained to me what he would like to do:

"I want to see all my friends at once; and I wish to have it so arranged that there shall be no one left out. I hope my friends will bring their young people who would like to come. Perhaps you may remember our friends better than I do; would you mind making out a list for me—so that we can send the invitations. Gunter can do the commissariat. Of course I should like to ask a few of our Lyceum audience who come much to the theatre. Some of them I know, but there are others from whom I have received endless courtesies and I want them to see that I look on them as friends."

I set to work on a list, and two days afterwards in the office he said to me:

"What about that list? We ought to be getting on with the invitations."

"No use," I said. "You can't give that party—not as you wish it!"

"Why not?" he asked amazed; he never liked to hear that anything he wished could not be done. I held up the sheets I had been working at.

"Here is the answer," I said. "There are too many!"

"Oh, nonsense, my dear fellow. You forget it is a huge garden." I shook my head.

"The other is huger. I am not half through yet, and they total up already over five thousand!"

And so that party never came off.

He had many many close friends whose names I should like to mention here, but to attempt a full list would not be possible. Such must be incomplete; and those so neglected might be pained. And so I venture to give in this book only the names of those who belong to the structure of the incident which I am recounting.

But Irving's social power was not merely in his hospitality. He was in request for all sorts and kinds of public and semi-public functions—the detailed list of them would be a serious one; of monuments that he has unveiled; of public dinners at which he has taken the chair or spoken; of foundation and memorial stones which he has laid; of flower shows, bazaars, theatres, libraries and public galleries that he has opened.

The public banquets to him have been many. The entertainments in his honour by clubs and other organisations were multitudinous.

And wherever he went on any such occasion,

whatever space there was—were it even in an open square or street—was crowded to the last point.

This very popularity entailed much work, both in preparation and execution, for he had always to make a speech. With him a speech meant writing it and having it printed so that he could read it—though he never appeared to do so.

All this opened many new ways for his successes in his art, and so aided in the growth of its honour. For instance, he was the first actor asked to speak at the annual banquet of the Royal Academy; thus through him a new toast was added to the restricted list of that very conservative body.

The "First Night" gatherings on the stage of the Lyceum after the play became almost historic; the list of the guests would form an index to those of note of the time.

There were similar gatherings of a certain national, and even international, importance; such as when the members of the Colonial Conference came *en masse;* when the Conference of Librarians attended the theatre; when ships of war of foreign nations sent glad contingents to the theatre; when the Guests of the Nation were made welcome.

Some of the latter groups are, I think, worthy to be told of in detail. I venture to give here—only as illustration of the range of his hospitalities at the Lyceum and elsewhere—some names which may be interesting. There are but few to whom they could all be known; but many of them are known either in London or locally. Occasionally, when opportunity permitted and memory served, I jotted down—often on my copy of the *menu*—the names of some of my fellow guests; and as I usually

SOME GUESTS

kept these interesting souvenirs, I am able to give a somewhat suggestive list. It is, of course, only partial—incomplete; by comparison meagre; representative rather than comprehensive. A complete list—were such possible—might be tiresome to the many, even though it should recall to individuals, as this of more than a thousand will, some delightful hours.

H.H. Prince Ibraham
Senator Chauncey Depew
Principal Story, Glasgow University
Mrs. and Misses Story
Sir Edward and Lady Russell
Mrs. Jack Gardner
Miss Genevieve Ward
Emma Nevada
Coquelin
Admiral Sir Harry Keppel
Mrs. Stirling (Lady Gregory)
Lord Chancellor Walker
Frederick Goodall, R.A.
Mrs. and Miss Goodall
Mr. and Mrs. Lawrence Barrett
Dr. Billings, U.S.A.
Judge and Mrs. McConnell
General Barnes (U.S.A.)
Edwin A. Ward
Dion Boucicault
Mr. and Mrs. E. Cramp
John Farrell
Sir William Robinson
The Ranee, Lady Brooke
Sir Ernest and Miss Cassel
Mr. and Mrs. J. H. Holmes
Sir Wm. Thomson, C.B.
Lady and Miss Thomson
W. T. Emmott
Judge Truax (New York)
Charles Santley
Mr. and Mrs. Margetson
Mr. and Mrs. Edmund Yates

Paderewski
Marquis of Worcester
Lord Burnham
Mr. and Mrs. Henry F. Dickens
The Misses Dickens
Miss Georgina Hogarth
Garnier
Hon. Sir S. Ponsonby-Fane
Alexander Salvini
Sir Charles Scotter
Richard Harding Davis
Sir C. and Lady Kinloch Cooke
Hon. Benjamin H. Brewster
Mr. and Mrs. C. Bradshaw
Albert Bierstadt
Stephen Fiske
Ernest Moore
James Albery
Dr. Keeley
Sir F. and Lady Lockwood
Fitzgerald Molloy
Sir Walter Gilbey, Bart.
Thomas Thorne
Sir James D. Linton, P.R.I.
Austin Brereton
Mr. and Mrs. Francis Wilson
Col. Mellor, M.P.
Mrs. and Mrs. Ernest Hawksley
General Sir Owen Lanyon
Charles Dickens (the younger)
James Orrock, R.I.
H. W. Massingham
C. W. McIlvaine
Montgomery Phister

Patti
Count Albert Mensdorff
J. G. Blaine
Joseph Jefferson
Admiral Lord C. Beresford
Mr., Mrs. and Miss Wirt Dexter
Judge Vanderpoel
Calvé
President Daniel Gilman, Johns Hopkins University
Francisque Sarcy
Lord Coleridge, L.C.J.
Mr. and Mrs. Edward J. Shaw
General Osborne (U.S.A.)
Louis F. Austin
Mr. and Mrs. Richard Mansfield
Mr. and Mrs. Edgar Pemberton
Haddon Chambers
President W. R. Harper, Chicago University
Mrs. Harper
Mr. and Mrs. Mortimer Mempes
Charles A. Dana
Coquelin cadet
Alfred Darbyshire
Mr. and Mrs. J. M. Barrie
C. Hamill
T. H. Bolton, M.P.
W. T. Arnold
Mr. and Mrs. George Henschel
Miss Greta Morritt
Montagu Williams, Q.C.
W. C. Bobbs
G. A. Redford
Judge Shea (New York)
Tom Taylor
Sir Walter Palmer, Bart.
Lady Palmer
W. Ordway Partridge
Peter A. B. Widener
Marion Crawford
Rt. Hon. and Mrs. H. H. Asquith
Henry Norman, M.P.
W. A. Purrington

Rt. Hon. A. J. Balfour
Mr. and Mrs. Frank Hill
Salvini
Anthony Hope Hawkins
Sir Campbell and Lady Clarke
Mrs. Tyson
The Duke of Fife
Signor Gennadius
Mr. and Mrs. J. Howard, Junr.
Seth Low
Dr. Charcot
Mrs. Gillespie
Dr. and Mrs. Davis
Mr. and Mrs. Bailey Aldrich
Mr. and Mrs. G. J. G. Lewis
John McCollough
Adolphe Brisson
Guy Boothby
Fraulein Haverland
Sarasate
Mr. and Mrs. Stewart Smith
Sir Morell and Lady Mackenzie
Mr. and Mrs. Wm. Edwards
Charles Major
Leonard Jerome
Dr. Edgar Browne
A. Howard Hinkle
Comte de Franqueville
Sir Harry Poland
Elsie de Wolf
Peixotto
Baillie Cleland
Mr. and Mrs. John B. Jeffery
E. F. S. Pigott
Sir Charles Cameron
Mr. and Mrs. George Grossmith
A. P. Burbank
Sir Charles and Lady Wyndham
Baillie Sorley
Dr. Graydon
W. J. Florence
Judge Harrison
Sir Wemyss Reid
Robert Taber

SOME GUESTS

Genl. Rt. Hon. Sir Dighton Probyn, V.C.
H.E. Genl. Horace Porter, Ambassador U.S.
Sir W. H. and Lady Russell
Captain Mimra
Mr. and Mrs. W. McMichael
George Boughton, R.A.
Mrs. Boughton
Mr., Mrs. and Miss J. L. Toole
Sarah Bernhardt
Maurice Bernhardt
Israel Zangwill
Mr. and Mrs. Melville Stone
Lord Randolph Churchill
Lady Randolph Churchill
William Warren
Mr. and Mrs. Brydges-Willyams
Senator Clarke
Miss Alice Goetz
Mr. and Mrs Perugini
John Northcott
General Miles (U.S.A.)
Judge Brady (N.Y.)
Mr. and Mrs. F. MacMillan
Judge N. Davis (New York)
John Ayling
H.E. Baghos Pacha Nubar
Mr. and Mrs. Bryan Lathrop
Mrs. W. K. Clifford
Mrs. Glover
James Hearn
Mr. and Mrs. E. T. Cook
Augustus Pitou
A. C. Calmour
James Fernandez
Angus Hamilton
Mrs. Craigie
Mr. and Mrs. Annan Bryce
Albert Bruce Joy
Jerome K. Jerome
Edwin Long, R.A.
John Hollingshead
Serjeant Ballantine
Mr. and Mrs. G. W. Smalley
Duke of Devonshire
Duchess of Devonshire
F. R. Lawrence
Richmond Ritchie
Mrs. Ritchie (Miss Thackeray)
Signor Yturbe
Mr. & Mrs. & Miss Hare
Lord and Lady Pirbright
Sir Henry Lawrence, Bart., and Lady Lawrence
M. L. Mayer
Sir John and Lady Monckton
Sydney Brooks
Mr. and Mrs. Phil May
Joseph Proctor
Mr. and Mrs. J. B. Partridge
Mr. and Mrs. B. Tilghman
Sir James and Lady Dewar
Mr. and Mrs. St. C. McKelway
Ludovic Goetz
Charles Klein
Mr. and Mrs. A. E. T. Watson
Miss Elizabeth Marbury
Wm. Woodall, M.P.
Sir John Tenniel
Genl. Hon. C. and Miss Thesiger
Mr. and Mrs. Beatty-Kingston
Genl. L. Fairchild (U.S.A.)
Seymour Hicks
Randegger
Wm. Heinemann
Mr. and Mrs. H. E. Abbey
C. F. Fearing
Tosti
D. F. Lowe, of Heriots
Major Lyon
Gilbert Farquhar
A. W. Dubourg
Hawes Craven
Julia Marlow
Mr. and Mrs. George Bancroft
R. Caldecott
Sir Whittaker Ellis
Mr. and Mrs. Ben Webster
Lord Justice FitzGibbon

Mr. and Mrs. Hall Caine
Duchess of St. Albans
Mr. and Mrs. Morton McMichael
H.H. The Raja of Kapurthala
Genl. Francis A. Walker (U.S.A.)
Mr. and Mrs. Henry Labouchere
Marshall Field
Edward Fitzgerald
Charles Cramp
Ludwig Barnay
P. T. Barnum
Sir Squire and Lady Bancroft
George Ade
Coquelin fils
Frank Dicksee, R.A.
Edward Terry
Alfred Gilbert, R.A.
Sir William Van Horne
Mr. and Mrs. J. W. Mackail
Mr., Mrs. and Misses T. Catling
Boito
Howard Carroll
Mrs. Ward
Sir Wm. Agnew, Bart.
Corney Grain
Edward Henry Palmer
"Barney" Barnato
Rt. Hon. George Wyndham
Countess Grosvenor
William Gillette
Dr. and Mrs. David Newman
Mr. and Mrs. E. Routledge
Admiral Gordon
Major W. H. Wiley
F. Anstey Guthrie
Miss Amy Leslie
W. P. Frith, R.A.
Mr. and Mrs. Thaddeus
J. Forbes-Robertson
Gertrude Elliott
Goodenough Taylor
Henry Hackett
James McHenry
E. Freiberger
John McNally
Edwin Booth and Miss Booth
Sir James Blyth, Bart.
Misses Blyth
Earl of Hardwicke
Mr., Mrs. and Miss Pullman
Justin and Miss McCarthy
" Uncle " George Bromley
Duchess of Manchester
Seymour Lucas, R.A.
Mrs. Lucas
Paul Mounet-Sully
James Whitcomb Riley
Mr. and Mrs. E. A. Bendall
Mrs. and Miss Cadwallader-Jones
Ilona Eibenschutz
Mr. and Mrs. Martin Harvey
Judge Adams
J. S. Metcalfe
Mrs. Allingham
Frank Thomson
Mary Moore
Sir Gilbert and Lady Parker
Edward Dicey
John Elderkin
Sir Maurice Fitzgerald (The Knight of Kerry)
Dr. Lambdin
A. G. R. Heward
Henry Harper
Solly Joel
Louis Becke
W. Griscom
S. Gatti
C. Hetherington
W. Padgett
Angus Campbell
J. McLure Hamilton
W. Lestocq
Col. Hughes
Senator Jones
Mr. and Mrs. G. B. Burgin
Horace Howard Furniss
Jules Claretie
Mr. and Mrs. C. A. Otis

SOME GUESTS

Dr. Nansen
Lord Glenesk
H.E. Charlemagne Tower, U.S. Ambassador
Mrs. Charlemagne Tower
Sir George Faudel-Phillips, Bart.
Lady and Misses Faudel-Phillips
Alfred Beit
Lord Ronald Gower
Charles Frohman
Lady Lister Kaye
W. A. Burdett-Coutts, M.P.
Right Hon. Baroness Burdett-Coutts
Leopold Teller
Sims Reeves
Mr. and Mrs. Talcott Williams
Archdeacon Sinclair
Abbé Liszt
Mr. and Mrs. Walter Pollock
Mr. and Mrs. Felix Moscheles
Mr. and Mrs. E. S. Willard
Albert Sterner
Roswell Field
Mr. and Mrs. Arthur à Beckett
F. M. Stanwood
Sir Frederick Pollock, Bart.
Lady Pollock
Commander Nazro (U.S.A.)
Miss Braddon (Mrs. Maxwell)
Mr. and Mrs. William Winter
Mr. and Mrs. J. E. C. Bodley
R. Weightman
Jacques Normand
Malcolm Watson
R. Stodart Walker
Mr. and Mrs. J. M. Francis
William Allan Lloyd-Davies
Mrs. Nettleship
Joseph Fisher
Mr. and Mrs. T. P. O'Connor
Genl. Sir F. de Winton
Mr. and Mrs. H. H. Kohlsaat
H.E. Whitelaw Reid, Ambassador U.S.
Capt. and Mrs. Egerton Castle
Lord Alcester
Mr. and Mrs. J. M. Le Sage
H.E. R. McCormick, U.S. Ambassador, & Mrs. McCormick
Mr. and Mrs. Knox D'Arcy
Mr. and Mrs. Arthur Lewis
Febvre
Lord and Lady Morris
Woodbury Langdon
The Dean of Manchester
Mr. and Mrs. J. Chute
Mr. and Mrs. Stannard
Sir James and Lady Henderson
Mr. and Mrs. J. B. Bishop
Mr. and Mrs. J. C. Parkinson
Samuel Bowles
R. Underwood Johnson
Professor Blackie
Mr. and Mrs. Fred Terry
Rev. Freeman Wills
Sir F. Pollock, Bart.
Lady Pollock
Mr. and Mrs. I. N. and Miss Ford
Mr. and Mrs. H. H. Furness, Junr.
Mrs. Langtry
H. L. Wagner
Mr. and Mrs. Harry Furniss
Mr. and Mrs. Clarke Davis
Joseph Skipsey
Robert Arthur
W. O. Bates
H. Guy Carleton
Sir Spencer St. John
Frank Bartlett
Count de Leyden
Mr. and Mrs. Clement Scott
Mr., Mrs. and Misses Hoyt
Frank Tyars
Archibald Clavering Gunter
Henry Kemble
Edgar Fawcett

Earl and Countess of Warwick
T. Reed (Speaker, U.S.A.)
Alfred de Rothschild
Sir Edward Burne-Jones, Bart.
Lady Burne-Jones
Mr., Mrs. and Miss Henri Riviere
Earl and Countess of Albemarle
Mr. W. L. Courtney
Mrs. and Misses Courtney
Earl of Lytton (" Owen Meredith ")
Darmont
Admiral Schröeder (German Navy)
Richard Butler
Sir James and Lady Knowles
Genl. Wesley Merritt (U.S.A.)
Nesper
Langdon Mitchell
Moy Thomas
Mr. Marcus Stone, R.A.
Mrs. Stone
Mr. Justice Sir James Mathew
Lady and Miss Mathew
G. L. Rives
Mr. and Mrs. F. W. Lawson
Col. Templar
Professor Jack
Maurice Minton
Mancinelli
Parke Godwin
J. N. Petrie
Frank Lloyd
Harold Frederic
J. C. Macdona, M.P.
Fred Kerr
Mr. and Mrs. Prescott Bigelow
Edward German
W. H. Rideing
W. Snape
Weedon Grossmith
Sir Andros de la Rue, Bart.
Lady de la Rue
Judge Daly (New York)
H.E. Joseph B. Choate, Ambassador U.S.
Mrs. and Miss Choate
H.E. Wayne McVeagh, U.S. Ambassador
Mrs. and Miss Wayne McVeagh
Rt. Hon. Sir Fred. Milner, Bart.
H.S.H. Duke of Saxe-Meinengen
Lord and Lady St. Helier
Daniel Burnham
Mr., Mrs. and Misses Casella Worms
H. H. Richardson
Captain Iwamoto (Japan Navy)
David Murray, R.A.
Governor Dorsheimer
Lord and Lady Northcliff
Heinrich Conreid
Senator Evarts
Charles Russell
David Belasco
Sir Francis Burnand
Lady and Misses Burnand
Miss Agnes Keyser
H.H. Maharaja the Gaekwar of Baroda
Callender Ross
Franklin Fyles
Sir W. and Lady Soulsby
Col. Ames
H. H. Anderson
Frank Richards
Major, Mr. and Mrs. Arthur Griffiths
Norman Hapgood
Mr. and Mrs. W. B. Scoones
E. A. Perry
Mr. and Mrs. (Kate Douglas Wiggin) Riggs
Mr. and Mrs. Passmore Edwards
E. W. Garden
Mr. and Mrs. W. E. Bryant
H. C. Duval

SOME GUESTS

John Uri Lloyd
F.M. Viscount Wolseley
Mr., Mrs. and Misses de Young
Sir Thornley and Lady Stoker
Lord and Lady Esher
Ange Galdemar
Theodore Watts-Dunton
Mr. and Mrs. W. M. Laffan
Sir A. and Lady Conan Doyle
Antoinette Sterling
H.E. T. F. Bayard, Ambassador U.S.
Edward Dowden
E. A. Abbey, R.A., and Mrs. Abbey
G. H. Schwab
Mr. and Mrs. Beerbohm Tree
Mr. and Mrs. James Methven
Sir C. V. and Lady Stanford
Professor Robinson
Sydney Grundy
Graham Robertson
Sir C. and Lady Euan Smith
Mr. and Mrs. Dixey
Lord Houghton
Daniel Frohman
Mr. and Mrs. Carlaw Martin
Arthur Durham
Vice-Admiral Gough
H. T. Chance
Hon. S. and Mrs. Coleridge
Ethel Barrymore
Dr. Dabbs
Fred Mouillot
Charles Dyall
E. M. Borrajo
Lord Currie
Lady Currie (" Violet Fane ")
Lady Agnes Cooke
Samuel Smiles
Mr. and Mrs. Littleton
Carl Hentschel
T. J. Keenan
John Swan, R.A., and Mrs. Swan
David James

Sir Coutts Lindsay, Bart.
Miss Matilda Levy
H.E. James Russell Lowell, Ambassador U.S.
Lord and Lady Tennyson
Prince Ernest of Hohenlohe-Langenburg
Mr. and Mrs. T. P. Fowler
Sidney Lee
Emile Moreau
E. L. Godkin
Miss Betty Webb
Damala
B. L. Farjeon
Mr. and Mrs. Bradley Martin
Charles Hallé
Mr. and Mrs. M. B. I. Goddard
Sir Augustus Harris
Hon. Harry and Mrs. Lawson
Mr. and Mrs. T. Donaldson
Arminius Vambéry
Henry Watterson
Dr. C. S. Fitzgerald
Sir W. and Lady M. Banks
Mr. and Mrs. J. B. Howard
Professor Remsen
Dr. Domville
Dr. and Mrs. Robson Roose
Mr. and Mrs. A. S. Wortley
Dr., Mrs. and Misses Langmaid
Mr. and Mrs. Arthur Frankau
General Foote (U.S.A.)
Mr., Mrs. and Miss John Drew
Mr. and Mrs. Arthur Warren
Lady Cicely Hamilton
Judge Russell (New York)
Percy Fitzgerald
Archdeacon Watkins
Lord and Lady Skelmersdale
Sir Baldwin Leighton, Bart.
Mr. and Mrs. J. Sargent Wise
A. Pencoast
Isidore De Lara
" Larry " Jerome
Ray Rockman

R. Watson Gilder
Senator and Mrs. Mark Hanna
Mr. and Mrs. Arthur Greenwood
Earl and Countess of Aberdeen
Mr. and Mrs. Bernard N. and Miss Baker
Mr. and Mrs. T. Nelson Page
Sir Richard Quain, Bart.
Lady and Miss Quain
Mrs. Keeley
H.E. E. J. Phelps, Ambassador U.S., and Mrs. Phelps
Rejane
Augustus St. Gaudens
Professor T. Gollanz
Mr. and Mrs. Laurence Hutton
David Law
Genl. Sir H. Macdonald
Admiral Baldwin (U.S.A.)
Julius Cahn
Mr. and Mrs. H. A. Jones
Sir John Ure Primrose, Bart.
Lady Primrose
Mrs. Gilbert
Wells J. Hawkes
Duke and Duchess of Sutherland
Rev. Henry Ward and Mrs. Beecher
Prof. and Mrs. R. Y. Tyrrell
Mrs. Cashel Hoey
Murat Halstead
J. Nicol Dunn
Col. and Mrs. Michie (U.S.A.)
Lena Ashwell
Lieut. W. S. Montgomery
Arthur Collins
Sir James Ritchie
Mrs. Brown Potter
Sir William Bailey
Norman Forbes
Sir Henry Thompson
Carl Rosa
Andrew Mudie
Dr. Nedley
Lord Farquhar
H.E. Robert Lincoln, Ambassador U.S.
Mrs. Lincoln
Sidney Colvin
Ada Rehan
Lord Russell of Killowen, L.C.J.
Lady Russell
T. Stoker, C.S.I., and Mrs. Stoker
Mr. and Mrs. F. Frankfort Moore
Esther Palliser
Joseph Knight
John Russell Young
Mr. and Mrs. E. E. Pinches
Mr. and Mrs. G. Alexander
Julian Hawthorne
Dean Farrar
Countess Narjac
Eugene Field
Herman Vezin
Mr. and Mrs. F. A. Marshall
Mr. and Mrs. Poultney Bigelow
Lewis Waller
Sir Anderson and Lady Critchett
J. McN. Whistler
W. B. Parsons
Mr. and Mrs. Duncan Mackellar
Mr. and Mrs. Augustin Daly
E. J. Broadfield
Sir Julius Benedict
Mr. and Mrs. C. W. Mathews
Howard Saxby
Mr. and Mrs. A. M. Palmer
Sir David Richmond, Bart.
Lady Richmond
H. W. Sprague
Judge Haydon
Jennie Eustace
Professor Ray Lankester
The Misses Gaskell
Senator Chandler
Phyllis Broughton

SOME GUESTS

George du Maurier
Mrs. and Misses du Maurier
H.E. Col. John Hay, Ambassador U.S.
Mrs. and Miss Hay
Lord Chancellor Ashbourne
Lady Ashbourne
Mr. and Mrs. Rafe Leycester
Elihu Root
Sir George Lewis, Bart.
Lady and Misses Lewis
Mounet-Sully
Alfred Austin, Poet Laureate
Mrs. Alfred Austin
Mr. and Mrs. Elwyn Barron
Samuel Story, M.P.
Hamilton Aide
W. L. Bull
Col. Arthur Lee, M.P.
Charles Dudley Warner
W. D. Howells
Earl of Crawford
J. A. Aitken, R.S.A.
Mrs. Aitken
M. P. Handy
Mr. and Mrs. Stuart Ogilvie
Cornelius Bliss
Sir D. and Lady Straight
J. W. Griggs (Attorney-General, U.S.A.)
Mr. and Mrs. Frank D. Millet
Col. Sinclair
Mr. and Mrs. Arthur Bourchier
David A. Munro
Admiral Schley (U.S.A.)
James Staats Forbes
Mr. and Mrs. John P. Marquand
General Sherman (U.S.A.)
Mr. and Mrs. E. Y. Lowne
Judge Morrow
Mr. and Mrs. T. Threlfall
R. Swain Giffard
Nellie Farren
Archibald Grove
Sir Henry M. and Lady Stanley
Earl of Carrington
Charles Lamb Kenney
Earl and Countess of Londesborough
Victor Maurel
Dr. George Stoker, C.M.G., and Mrs. Stoker
John Mackay
Wilson Barrett
Rose Le Clerc
Col. North
Rt. Hon. John and Mrs. Burns
J. G. Simmons
Cronegk
Mr. and Mrs. Fred Wyndham
Mr. and Mrs. Slason Thompson
Marion Terry
Earl of Dunraven
George F. Shaw
Colonel Fitz-George
B. H. Barrows
E. Blashfield
Mr. and Mrs. H. D. Traill
W. H. Grenfell
Sir Alexander C. Mackenzie
Lady and Miss Mackenzie
Mr. and Mrs. G. W. Childs
Lady Dorothy Nevill
Mr. and Mrs. Will. J. Davis
Sir Bruce Seton, Bart.
Lady Seton
F. Inderwick, Q.C.
Mrs. and Miss Inderwick
Mr. and Mrs. Stanford White
Mr. and Mrs. Walter Ellis
Colonel McClure
Mr., Mrs. and Miss Comyns Carr
J. L. Lyell
Mr. and Mrs. Tinsley Linley
Mr., Mrs. and Miss F. Wicks
Thomas Hardy
Mr. and Mrs. E. H. Clement
Lilian Braithwaite
" Max Eliot " (Mrs. Ellis)
General Louis Merrill (U.S.A.)

Duca and Duchessa del Balzo
F.M. Sir Frederick Haines
Mr. and Mrs. Henry Gilbey
Mr. and Mrs. A. W. Pinero
Hon. Lady Hamilton-Gordon
Lord and Lady Pirrie
Mr. and Mrs. G. A. Sala
John Sargent, R.A.
Ellen Terry
Lord and Lady Sandhurst
Charles Major
Judge and Mrs. Parry
Sir William Pearce, Bart.
Sir Arthur Sullivan
Victor Mapes
The Countess of Bective
Genl. Hon. W. F. Cody (U.S.A.)
Lord and Lady A. Campbell
Mr., Mrs. and Misses Hatton
Wilson King
Sir Richard and Lady Burton
H. Chance Newton
Minnie Hauck
J. H. Meltzer
C. R. Hosmer
Booth Tarkington
Col. Collins
Henry Howe
Col. John C. New (U.S.A.)
Sir William Windyer
Mrs. Sherwood
David Heilbron
Col. C. Edwards (U.S.A.)
A. J. Dixon
Jacob Bright
Earl and Countess of Radnor
Max O'Rell
W. Q. Orchardson, R.A.
Sir Edward Hulse, Bart.
Hon. Lady Hulse
Lord Justice Barry
Mr. and Mrs. Humphry Ward
Arthur Chappell
Val Prinsep, R.A., and Mrs. Prinsep
S. L. Clemens ("Mark Twain")
Mrs. and Misses S. L. Clemens
Ames Van Wart
Prince Edward of Saxe-Weimar
Duse
Baron Huddleston
Lady Diana Huddleston
Mr., Mrs. and Misses H. A. Blyth
The Bishop of Ripon, and Mrs. Boyd-Carpenter
Col. and Mrs. Bass (U.S.A.)
Mr. & Mrs. John & Misses Fiske
Thomas Reid
Dr., Mrs. and Misses Pryde
Mr., Mrs. and Miss C. Fairchild
Mr. and Mrs. Herman Merivale
Mr. and Mrs. Ballard Smith
Mrs. Charles Mathews
William Carey
H. W. Lucy ("Toby, M.P.")
Mrs. Lucy
Lord Knollys
Mrs. Van Aucken
Major Ricarde-Seaver
Dr. Porteous
Col. Harvey
Joseph Grego
W. H. Bartlett
Gerald Lawrence
Fay Davis
Rudolph Lehmann
Earl and Countess of Onslow
Mr. and Mrs. Robert Crawford
General Collis (U.S.)
J. F. Graham
Dr. Andrew Wilson
Mr. and Mrs. Arthur Stirling
E. Hamilton Bell
John Pettie, R.A.
Mr. and Mrs. Seymour Trower
Dr. and Mrs. Playfair
Beatrice Harraden
Judge Madden

SOME GUESTS

E. Onslow Ford, R.A., and Mrs. Ford
Lord Goschen
James Creelman
M. Porel
Right Hon. W. E. Gladstone and Mrs. Gladstone
H. C. Fahnstock
Sir Theodore Martin
Lady Martin ("Helen Faucit")
Capt. Emery (U.S.A.)
John Fox, Junr.
Sir William, Lady and Misses Hardman
Mr. and Mrs. Navarro (Mary Anderson)
Admiral Erben (U.S.A.)
Mr. and Mrs. W. M. Gilbert
W. W. Jacobs
Earl of Cawdor
John Hart
Mr. and Mrs. Alfred Waite
Justin Huntly McCarthy
Nat Godwin
Maxine Elliot
Mr. and Mrs. J. I. C. Clarke
Ralph Caine
Wolf Joel
Mr. and Mrs. W. H. Tailer
Mr. and Mrs. T. McKenna
Sir John R. Robinson
Col. Tom Ochiltree (U.S.A.)
Dr. John Marshall
Fred Leslie
Mrs. Campbell Praed
Louis N. Parker
Lady Mabel Egerton
Judge and Mrs. Tom Hughes
Mr. and Mrs. W. P. Byles
Alfred Parsons, A.R.A.
Mr. and Miss Stone Benedict
James R. Osgood
Mr. and Mrs. Linley Sambourne
Mr. and Mrs. C. Moberley Bell
Mr. and Mrs. John B. Carson
H.S.H. Prince Leiningen
Lord Strathcona
Tamagno
The Duke of Beaufort
Mr. and Mrs. Brandon Thomas
T. Russell Sullivan
Sir Luke Fildes, R.A.
Lady Fildes
J. H. Rhoades
T. H. S. Escott
Gounod
Alfred Scott-Gatty
Mr. and Mrs. Jopling Rowe
Mr. and Mrs. W. F. Fladgate
Robert Hichens
Mr. and Mrs. John Foord
Mackenzie Bell
General Duplat
Richard Garnett
Mr. and Mrs. S. Heilbut
Sir Philip Burne-Jones, Bart.
General Dumont
Keeley Halswelle
Mr. and Mrs. Yerkes
G. R. Blanchard
Sir Thomas and Lady Fardell
Wm. Bliss
Earl and Countess of Ribblesdale
Mr. Coudert
Pamela Colman Smith
Mr. and Mrs. Lawson Tait
H. J. Byron
Prof. Brodsky
Irene Vanbrugh
Whitworth Wallis
C. H. Ross
Carlo Pellegrini
Sir Laurence Alma-Tadema, R.A.
Lady and Misses Alma-Tadema
Sydney Valentine
Mr. and Mrs. Cyril Maude
Mr. and Mrs. Frederick Myers
David James

Sir Henry and Lady Blake
Perry Belmont
Charles Warner
Mr. and Mrs. Sydney Pawling
Flag-Lieut. Potter, U.S.N.
Gaston Mayer
C. M. Lowne
Dr. Du Bois, U.S.N.
Earl and Countess of Winchilsea
Louis Engel
Philip Carr
H. C. Horton
Gerald Maxwell
Lady Marjorie Gordon
Mrs. Tennant
G. Shelton
Mrs. Franklin
Thomas Nast
Sir John Hassard
W. G. Wills
Sir Lepel and Lady Griffin
Dr. and Mrs. Todhunter
Lady Alix Egerton
J. W. Arrowsmith
William Telbin
George Derlacher
Mr. and Mrs. Dion Boucicault
Edith Craig
Lieut. Bailey, U.S.N.
Maurice Grau
Joseph Bennett
Mr. and Mrs. Gilbert Hare
Lord Emlyn
T. Reynolds
Mr. and Mrs. Cecil Raleigh
Mr. and Mrs. F. Tennant
Mr. and Mrs. F. Tyars
Mr. and Mrs. H. B. Stanford
Julian Ralph
John T. Raymond
Lady Blomfeld
Misses Hepworth Dixon
Herbert Schmalz
Dutton Cook
Sir Arnold White
James Mortimer
Colin Hunter, A.R.A., and Mrs. Hunter
Thomas MacQuoid
Katherine S. MacQuoid
Forbes Winslow
Sir Edwin Arnold
W. B. Maxwell
Commander Hodge, U.S.N.
J. D. Beveridge
Samuel Elliott

XXXV

VISITS OF FOREIGN WARSHIPS

I

WHEN, in May 1894, the United States cruiser *Chicago* came to London whilst making her cruise of friendly intent, there was of course a warm-hearted greeting. Admiral Erben was the very soul of geniality and Captain Mahan was, through his great work on *The Sea Power of England*, himself a maker of history. At the banquet given to them in St. James's Hall, Irving, though nominally present, was unable to attend as he had to play at the Lyceum, but he made a point of my going. He felt that all that could possibly be done to cement the good feeling between Great Britain and America was the duty of every Englishman—even the least of them.

At the banquet, on the end of the hall was the legend in gigantic letters:

"BLOOD IS THICKER THAN WATER"

—the phrase that became historic when Admiral Erben was in China. It will be remembered that whilst a flotilla of British boats were attacking a fort on the river and had met a reverse they were aided by the crew of the American ship of war. They were on a mud flat at the mercy of the

Chinese, who were wiping them out. But the crew of the neutral vessel—unaided by their officers, who had of course to show an appearance of neutrality in accord with the wisdom of international law—put off their boats and took them off. On protest being made, the answer was given in the above phrase.

Through me Irving conveyed a warm invitation to all the officers to come to the Lyceum to see the play and stop for supper in the Beefsteak Room. They all came except Captain Mahan, who had to be away at an engagement out of London. It was a delightful evening for us all and many a new friendship began.

In addition to the officers, Irving had asked the whole crew of the *Chicago* to come to the play in such numbers and on such nights as might be possible. They came on three different nights. Each party came round to the office to have a drink—and a very remarkable thing it was considering that, except the petty officers, they were all ordinary seamen, marines and stokers, though they had everything that was drinkable to choose from—for Irving wished them to have full choice of the best—no man would take a second drink! They had evidently made some rule of good manners amongst themselves. A fine and hearty body of men they were—and with good memories one and all. For ten years afterwards—right up to the end of our last tour—there was hardly a week during our American touring that some of that crew did not come to make his greeting.

The return party to the ship came on Sunday, June 3, when we went to lunch on board the

Chicago. Irving took with him Toole, Major Ricarde-Seaver and Thomas Nast, the American cartoonist, who had been at the supper at the Lyceum. We went down to Gravesend, where the vessel lay, and were met by the younger officers who brought us on board. There welcome reigned. It shone in the eyes of every man on the ship, from the Admiral down. The men on parade looked as if only the hold of discipline restrained them as Irving passed by with words of kindly greeting. We had a delightful time. One little incident in which I was myself a participant marked a certain difference in the discipline of the navies of Britain and America. At lunch when I refused wine—being gouty—I was asked what I would like. When I said a whisky-and-soda, the officer, in whose charge I was, said with his face fallen:

"I am very sorry old chap, but you can't have that. Spirits are not allowed to be drunk in our Navy." Of course I said it did not matter; that I would take a glass of wine. This was poured out for me and stood by me. We were speaking of something else when the officer on the other side of me said suddenly:

"Look here, what's wrong with you? You are quite pale! Are you not well?" I certainly felt anything but pale on that burning June day. The heat of the sun on the water seemed to make its way in through the open ports. But when he said I was, I waited developments. The officer, who was regarding me with much concern, turned to the man who was waiting on us and said:

"Tell the Quarter-master to ask the doctor to

come here!" The doctor came. "I am afraid Bram Stoker is not well," he said. "Hadn't you better look to him!" The doctor felt my pulse, and with a glance at the as yet untouched wine beside me took out his note-book and wrote a prescription which he handed to the Quartermaster to have sent to the Apothecary.

Presently the dose was brought to me. I don't of course know what it was, but it *tasted* exceedingly like whisky-and-soda! In justice to the skill of my physician and the concern of my hosts I may say that I certainly felt better after I had, by degrees, swallowed it.

When late in the afternoon we were returning on shore, the whole crew were on deck. I do not believe there was a man on board who was not there. If the greeting was hearty, the farewell was touching. We had got into the boat and were just clearing the vessel, we waving our hats to those behind, when there burst out a mighty cheer, which seemed to rend the air like thunder. It pealed over the water that still Sabbath afternoon and startled the quiet folk on the frontages at Gravesend. Cheer after cheer came ringing and resonant with a heartiness that made one's blood leap. For there is no such sound in the world as that full-throated Anglo-Saxon cheer which begins at the heart—that inspiring, resolute, intentional cheer which has through the memory of ten thousand victories and endless moments of stress and daring become the heritage of the race.

Before the *Chicago* left London, a little deputation came one evening to the Lyceum from the crew. To Irving they presented a fine drawing in water-colour of their ship, together with a silver box with an Address written and illuminated by themselves. It was a hearty document, redolent of the memories of crossing the Line and such quaint conceits as the deep water seaman loves.

I value dearly their gift to myself; a beautiful walking-stick of zebra-wood and silver, of which the inscription runs:

> "Presented to Bram Stoker, Esq.
> By the crew of U.S. *Chicago*, 1894."

II

Three years after the visit of the *Chicago*—1897—another warship came on a similar friendly mission.

This was the battleship *Fuji*, of the Japanese Navy. In those days Japan was just beginning to step from her sun-lit shores down into the great world. She had awakened to the need for self-protection and had manifested her fighting power with modern weapons in the capture of Port Arthur. Captain Mimra, who commanded the *Fuji*, had been appointed Commandant of the fortress-city after the capture.

Irving thought it would be hospitable to ask the visitors to the play. On the night of April 2, Captain Mimra and his officers came. The play then running, *Richard III.*, was one that took up Irving's time from first to last during the evening so that it was not possible for him to have the privilege of meeting his guests personally. So I had to be deputy host. The party sat in the

Royal box and the one next to it, the two boxes having been made into one for the occasion. After the third act of the play we all went into the " Prince of Wales's Room "—the drawing-room attached to the Royal box—and drank a glass of wine together to a toast which was prophetic :

" England and Japan ! "

XXXVI

IRVING'S LAST RECEPTION AT THE LYCEUM

The Queen's Jubilee, 1887—The Diamond Jubilee, 1889— The King's Coronation, 1902

I

AT the time of the Queen's Jubilee in 1887, Irving had something to do in the celebration in a histrionic way. He was able to make welcome at the Lyceum and to entertain individually many of those who came from over seas to do honour to the occasion. The only act of general service which came within his power was to lend the bells which were played in Hyde Park on the occasion of the Children's Jubilee. These were the "hemispherical" bells which had been founded for the production of *Faust*, and were the largest of the kind that had ever been made. On that day it seemed as though the carillon sounded all over London.

II

Ten years later, when the "Diamond" Jubilee was kept, much more attention was paid to the

Colonial and Indian guests than had ever been done before. The Nation had waked to the importance of the "Dependencies," and the representatives of these were treated with all due honour. Irving, thinking like many others that it would be well that private hospitalities given in general form might suppliment the public functions, gave a special *matinée* performance on June 25 for the troops of all kinds which had been sent to represent the various parts of the Empire. The authorities fell in with the plan so thoroughly that he was encouraged to add to his service of hospitality a reception on the stage after the play on the night of June 28. To this came all the Colonial Premiers, and all those Indian Princes and such persons of local distinction throughout the world as had been named on the official lists, and all the officers taking a part in the proceedings. Besides these were a host of others, amongst whom were a large number of representatives of literature and the various arts.

III

When, in 1902, the time of the Coronation was approaching and matters were being organised for a fitting welcome to the guests of the nation, Irving, remembering the success of his little effort of five years before and the official approval of it, wrote to the Lord Chamberlain to ask if it would be in accordance with the King's wishes that the stage reception should be repeated. His Majesty not only approved of the idea, but commanded that the matter should be taken up

CORONATION FESTIVITIES

by the Indian and the Colonial Offices, so that those high officials in charge of the public arrangements might have the date of the reception placed on the official list of "informal formalities." This meant that a special date was to be made certain for the occasion and that the nation's guests would attend in force. There were so many events of social importance close to the time fixed for the Coronation that there was a certain struggle for dates. Those hosts were supposed to be happy who secured that which they wished. Our date was fixed for the night of Thursday, July 3.

When, on June 26, the ceremony of the Coronation was postponed on account of the dangerous illness of the King, it was made known formally that it was His Majesty's expressed wish that all the functions of hospitality to the guests should go on as arranged. In Irving's case much pains had been taken officially. Sir William Curzon Wyllie, of the Political Department of the India Office, and Sir William Baillie-Hamilton, at the Colonial Office, arranged matters.

When the night of July 3 arrived all possible preparations had been made at the Lyceum. As the function was to take place after the audience had gone there would be little time to spare and we had to provide against accidents and hitches of all kinds.

The play began at eight o'clock and there was an immense audience. At ten minutes to eleven the curtain fell; and then began one of the finest pieces of carefully organised work I have ever seen. Everything had been planned out, every man was in his place, and throughout there was no scrambling or interfering with each other although the haste was positively terrific. All was done in silence, and each gang knew how to wait till their moment for exertion came.

As the audience filed out of the stalls and pit a host of carpenters edged in behind them and began to unscrew the chairs and benches. So fast did they work that as the audience left the proscenium the blocks of seats followed close behind them to the waiting carts. Following the carpenters came an array of sturdy women cleaners, who used broom and duster with an almost frantic energy, moving in a nimbus of dust of their own making. All the windows in the house had been opened the instant the curtain fell, so that the place was being aired whilst the work was going on. Behind the cleaners came a force of upholsterers with great bales of red cloth, which had already been prepared and fitted, so that an incredibly short time saw the floor of the house looking twice its usual size in its splendour of crimson. By this time the curtain had gone up showing the stage clear from front to back and from side to side. A train of carts had been waiting, and as there was a great force of men on the stage the scenes and properties seemed to move of their own accord out of the great doors at the back of the stage. On the walls right and left of the stage and at the back hung great curtains of crimson velvet and painted satin which we used in various plays. The stage was covered with crimson cloth. At each side of the orchestra was lifted in a staircase ready prepared, some six feet wide, carpeted with crimson and with handrails covered with crimson velvet. A rail covered with velvet of the same colour protected unthinking guests from walking into the orchestra. Then came the florists. An endless train of palms and shrubs and flowers in pots seemed to move in and disperse themselves about the theatre. The boxes were filled with them and all along the front of the circles they stood in serried lines till the whole place was in waves of greenery and flowers. The orchestra was filled with palms which rose a foot or two over the place of the footlights. In the meantime the caterer's little army had brought in tables which they placed in the back of the pit, the walls of which had during the time been covered in Turkey red.

All the while another army of electricians had been at work. They had fixed some great chandeliers over the stage and had put up the "set pieces" arranged for the proscenium. These were a vast Union Jack composed of thousands of coloured lights which hung over the dress circle, and an enormous crown placed over the upper circle. I never in my life saw anything so magnificently effective as these lights. They seemed to blaze like titanic jewels, and filled the place with a glory of light.

While all this was going on, we had the whole house searched from roof to cellar by our own servants and a force of detectives sent for the purpose. It did not do to neglect precautions on such an occasion when the spirit of anarchy stalked abroad. When this was done the detectives took their places all round the theatre, and the coming guests had to pass through a line of them. This was necessary to avoid the possibility of expert thieves gaining admission. Some of these guests were known to wear, when in State costume; jewels of great value. In fact one of the Indian Princes who was present that night wore jewels of the value of half a million sterling.

All this preparation had been made within the space of *forty minutes*. When the guests began to arrive a few minutes before half-past eleven, for which hour they had been bidden, all was in order. Some of them, who had been present at the play and had waited in the vestibule could hardly believe their eyes when they saw the change.

Irving stood in the centre of the stage, for there were three doors of entry, one at the back of the stage, the private door O.P., and the stage door which was on the prompt side. Only one door, that at the back of the stage, had been arranged, but the guests came so fast—and so many of them were of a class so distinguished as not to be accustomed to wait—that we found it necessary to open the others as well. Servants trained to announce the names of guests had been put on duty, but their task was no easy one, and there were some strange mispronunciations. I give some of the names of the thousand guests, from which the difficulty may be inferred:

His Highness Maharaj Adhiraj Sir Madho Rao Scindia, Maharaja of Gwalior.

His Highness Maharaja Sir Ganga Singh, Maharaja of Bikaner.

His Highness Sir Pertab Singh, Maharaja of Idar.

His Highness Maharaj Adhiraj Sawai Sir Mahdo Singh, Maharaja of Jeypore.

DIFFICULT ANNOUNCING

His Highness the Maharaja of Kohlapur.
Maharaja Kunwar Dolat Singh.
His Highness the Maharaja of Kooch Bahar.
Maharaj Kunwar Prodyot Kumar Tagore.
Sir Jamsetjee Jeejeebhai.
Raja Sir Savalai Ramaswami Mudaliyar.
Maharaja Sri Rao the Hon. Sir Venkalasvetachalapati Ranga Ras Bahadur, Raja of Bobbili.
Meherban Ganpatrao Madhavrao Vinchwikar.
The Hon. Asif Kadr Saiyid Wasif Ali Mirza, of Murshidabad.
The Hon. Nawab Mumtaz-ud-daula Muhamad Faiyaz Ali Khan, of Pahasu Bulandshahr.
Nawab Fateh Ali Khan, Kizilbash.
Gangadhar Madho Chitnavis.
Rai Jagannath Barua Bahadur.
Maung On Gaing.
Lieut.-Colonel Nawab Mahomed Aslam Khan, Khan Bahadur.
The Sultan of Perak.
King Lewanika.
H.R.H. The Crown Prince of Siam.
The Datoh Panglima Kinta.
The Datoh Sedelia Rab.
Sri Baba Khem Singh, Bedi of Kullar.

They were from every part of the world and of every race under the sun. In type and colour they would have illustrated a discourse on ethnology, or craniology. Some were from the centre of wildest Africa, not long come under the dominion of Britain. Of one of them, a king whose blackness of skin was beyond belief, I was told an anecdote. Just after his arrival in London, he had been driving out with the nobleman to whose tutelage he had been trusted. In one of the suburban squares a toxophilite society was meeting. The king stopped the carriage and turning to his companion said:

"Bows and arrows here in the heart of London! And I assure you that for more than a year I have prohibited them in my dominions."

The Premiers of all the great Colonies were present, and a host of lesser representatives of King Edward's dominions. Also a vast number of peers and peeresses and other representatives of the nation—statesmen, ecclesiastics, soldiers, authors, artists, men of science and commerce.

The most gorgeous of all the guests were of course the Indian Princes. Each was dressed in the fullest dress of his nationality, state and creed. The amount of jewels they wore, cut and uncut, was perfectly astonishing.

It was very hard to keep Irving in the spot which he had chosen for himself; for as the great crowd streamed in on three sides he kept shifting a little every moment to greet some old friend, and had to be brought back to the point where he could meet all. In such cases he was always amenable to a delightful degree. Seeing the difficulty to himself he asked me to get two or three important friends to stand with him. He named Lord Aberdeen and the late Right Hon. Richard Seddon, the Premier of New Zealand. These came and stood with him, and the nucleus protected him from movement.

Lord Aberdeen was an old friend and had, when he was Governor-General of Canada, shown Irving the most conspicuous courtesy. I remember well the evening when we were leaving Toronto for Montreal after the *matinée*, February 21, 1894. We had got into the train and the workmen were loading up the scenery and luggage when there was a great clatter of horsemen coming at the gallop and up rode the Governor-General with his escort. His courtesy to the distinguished guest was very pleasing to the warm-hearted Canadians.

"Dick" Seddon Irving had met five years before at the great party which Lord Northcliff—then Mr. Alfred Harmsworth—had given in his new house in Berkeley Square on the night before the Diamond Jubilee—June 21, 1897. When Irving and I arrived we followed immediately after the Colonial Premiers—I think there were eight of them—who had that day received the honour of Privy Councillorship and wore their Court dress. Mr. Seddon asked to be introduced to Irving, and at once took him away to the corner of a room where they could talk freely. I was afterwards told that when he had gone to the Opera in Covent Garden a few days before—where with his family he was given the Royal box—he asked when the opera had gone on for a good while:

"But where is Irving? He is the man I want to see most!"

That Coronation reception was certainly a most magnificent sight. Many who were at both functions said that it was even finer than the reception at the India Office, which was a spectacle to remember. But of course the theatre had an advantage in shape and its rising tiers. When one entered at the back of the stage the *coup d'œil* was magnificent. The place looked of vast size; the many lights and the red seats of the tiers making for infinite distance as they gleamed through the banks of foliage. The great crown and Union Jack seeming to flame over all; the moving mass of men and women, nearly all the men in gorgeous raiment, in uniform or Court dress, the women all brilliantly dressed and flashing with gems; with here and there many of the Ranees and others of various nationalities in their beautiful robes. Everywhere ribbons and orders, each of which meant some lofty distinction of some kind. Everywhere a sense of the unity and the glory of Empire. Dominating it all, as though it was floating on light and sound and form and colour, the thrilling sense that there, in all its bewildering myriad beauty, was the spirit mastering the heart-beat of that great Empire on which the sun never sets.

That night was the swan-song of the old Lyceum, and was a fitting one; for such a wonderful spectacle none of our generation shall ever see again. As a function it crowned Irving's reign as Master and Host.

Two weeks later the old Lyceum as a dramatic theatre closed its doors—for ever.

XXXVII

THE VOICE OF ENGLAND

In August 1880, Irving and I went on a short holiday to the Isle of Wight, where later Loveday joined us. One evening at Shanklin we went out for a stroll after dinner. It was late when we returned; but the night was so lovely that we sat for a while under a big tree at the entrance to the Chine. It was a dark night and under the tree it was inky black; only the red tips of our cigars were to be seen. Those were early days in the Home Rule movement, and as I was a believer in it Irving was always chaffing me about it. It was not that he had any politics himself—certainly in a party sense; the nearest point to politics he ever got, so far as I know, was when he accepted his election to the Reform Club. But he loved to "draw out" any one about anything, and would at times go quite a long way about to do it. We had been talking Home Rule and he had, of course for his purpose, taken the violently opposite side to me. Presently we heard the slow, regular, heavy tramp of a policeman coming down the road; there is no mistaking the sound to any one who has ever lived in a city. Irving turned to me—I could tell the movement by his cigar—and said with an affected intensity which I had come to identify and understand:

"How calm and silent all this is! Very different, my boy, from the hideous strife of politics. It ought to be a lesson to you! Here in this quiet place, away from the roar of cities and on the very edge of the peaceful sea, there is opportunity for thought! You will not find here men galling their tempers and shortening their lives by bitter thoughts and violent deeds. Believe me, here in rural England is to be found the true inwardness of British opinion!"

I said nothing; I knew the game. Then the heavy, placid step drew closer. Irving went on:

"Here comes the Voice of England. Just listen to it and learn!" Then in a cheery, friendly voice he said to the invisible policeman:

"Tell me, officer, what is your opinion as to this trouble in Ireland?" The answer came at once, stern and full of pent-up feeling, and in an accent there was no possibility of mistaking:

"Ah, begob, it's all the fault iv the dirty Gover'mint!" His brogue might have been cut with a hatchet. From his later conversation—for of course after that little utterance Irving led him on—one might have thought that the actor was an ardent and remorseless rebel. I came to the conclusion that Home Rule was of little moment to that guardian of the law; he was an out and out Fenian.

For many a day afterwards I managed to bring in the "Voice of England" whenever Irving began to chaff about Home Rule.

XXXVIII

RIVAL TOWNS

In the course of our tour in the Far West of America in 1893-4 we had an experience which Irving now and again told with great enjoyment to his friends. From San Francisco we went to Tacoma and Seattle, two towns on Puget Sound between which is a mighty rivalry. In Seattle we were walking along the main street when we saw a crowd outside the window of a drug store and went over to see the cause. The whole window-space was cleared and covered with sheets of white paper. In the centre, raised on a little platform, was an immense Tropical American horned beetle quite three inches from feelers to tail. Behind it was propped up a huge card on which was printed in ink with a brush in large letters:

"ORDINARY BED-BUG CAPTURED IN TACOMA."

XXXIX

TWO STORIES

I

NATURALLY the form of humour that appealed most to Irving was that based on human character. This feeling he shared with Tennyson—indeed with all in whom a deep knowledge of the "essential difference" of character is a necessity of their art. Perhaps the two following stories, of which he was exceedingly fond, will illustrate the bent of his mind. The first, having heard from some one else, he told me; the second I told him. I have heard him tell them both several times in his own peculiar way.

II

The first was of an English excursionist who was up near Balmoral in the later days of Queen Victoria. The day being hot, he went into a cottage to get a glass of water. He sat mopping his forehead, whilst the guid-wife was polishing the glass and getting fresh water from the well. He commenced to talk cheerfully:

"So the Queen is a neighbour of yours!"

AN UNCOMPROMISING SABBATARIAN

" Ooh, aye ! "

" And she is quite neighbourly, isn't she ? And comes to visit you here in your own cottages ? "

" Ooh, aye ! She's weel eneuch ! "

" And she asks you to tea sometimes at Balmoral ? "

" Ooh, aye ! She's nae that bad ! " The tourist was rather struck with the want of enthusiasm shown and ventured to comment on it inquiringly :

" Look here, ma'am ; you don't seem very satisfied with Her Majesty ! May I ask you why ? "

" Weel, I'll tell ye if ye wish. The fac' is we don't leik the gangin's on at the Caastle."

" Oh, indeed, ma'am ! How is that ? What is it that displeases you ? "

" We don't leik the way they keep—or don't keep—the Sawbath. Goin' oot in bo-ats an' rowin' on the Sawbath day ! " The tourist tried to appease her and suggested :

" Oh, well ! after all ma'am, you know there is a precedent for that. You remember Our Lord, too, went out on the Sabbath——" She interrupted him :

" Ooh, aye ! I ken it weel eneuch. Ye canna' tell me aught aboot Hem that I dinna ken a'ready. An' I can tell ye this : we don't think any moor o' Hem for it either ! "

III

The other story was of the funeral in Dublin of a young married woman. The undertaker, after the wont of his craft, was arranging the whole affair according to the completest local rules of mortuary etiquette. He bustled up to the widower saying :

" You, sir, will of course go in the carriage with the mother of the deceased."

" What ! Me go in the carriage with me mother-in-law ! Not likely ! "

" Oh, sir, but I assure you it is necessary. The rule is an inviolable one, established by precedents beyond all cavil ! " expostulated the horrified undertaker. But the widower was obdurate.

" I won't go. That's flat ! "

" Oh, but my good sir. Remember the gravity of the occasion—the publicity—the—the—possibility—scandal." His voice faded into a gasp. The widower stuck to his resolution and so the undertaker laid the matter before some of his intimate friends who were waiting instructions. These surrounded the chief mourner and began to remonstrate with him :

" You really must, old chap ; it is necessary."

" I'll not ! Go with me mother-in-law !—Rot ! "

" But look here, old chap——"

" I'll not I tell ye—I'll go in any other carriage that ye wish ; but not in that."

" Oh, of course, if ye won't, ye won't. But remember it beforehand that afterwards when it'll be thrown up against ye, that it'll be construed into an affront on the poor girl that's gone. Ye loved her Jack, we all know, an' ye wouldn't like *that !* "

This argument prevailed. He signed to the undertaker and began to pull on his black gloves.

As he began to move towards the carriage he turned to his friends and said in a low voice :
"I'm doin' it because ye say I ought to, and for the poor girl that's gone. But ye'll spoil me day ! "

XL

SIR RICHARD BURTON

A Face of steel—Some pleasant suppers—Lord Houghton —Searching for Patriarchs—Edmund Henry Palmer— Desert law—The " Arabian Nights"

I

WHEN in the early morning of August 13, 1878, Irving arrived in Dublin, on his way to Belfast to give a Reading for the Samaritan Hospital, I met him at Westland Row Station. He had arranged to stay for a couple of days with my brother before going north. When the train drew up, hastening to greet him I entered the carriage. There were two other people in the compartment, a lady and gentleman. When we had shaken hands, Irving said to his *compagnons de voyage*:

" Oh, let me introduce my friend Bram Stoker ! " They both shook hands with me very cordially. I had not come to meet strangers; Irving was my objective. Nevertheless, I could not but be struck by the strangers. The lady was a big, handsome blonde woman, clever-looking and capable. But the man riveted my attention. He was dark, and forceful, and masterful, and ruthless. I have never seen so iron a countenance. I did not have much time to analyse the face; the bustle of arrival prevented that. But an instant was enough to make up my mind about him. We separated in the carriage after cordial wishes that we might meet again. When we were on the platform, I asked Irving:

"Who is that man?"

"Why," he said, "I thought I introduced you!"

"So you did, but you did not mention the names of the others!" He looked at me for an instant and said inquiringly as though something had struck him:

"Tell me, why do you want to know?"

"Because," I answered, "I never saw any one like him. He is steel! He would go through you like a sword!"

"You are right!" he said. "But I thought you knew him. That is Burton—Captain Burton who went to Mecca!"

The Burtons were then paying a short visit to Lord Talbot de Malahide. After Irving went back to London, I was very busy and did not ever come across either of them. That autumn I joined Irving and went to live in London.

II

In January of next year, 1879, I met the Burtons again. They had come to London for a holiday.

The first meeting I had then with Burton was at supper with Irving in the Green Room Club— these were occasional suppers where a sort of smoking-concert followed the removal of the dishes. I sat between Burton and James Knowles, who was also Irving's guest. It was a great pleasure to me to meet Burton familiarly, for I had been hearing about him and his wonderful exploits as long as I could remember. He talked very freely and very frankly about all sorts of things, but that night there was nothing on the *tapis* of an exceptionally interesting nature.

That night, by the way, I heard Irving recite *The Captive* for the first time. He also did *Gemini and Virgo;* but that I had heard him do in Trinity College, Dublin.

The Burtons remained in London till the end of February, in which month we met at supper several times. The first supper was at Irving's rooms in Grafton Street, on the night of Saturday, February 8, the other member of the party being Mr. Aubertin. The subdued light and the quietude gave me a better opportunity of studying Burton's face; in addition to the fact that this time I sat opposite to him and not beside him. The predominant characteristics were the darkness of the face—the desert burning; the strong mouth and nose, and jaw and forehead—the latter somewhat bold—and the strong, deep, resonant voice. My first impression of the man as of steel was consolidated and enhanced. He told us, amongst other things, of the work he had in hand. Three great books were partially done. The translation of the *Arabian Nights*, the metrical translation of Camoëns, and the *Book of the Sword*. These were all works of vast magnitude and requiring endless research. But he lived to complete them all.

Our next meeting was just a week later, Saturday, February 15. This time Mr. Aubertin was host and there was a new member of the party, Lord Houghton, whom I then met for the first time. I remember that amongst other good things which we had that night was some exceedingly fine old white port, to which I think we all did justice—in a decorous way. The talk that evening kept on three subjects: fencing, the life of Lord Byron, and Shakespeare. Burton was an expert and an authority on all connected with the sword; Lord Houghton was then the only man living— I think that Trelawny, who had been the only other within years, had just died—who knew Byron in his youth, so that the subject was at once an interesting one. They all knew and had ideas of Shakespeare and there was no lack of variety of opinion. Amongst other things, Burton told us that night of his life on the West Coast of Africa—" the Gold Coast "—where he was Consul and where he kept himself alive and in good health for a whole year by never going out in the midday sun if he could help it, and by drinking a whole flask of brandy every day! He also spoke of his life in South America and of the endurance based on self-control which it required.

The third supper was one given on February 21, at Bailey's Hotel, South Kensington, by Mr. Mullen the publisher. Arthur Sketchley was this time added to the party. The occasion was to celebrate the birthday of Mrs. Burton's book of travel, *A.E.I.* (Arabia, Egypt, India), a big book of some five hundred pages. We were each presented with a copy laid before us on the table. I sat between Lord Houghton and Burton. They were old friends—had been since boyhood. Each called the other Richard. Houghton, be it remembered, was Richard Monckton Milnes before he got his peerage in 1863. The conversation was very interesting, especially when Burton was mentioning experiences, or expounding some matters of his knowledge, or giving grounds for some theory which he held. The following fragment of conversation will explain something of his intellectual attitude:

Burton had been mentioning some of his explorations amongst old tombs and Houghton asked him if he knew the tomb of Moses. He replied that he did not know it though of course he knew its whereabouts.

"It must be found if sought for within a few years!" he added. "We know that he was buried at Shekem." (I do not vouch for names or details—such do not matter here. I take it that Burton knew his subject and was correct in what he did say.) "The valley is narrow, and only at one side and in one place would a tomb be possible. It wouldn't take long to explore that entire place if one went at it earnestly." Again Houghton asked him:

"Do you know exactly where any of the Patriarchs are buried?"

"Not exactly! But I could come near some of them."

"Do you think you could undertake to find any one of them?" Burton answered slowly and thoughtfully—to this day I can seem to hear the deep vibration of his voice:

"Well, of course I am not quite certain; and I should not like to promise anything in a matter which is, and must be, purely problematical. But

I think—yes! I think I could put my hand on Joseph!" As he stopped there and did not seem as though he was going to enlarge on the subject, I said quietly as though to myself:

"There's nothing new or odd in that!" Burton turned to me quickly:

"Do you know of any one attempting it? Has it been tried before? Do you know the explorer?"

"Yes!" I said, feeling that I was in for it, "but only by name. I cannot claim a personal acquaintance."

"Who was it?"—this spoken eagerly.

"Mrs. Potiphar!"

The two cynics laughed heartily. The laughter of each was very characteristic. Lord Houghton's face broadened as though he had suddenly grown fatter. On the other hand Burton's face seemed to lengthen when he laughed; the upper lip rising instinctively and showing the right canine tooth. This was always a characteristic of his enjoyment. As he loved fighting, I can fancy that in the midst of such stress it would be even more marked than under more peaceful conditions.

The last time we met Captain Burton during that visit was on the next night, February 22, 1879, at supper with Mrs. Burton's sister, Mrs. Van Tellen.

He was going back almost immediately to Trieste, of which he held the consulship. In those days this consulship was a pleasant sinecure—an easy berth with a fairly good salary. It was looked on as a resting-place for men of letters. Charles Lever held it before Burton. In the old days of Austrian domination Trieste was an important place and the consulship an important one. But its commercial prosperity began to wane after the cry *Italia irredenta* had been efficacious. The only thing of importance regarding the office that remained was the salary.

III

Six years elapsed before we met again. This was on June 27, 1885. The Burtons had just come to London and had asked Irving and me to take supper with them at the Café Royal after the play, *Olivia*. That night was something of a disappointment. All of our little *partie carrée* had made up our minds for a long and interesting —and thus an enjoyable—evening.

Chiefest amongst the things which Irving was longing to hear him speak of was that of the death of Edmund Henry Palmer three years before. Palmer had been a friend of Irving's long before, the two men having been made known to each other by Palmer's cousin, Edward Russell, then in Irving's service. When Arabi's revolt broke out in Egypt, Palmer was sent by the British Government on a special service to gather the friendly tribes and persuade them to protect the Canal. This, by extraordinary daring and with heroic devotion, he accomplished; but he was slain treacherously by some marauders. Burton was then sent out to bring back his body and to mete out justice to the murderers—so far as such could be done.

Just before that time Burton had in hand a work from which he expected to win great fortune both for himself and his employer, the Khedive. This was to re-open the old Midian gold mines. He had long before, with endless research, discovered their locality, which had long been lost and forgotten. He had been already organising an expedition, and I had asked him to take with him my younger brother George, who wished for further adventure. He had met my suggestion very favourably, and having examined my brother's record was keen on his joining him. He wanted a doctor for his party; and a doctor who was adventurous and skilled in resource at once appealed to him. Arabi's revolt postponed such an undertaking; in Burton's case the postponement was for ever.

Our new civic brooms had been at work in London and new ordinances had been established. Punctually at midnight we were inexorably turned out. Protests, cajoleries, or bribes were of no avail. Out we had to go! I had a sort of feeling that Burton's annoyance was only restrained from adequate expression by his sense of humour. He certainly could be "adequate"—and in many languages which naturally lend themselves to invective—when he laid himself out for it. The Fates were more propitious a few months later, when Irving had a supper at the Continental Hotel, on July 30—the last night of the season and Benefit of Ellen Terry. By this time we understood the licensing law and knew what to do. Irving took a bed at the hotel and his guests were allowed to remain; this was the merit of a hotel as distinguished from a restaurant. There was plenty of material for pleasant talk in addition to Captain and Mrs. Burton, for amongst the guests was James McHenry, J. L. Toole, Beatty Kingston (the war correspondent of the *Daily Telegraph*), Willie Winter, Mr. Marquand of New York, and Richard Mansfield. All was very pleasant, but there was not the charm of personal reminiscence, which could not be in so large a gathering.

IV

The following year, 1886, however, whilst the Burtons were again in London, we had two other delightful meetings. On July 9, 1886, Irving had Sir Richard and Lady Burton—he had been knighted in the meantime—to supper in the Beefsteak Room after the play, *Faust*. This was another *partie carrée*; just Sir Richard and Lady Burton, Irving and myself. That night we talked of many things, chiefly of home interest. Burton was looking forward to his retirement and was anxious that there should not be any hitch. He knew well that there were many hands against him and that if opportunity served he would not be spared. There were passages in his life which set many people against him. I remember when a lad hearing of how at a London dinner-party he told of his journey to Mecca. It was a wonderful feat, for he had to pass as a Muhammedan; the slightest breach of the multitudinous observances of that creed would call attention, and suspicion at such a time and place would be instant death. In a moment of forgetfulness, or rather inattention, he made some small breach of rule.

He saw that a lad had noticed him and was quietly stealing away. He faced the situation at once, and coming after the lad in such a way as not to arouse his suspicion suddenly stuck his knife into his heart. When at the dinner he told this, some got up from the table and left the room. It was never forgotten. I asked him once about the circumstance—not the dinner-party, but the killing. He said it was quite true, and that it had never troubled him from that day to the moment at which he was speaking. Said he:

"The desert has its own laws, and there—supremely of all the East—to kill is a small offence. In any case what could I do? It had to be his life or mine!"

As he spoke the upper lip rose and his canine tooth showed its full length like the gleam of a dagger. Then he went on to say that such explorations as he had undertaken were not to be entered lightly if one had qualms as to taking life. That the explorer in savage places holds, day and night, his life in his hand; and if he is not prepared for every emergency, he should not attempt such adventures.

Though he had no fear in the ordinary sense of the word, he was afraid that if any attack were made on him *apropos* of this it might militate against his getting the pension for which he was then looking and on which he largely depended. We spoke of the matter quite freely that evening. At that time he was not well off. For years he had lived on his earnings and had not been able to put by much. The *Arabian Nights* brought out the year before, 1885, produced ten thousand pounds.

There were only a thousand copies issued at a cost of ten guineas each. The entire edition was subscribed, the amounts being paid in full and direct to Coutts and Co., so that there were no fees or discounts. The only charge against the receipts was that of manufacturing the book. This could not have amounted to any considerable sum for the paper was poor, the ink inferior, and the binding cheap. Burton had then in hand another set of five volumes of *Persian Tales* to be subscribed in the same way. Neither of the sets of books were "published" in the literal way. The issue was absolutely a private one. All Burton's friends, myself included, thought it necessary to subscribe. Irving had two sets. The net profits of these fifteen volumes could hardly have exceeded thirteen thousand pounds.

V

Our next meeting was on September 18, 1886, when we were all Irving's guests at the Continental once again—another *partie carrée*.

On this occasion the conversation was chiefly of plays. Both Sir Richard and Lady Burton impressed on Irving how much might be done with a play taken from some story, or group of stories, in the *Arabian Nights*. Burton had a most vivid way of putting things—especially of the East. He had both a fine imaginative power and a memory richly stored not only from study but from personal experience. As he talked, fancy seemed to run riot in its alluring power; and the whole world of thought seemed to flame with gorgeous colour. Burton *knew* the East. Its brilliant dawns and sunsets; its rich tropic vegetation, and its arid fiery deserts; its cool, dark mosques and temples; its crowded bazaars; its narrow streets; its windows guarded for out-looking and from in-looking eyes; the pride and swagger of its passionate men, and the mysteries of its veiled women; its romances; its beauty; its horrors. Irving grew fired as the night wore on, and it became evident that he had it in his mind from that time to produce some such play as the Burtons suggested should occasion serve. It was probably the recollection of that night that brought back to him, so closely as to be an incentive to possibility, his own glimpse of the East as seen in Morocco and the Levant seven years before. When De Bornier published his *Mahomet* in Paris some few years later he was in the receptive mood to consider it as a production.

I asked Lady Burton to get me a picture of her husband. She said he had a rooted dislike to letting any one have his picture, but said she would ask him. Presently she sent me one, and with it a kindly word: " Dick said he would give it you, because it was you; but that he wouldn't have given it to any one else!"

XLI

SIR HENRY MORTON STANLEY

An interesting dinner—"Doubting Thomases" The lesson of exploration—"Through the Dark Continent" —Dinner—Du Chaillu—The price of fame

I

ON October 22, 1882, Irving gave a little dinner to H. M. Stanley in the small private dining-room of the Garrick Club. The other guests were George Augustus Sala, Edmund Yates, Col. E. A. Buck of New York, Mr. Bigelow (then British agent of the U.S. Treasury), H. D. Traill, Clement Scott, Joseph Hatton, T. H. S. Escott, Frank C. Burnand, W. A. Burdett-Coutts, J. L. Toole, and myself—fourteen in all.

The time was after Stanley had made his expedition in Africa, which he afterwards chronicled under the name of *In Darkest Africa*, and had gone out again to explore the region of the Congo for the Brussels African International Association. He had returned for a short visit to Brussels and London. He had been much in Belgium in consultation with the King regarding the foundation of the Congo Free State. Every one present was anxious to hear what he had to say; and Irving, who, when he chose, was most excellent in drawing any one out, took care that he had a good leading. Indeed it was a notable evening, for we sat there after dinner till four o'clock in the morning and for most of the time he held the floor. He was always interesting and at times kept us all enthralled. He had a peculiar manner, though less marked then than it became in later years. He was slow and deliberate of speech; the habit of watchful self-control seemed even then to have eaten into the very marrow of his bones. His dark face, through which the eyes seemed by contrast to shine like jewels, emphasised his slow speech and measured accents. His eyes were very comprehensive, and, in a quiet way, without appearing to rove, took in everything. He seemed to have that faculty of sight which my father had described to me of Robert Houdin, the great conjurer. At a single glance Stanley took in everything, received facts and assimilated them; gauged character in its height, and breadth, and depth, and specific gravity; formed opinion so quickly and so unerringly to the full extent of his capacity that intention based on what he saw seemed not to follow receptivity but to go hand in hand with it. Let me give an instance :

At least two of those present did not seem prepared to accept his statements in simple faith. Of course not a word was said by either to jar the harmony of the occasion or to convey doubt. But doubt at least there was; one felt it without evidence. I knew both men well and felt that it was only the consistent expression of their attitude towards the unknown. Both, so far as I knew—or know now—were strangers to him, though of course their names were familiar. I knew from Irving's glance at me where I sat across the table from him that he understood. Irving and I were so much together that after a few years we could almost read a thought of the other; we could certainly read a glance or an expression. I have sometimes seen the same capacity in a husband and wife who have lived together for long and who are good friends, accustomed to work together and to understand each other. He had a quiet sardonic humour, and this combined with an intuitive faculty of reasoning out *data* before their issue was declared—together with his glance to my right where the two men sat—seemed to say:

"Look at Yates and Burnand. Stanley will be on to them presently!"

And surely enough he was on to them, and in a remarkable way. He was describing some meeting with the King of the Belgians regarding the finances of the new State, and how of those present a small section of the financiers were making negative difficulties. The way he spoke was thus:

"Amongst them two 'doubting Thomases'— as it might be you and you"—making as he spoke a casual wave of his hand without looking at either, as though choosing at random, but so manifestly meaning it that all the other men laughed in an instantaneous chorus.

Somehow that seemed to clear the air for him; and having established a position which was manifestly accepted by all, he went on to speak more earnestly.

I shall never forget that description which he gave us of the reaching that furthest point on Lake

Leopold II. that white men had ever reached. He wrote of it all afterwards in his book on the Congo, though the incident which he then described differed slightly from the account in his book produced three years afterwards. No written words could convey the picturesque convincing force of that quiet utterance, with the searching still eyes to add to its power. How as the little steamer drew in shore the natives had rushed in clustering masses ready to do battle. How one nimble giant had leaped far out on an isolated rock that just showed its top above the still water, and poised thereon for an instant had hurled a spear with such force and skill that it passed the limit they had fixed as the furthest that a missile could reach them and where they held the boat in safety. How he himself had peremptorily checked in a whisper one beside him who was preparing to shoot, and he himself took a gun and fired high in the air just to show the savages that he too had power and greater power than their own should they choose to use it. How, awed by the sound and by the steamer, the natives made signs of obeisance; whereupon he brought the boat close to the rock whence the warrior had launched his spear and laid thereon offerings of beads and coloured stuffs and implements of steel, saying as he prepared to move away:

"We shall come again!"

Then he told of the wonder of the savages; their reverence; their complete submission! How the canoe moved away in that glory of wonder which would in time grow to a legend, and then to a belief that some day white Gods who brought gifts would come to them bringing unknown good.

It was an idyll of peace; a lesson in beneficent pioneering; a page of the great book of England's wise kindliness in the civilisation of the savage which as yet has been written but in part. We all sat spellbound. There was no " doubting Thomas " then. I think, one and all, we held high regard and affection for the man who spoke.

Then encouraged by the reception of his words —and after all it was a noble audience, in kind if not in quantity, for any man to speak to—he went on at Irving's request to re-tell to us the story of his finding of Livingstone. Here he did not object to any direct questioning, even when one man asked him if the report was exact of his taking off his helmet and bowing when he met the lost explorer with the memorable address:

" Dr. Livingstone, I believe ? "

He laughed quietly as he answered affirmatively —a strange thing to see in that dark, still face, where toil and danger and horror had set their seals. But it seemed to light up the man from within and show a new and quite different side to his character.

Somehow there is, I suppose—indeed must be— some subtle emanation from both character and experience. The propulsive power of the individuality takes something from the storage of the mind. Certainly some persons who have been down in deep waters of any kind convey to those who see or hear them something of the dominating note of their experience. Stanley had not only the traveller's look—the explorer's look; he seemed one whose goings had been under shadow.

It may of course have been that the dark face and the still eyes and that irregular white of the hair which speaks of premature stress on vitality conveyed by inference their own lesson; but most assuredly Henry Stanley had a look of the forest gloom as marked as Dante's contemporaries described of him: that of one who had traversed Heaven and Hell.

After a long time we broke up the set formation of the dinner table, and one by one in informal turn we each had a chat with the great explorer. He told us that he wanted some strong, brave, young men to go with him to Africa, and offered to accept any one whom I could recommend.

II

The next year, on September 14, we met again when Irving had a large dinner-party—sixty-four people—at the Continental Hotel. Of course in so large a party there was little opportunity of general conversation. All that any one—except a very favoured few who sat close at hand—could speak or hear was of the commonplace of life—parting and meeting.

I did not meet Stanley again for six years, but Irving met him several times, and at one of their meetings there was a little matter which gave me much pleasure:

When we had gone to America in 1883 I had found myself so absolutely ignorant of everything regarding that great country that I took some pains to post myself up in things exclusively and characteristically American. Our tour of 1883-4 was followed by another in 1884-5, so that in the space of a year which the two visits covered I had fine opportunities of study. In those days Professor James Bryce's book on *The American Commonwealth* had not been written—published at all events. And there was no standard source from which an absolutely ignorant stranger could draw information. I found some difficulty then in buying a copy of an Act of Congress so that I might study its form; and it was many months before I could get a copy of the Sessional Orders of Congress. However, before we left at the conclusion of our second visit I had accumulated a lot of books—histories, works on the constitution, statistics, census, school books, books of etiquette for a number of years back, Congressional reports on various subjects—in fact all the means of reference and of more elaborate study. When I had studied sufficiently—having all through the tour consulted all sorts of persons—professors, statesmen, bankers, &c.—I wrote a lecture, which I gave at the Birkbeck Institution in 1885 and elsewhere. This I published as a pamphlet in 1886, as *A Glimpse of America*. Stanley had evidently got hold of it, for one night when we were in Manchester, June 4, 1890, I had supper alone with Irving and he told me that the last time he had met him, Stanley had mentioned my little book on America as admirable. He had said that I had mistaken my vocation—that I should be a literary man! Of course such praise from such a man gave me a great pleasure.

Strangely enough I had a ratification of this a year later. On March 30, 1891, I met at luncheon, in the house of the Duchess of St. Albans, Dr. Parke, who had been with Stanley on his journey *Through the Dark Continent ;* I had met him before at Edward Marston's dinner, but we had not had much opportunity of talking together. He told me that it was one of the very few books that Stanley had brought with him in his perilous journey across Africa, and that he had told him that it " had in it more information about America than any other book that had ever been written."

III

The dinner given to Stanley by Edward Marston, the publisher, on the eve of bringing out Stanley's great book, *Through the Dark Continent*—June 26, 1890—was a memorable affair. Marston had then published two books of mine, *Under the Sunset*, and the little book on America, and as " one of his authors" I was a guest at the dinner. Irving was asked, but he could not go as he was then out of town on a short holiday, previous to commencing an engagement of two weeks at the Grand Theatre, Islington, whilst the Lyceum was occupied by Mr. Augustin Daly's company from New York. At the dinner I sat at an inside corner close to Sir Harry (then Mr.) Johnston, the explorer and administrator, and to Paul B. du Chaillu, the African explorer who had discovered gorillas. I had met both these gentlemen before; the first in London several times; the latter in New York, in December 1884, in the house of Mr. and Mrs. Tailer, who that night were entertaining Irving and Ellen Terry. There we had sat together at supper and he had told me much of his African experience and of his adventures with gorillas. I had of course read his books, but it was interesting to hear the stories under the magic of the adventurer's own voice and in his characteristic semi-French intonation. In the course of conversation he had said to me something which I have never forgotten—it spoke volumes:

"When I was young nothing would keep me out of Africa. Now nothing would make me go there!"

In reply to the toast of his health, Stanley spoke well and said some very interesting things:

"In my book that is coming out I have said as little as possible about Emin Pasha. He was to me a study of character. I never met the same kind of character." Again:

"I have not gone into details of the forest march and return to the sea. It was too dreary and too horrible. It will require years of time to be able to think of its picturesque side."

At that time Stanley looked dreadfully worn, and much older than when I had seen him last. The six years had more than their tally of wear for him, and had multiplied themselves. He was darker of skin than ever; and this was emphasised by the whitening of his hair. He was then under fifty years of age, but he looked nearer to eighty than fifty. His face had become more set and drawn—had more of that look of slight distortion which comes with suffering and over-long anxiety.

There were times when he looked more like a dead man than a living one. Truly the wilderness had revenged upon him the exposal of its mysteries.

XLII

ARMINIUS VAMBÉRY

A Defence against torture—How to Travel in Central Asia—An Orator

AMONGST the interesting visitors to the Lyceum and the Beefsteak Room was Arminius Vambéry, Professor at the University of Buda-Pesth. On April 30, 1890, he came to see the play, *The Dead Heart*, and remained to supper. He was most interesting and Irving was delighted with him. He had been to Central Asia, following after centuries the track of Marco Polo and was full of experiences fascinating to hear. I asked him if when in Thibet he never felt any fear. He answered :

" Fear of death—no ; but I am afraid of torture. I protected myself against that, however ! "

" However did you manage that ? "

" I had always a poison pill fastened here, where the lappet of my coat now is. This I could always reach with my mouth in case my hands were tied. I knew they could not torture me, and then I did not care ! "

He is a wonderful linguist, writes twelve languages, speaks freely sixteen, and knows over twenty. He told us once that when the Empress

Eugenie remarked to him that it was odd that he who was lame should have walked so much, he replied:

"Ah, Madam, in Central Asia we travel not on the feet but on the tongue."

We saw him again two years later, when he was being given a Degree at the Tercentenary of Dublin University. On the day on which the delegates from the various Universities of the world spoke, he shone out as a star. He soared above all the speakers, making one of the finest speeches I have ever heard. Be sure that he spoke loudly against Russian aggression—a subject to which he had largely devoted himself.